# A Book of Salvias

# A Book of Salvias
## Sages for Every Garden

Betsy Clebsch

Drawings by
Carol D. Barner

Timber Press
Portland, Oregon

Reprinted 1997


Printed in Hong Kong



Timber Press, Inc.
The Haseltine Building
133 S.W. Second Avenue, Suite 450
Portland, Oregon 97204, U.S.A.

Library of Congress Cataloging-in-Publication Data

Clebsch, Betsy.
    A book of salvias : sages for every garden / Betsy Clebsch ;
drawings by Carol D. Barner.
        p.    cm.
    Includes bibliographical references and index.
    ISBN 0-88192-369-9
    1. Salvia.    I. Title.
SB413.S22C58    1997
635.9'3387–dc20                                                                96-22160
                                                                                        CIP

# TO *SALVIA*

In these times of fashionable rages
Let us honor enduring sages.
Known to cure, to mend, to ease;
Companions to cooks; splendid teas.
Hundreds of species our world adorn,
Richly diverse in flower and form.
Hail to *Salvia*, that scented salvation,
Worthy of study and our admiration.

—Andy Doty

# Contents

*Color plates follow page 64*

# Acknowledgments

My profound thanks go to all the following, friends old and new, a few no longer with us, who have generously shared their knowledge and resources while enthusiastically encouraging my efforts by word and deed.

My research would have foundered long ago but for the generous help of these and many other people:

Frank Almeda, Sherrie Althouse, Christine Andrews, Carol Barner, Dennis Breedlove, Fred Boutin, Ed Carman, Bill Clebsch, James Compton, Jean Coria, Andy Doty, Richard Dufresne, John R. Dunmire, John Fairey, Martin Grantham, Gerda Isenberg, Barbara Keller, Robert Kourik, John MacGregor, David Madison, Don Mahoney, Virginia Mann, William A. McNamara, Pat McNeal, Bart O'Brien, Adam Reyes, Jeff Rosendale, Carl Schoenfeld, M. Nevin Smith, Greg Starr, John Hunter Thomas, and Philip Van Soelen, also, Sarah Veblen, who asked the first questions, and my ever-helpful editors, Neal Maillet and Ruth Steckel. A special word of thanks is due Ginny Hunt, who propagated scores of salvias and found time to proofread the manuscript at many different stages.

# Preface

Few groups of plants add as much to a garden as salvias. They are as diverse in fragrance as they are in bloom, habit, and color. I was first drawn to salvias because of the exquisite scents of the leaves of California's native coastal species. Later, I came to appreciate their beauty in flower and their value as a nectar source for hummingbirds. I believe that once you have grown salvias you will always have space for a few in your garden. Strong herbal fragrances are usually an element of native habitats, and salvias are essential garden ingredients if you wish to recapture the complete sensory experience of natural settings.

In recent years, many subtropical salvias have become available, greatly expanding the ranges of color, texture, and leaf fragrance that are now accessible to the gardener. The genus *Salvia* has arguably the truest blues and brightest reds of any group of plants, and some species also have strikingly large flowers. It has been great fun to watch the expanded use of these plants in garden landscapes throughout the San Francisco Bay Area where Betsy Clebsch makes her home. The increased availability of superior plant forms in nurseries has been helped by her influence. Now, with this book, we have descriptions as well as cultural information on many species and cultivars that can be widely incorporated into the garden.

One of my favorite personal pursuits is the encouragement of urban wildlife, in particular, birds and butterflies. Salvias are a major source of nectar for hummingbirds, and those with red blooms are the ideal lure with their long, tubular flowers. Many species of butterflies feed on salvia nectar and pollen, while birds such as goldfinches relish the nutritious seeds.

For years botanical gardens and arboreta have cultivated many of the salvias described in this book, but their introduction to the gardening public has been slow because of the lack of cultural information. Betsy has observed the successes and failures of these numerous plantings and has cultivated both common and rare salvias in her own wonderful garden in the Santa Cruz Mountains. A wealth of information will finally be available to all of us with the publication of this book.

Don Mahoney

# Introduction

Plants of innate beauty and bearing, salvias have been especially popular since the 1970s with those who garden for pleasure. Gardening has become a widespread avocation throughout the English speaking world and Europe, and those who have chosen to grow salvias have found them handsome and dependable plants that are, by and large, easy to grow. Rapid and reliable transportation now makes it possible for many species and selections of *Salvia* to be introduced to horticulture from the wild. Nursery stock also benefits from modern transportation because of the reduced chance of injury to plants. My hope is that this book will not only help gardeners in selecting from the impressive, sometimes overwhelming, array of salvias, but that it will stimulate and encourage the study of these plants.

The Roman scientist and historian Pliny the Elder was the first to use the Latin name *Salvia*. The name derives from *salvare*, to heal or save, and *salvus*, uninjured or whole, referring to the several species of *Salvia* with medicinal properties. Pliny's interest in plants was utilitarian, and his encyclopedic compilation, *Natural History*, included salvias in the vegetable kingdom. In his botanical writing he dealt almost exclusively with the agricultural and medical attributes of plants.

Information on the virtues of sages is also to be found in the old herbals of medieval and renaissance Europe, usually illustrated with woodcuts or engravings. Not only are medicinal recipes given, but charms and spells are described. The common name *sage* originated in England and is probably a corruption of the old French *sauge*. Sage refers specifically to *Salvia officinalis*, a plant widely used long ago as a "simple," or household remedy. This well-known herb was highly touted, and popular sayings such as the following were widespread in England and on the continent:

> Sage helps the nerves and by its powerful might
> Palsy is cured and fever put to flight.

The early herbals contain entries for many different species of *Salvia*, coming from far and wide. Their description and cultivation, as well as their medicinal and other uses, received careful attention through word and picture.

Salvias are members of the mint family, Lamiaceae, and comprise the largest genus in that family. The fragrant foliage of many salvias has been used for over twenty centuries to heal the minds and bodies of people of many different climates and cultures. Salvias may be described by growth habit as perennial, biennial, or annual herbs, or as evergreen or deciduous shrubs. Some species are scandent and appear to climb, but they lack organs such as tendrils for support. The genus is distributed throughout the temperate and sub-tropical regions of the world, occurring from sea level to elevations of 11,000 ft (3400 m) or more. The temperature ranges where they are found is equally great. Some habitats experience 0° F (−18° C) or lower, while others may have readings of over 100° F (38° C). One can only marvel at the complex and rich diversity of the genus and at humankind's discovery of the healing or soothing qualities of different species occurring in regions spread throughout the world.

How can a gardener be positive that a plant is a salvia? Is there a simple set of easily observed characters that will help assure a reliable decision? First, look for opposite leaves and square stems that with age sometimes become round. Next, observe an individual flower closely. The corolla, the colorful tube, can have a variety of shapes, as the botanical drawings throughout this book will illustrate, but it must have two lips of unequal length; the upper lip is variable in shape and the lower lip is usually spreading. The calyx must also be two-lipped. The upper lip can have two or three teeth or may be undivided. The lower lip is often two-toothed. There are always two fertile stamens and sometimes two infertile ones called staminodes. Usually four seeds are produced; they are frequently mucilaginous when dampened. Botanists use many technical characters in describing salvias or any other plant, but only a few specific characters will be referred to in the salvia portraits in this book.

Over 900 species of *Salvia* exist worldwide, with well over half occurring in the Americas but none in Australasia. Add to that number natural hybrids (from the wild and from gardens) and cultivated hybrids, and the total figure increases by several hundred or more. Selected cultivars also raise the total significantly. Because of the large number of species and their diverse native locations, botanists have been unable to treat them in a single work. Luckily, monographs and floras for a number of geographical areas do exist, representing many years of work by competent authorities. Regional floras give essential information as to identification, geographical location, and habitat, and quite a number are available, particularly for areas within the United States. Monographs give a wealth of information that is restricted to a genus within a specific location. An example is *A Revision of* Salvia *in Africa Including Madagascar and the Canary Islands* (1974) by Professor I. C. Hedge of the Royal Botanic Garden, Edinburgh. This imposing work not only describes 59 species, but Professor Hedge's introductory remarks are rich with information as to *Salvia* characters, geography, and groupings. Botanical drawings of many species are also included.

California has a rich history of botanists and botanical exploration. To name a few, LeRoy Abrams, Carl Epling, Willis Linn Jepson, and Philip A. Munz have participated in this tradition. Epling's definitive work (1938) on California salvias defines the geographical distribution and speciation of the genus. It is interesting to note that all of the 17 salvia species that occur in California, including both annuals and perennials, freely hybridize with one another. Epling clearly states this fact and places all California salvias in a section called Audibertia. Nearly 500 salvia species are native to Mexico and Central and South America. This vast group is placed in a section named Calosphace and, according to Epling, only two species within this large group suggest any connection with the section Audibertia. Gardeners know from first-hand experience the ability of certain species within the section Calosphace to freely produce hybrids.

A year after his work on California salvias, Epling's sweeping monograph (1939) followed, describing salvias from the geographical areas in the United States bordering Mexico, through Mexico and Central America, and throughout South America. Many other invaluable monographs, floras, and articles are set out in the bibliography.

Since the 17th century, the British, with their profound interest in natural history and deep desire to learn about the world, have explored the world. From these far ranging explorations have come field notes and drawings with priceless plant information and specific botanical information in the form of plants, seed, and herbarium specimens. Growing and distributing plants has also been of prime importance. The Royal Botanic Garden, Kew, and the Royal Horticultural Society's garden at Wisley have been and remain at the center of this activity, and the tradition of plant exploration continues today along with the conservation and distribution of plants. Great Britain has three national salvia collections today. (See *Where To See Salvias*.)

Both private and public gardens along the French and Italian Riviera have long exhibited an interest in the collection and cultivation of salvias. By the year 1889 over 60 species were being grown in that region. At present, Gabriel Alziar, the director of the Jardin Botanique in Nice, France, is carrying on this tradition by continuing his study and work on *Salvia*. The botanic garden contains an impressive number of salvias representing many geographical regions. Over a period of six years, beginning in 1988, Professor Alziar published a catalog of all recorded salvias indicating habit, flower color, distribution, bibliography, and, perhaps most important of all, synonymy.

Through his intensive study Professor Alziar puts the number of salvia species between 600 and 700. This is considerably fewer than the more frequently cited 900.

In France, quite near the Mediterranean, Marie-Thérèse and Yols Herve supervise the French National Collection at Pépinière de la Foux in Le Pradet. It was a great pleasure for me to be able to visit them in 1995 and to be introduced to many salvias new to my eyes. Because of the gentle climate, I was also able to see old favorites growing luxuriously with companion plants that, in my garden, require shade.

Gardening has been a thread pulled tight throughout my life, a steady interest that binds the pages that follow. I have made and tended five gardens; the first in Virginia, the second in Texas, the following three in California. In my second California garden the handsome evergreen foliage and striking flowers of a large number of distinctly different salvias led me to grow them. This garden was a country retreat, and frequently several weeks would pass between visits. Plants had to be sturdy and able to survive with irregular care and water. Many salvias, the majority from Mexico, flourished, but although they gave me pleasure, they were perplexing at the same time. Frequently, they had no name or else the ubiquitous "sp." (species undetermined) designation. Sometimes two dissimilar plants would have the same name—a confusing situation indeed. I sought accurate information from reliable sources, and nursery people and botanists who visited the garden gave invaluable information as to a plant's source and who had grown it. The next stage of my search involved visiting botanic gardens and arboreta to see salvias that had been collected in their native habitats and to gather data about those collections. This activity put me in touch with many professional people who showed great interest in salvias in general and who have given me enthusiastic support in this project over the years.

In selecting plants to be described in this book, I have chosen those that are, in my experience, both beautiful and interesting garden subjects. With practical cultural information each salvia described can be grown well and, with nurturing, will thrive for some time. Obviously, some salvias are not appropriate for specific gardens because of temperature range, light patterns, or soil conditions. The descriptions should allow the gardener to make choices based on his own specific garden conditions. A very few plants that are as difficult to grow as they are hard to find, such as *Salvia cedrosensis*, are included. These exceptional salvias are described for the benefit of collectors and to draw attention to the tremendous diversity of the genus.

I wish I were able to say that I have grown all the salvias that have horticultural merit, but that is far from being the case. Securing seed or cuttings of little known or rarely grown salvias is exceedingly difficult. Species that are frequently grown abroad may be unknown or unavailable in the United States. I continually seek and incorporate into the garden salvias that are new to me. For example, seed of salvias from China, Japan, and India is being sent to this country and England through botanical exploration, and the adventurous gardener will be able to look forward to new lists from the Far East from which to choose as nurseries grow and propagate these exciting newcomers.

Writing about the culture of salvias would not have been possible had I not had a large garden in which to grow, observe, and enjoy the plants. My home and garden, Jardin del Viento, are in the Santa Cruz Mountains of California, thirty miles south of San Francisco at an elevation of 2000 ft (600 m). The garden is on a due south facing slope with the Pacific Ocean twelve miles distant as the crow flies. Nothing protects the garden from the storms that come directly from the ocean, and gusty 50 mph winds are common. As the name implies, Jardin del Viento was dedicated to the winds in the hope of appeasing their winter violence. The soil is friable, a medium clay that is easily amended. Two fences, 4 ft (1.2 m) in height and 5 ft (1.5 m) apart, surround the garden to protect plants from deer predation. Jardin del Viento has good drainage, an adequate water supply, and excellent airflow. Temperatures rarely reach the low 20°s F (around −6° C) or high 90°s F (around 33° C). The garden is alive with the activity of numerous pollinators: several species of hummingbirds, butterflies, moths, bees, flies, ants, and bats gather pollen and nectar throughout the year. I have referred to the garden throughout the book and think of it not only as a place in which to find comfort and stimulation but as a much needed workroom where plants are observed by myself and others.

It has been my good fortune to be able to see many species of *Salvia* in their native habitat. To walk on the desert and watch *Salvia carduacea* standing 2.5 ft (80 cm) high among tall grasses, all waving in the wind, is to experience a heady delight. Hover moths and insects add to the activity of the scene while one enjoys the scents that are carried on the breeze. A completely different experience is to walk in the cloud forest habitat of *S. holwayi* in Chiapas, Mexico. When flowering, this salvia adds a subtle splash of deep rusty red to a sea of green. An understory plant, it covers the ground and shrubs as it weaves its innumerable stems, with trusses of flowers all about.

Within this book, the salvias I have selected are treated alphabetically. References are given to color drawings or photographs as appropriate. In dealing with each species I have given the name of the plant and have cited a synonym when a name change has caused confusion. Information about the meaning of the plant's scientific name and the plant's native habitat, including elevation ranges and temperature tolerance, are provided. A description of each salvia is given, along with appraisals of cultivars and hybrids. Simple and straightforward cultural practices that have proved successful are described, including pruning. Suggestions for companion plantings are given to help readers envision their own combination of well-liked plants that require similar culture. Of prime importance is the initial placement of the salvia in the garden, and the gardener's subsequent observation will help ensure its well being.

Few, if any, cardinal rules can be made as to the culture of all salvias. The need for soil with good drainage applies to the plants discussed in this book even though *Salvia uliginosa*, as its name implies, grows in wet and marshy places. I have found well-drained soil to be especially advantageous during the dark and cold months of winter. Water-logged clay soil spells disaster and a hasty demise by drowning or disease. Soil that drains rapidly prevents fungal problems and promotes the circulation of air around the root cavities, an essential condition for healthy plants. Friable soil is usually recommended for all species, and attention is drawn to those plants needing very sharp drainage and to lime or humus loving species.

Although not prone to disease, occasionally plants are struck by fungal attack, and wilt and die. I know of no remedy for this. It occurs so seldom it has never been a problem in my garden. However, good air circulation will help in general with the overall health of the garden. I believe the volatile leaf oils and other chemicals in salvias not only encourage good health but discourage predation by insects, butterflies, snails, slugs, birds, even deer. Dr. Arthur O. Tucker, of Delaware State University, has defined and continues to define and quantify the foliar essential oils found in salvias occurring in California. The components of the oils are numerous and differ in number and quantity from species to species. Work of this nature is being carried out on salvias from many floristic provinces throughout the world.

Propagation of annuals and of biennials and perennials that mature as quickly as annuals is by seed that is usually sown outdoors. I sow seed in pots in late spring after both day and night air temperatures have warmed. At all times seedlings must be protected from birds. Herbaceous and woody perennials and shrub species are sown from late spring through early summer, allowing ample time for the plant's root system to become established before frost. Cuttings are sometimes a faster means of establishing a new plant, and woody perennials and shrubs respond well to this method. I have used a greenhouse for propagation, but because of white fly and aphid attacks, I have found a shaded area in the garden where cuttings can be closely watched to be convenient and satisfactory.

Color is close to the heart of the gardener and, at the same time, very ephemeral. Seeing and describing color is as elusive as planting and tending the plant is tangible. The quality or strength of light on a given plant determines our perception of its colors as does the time of day or time of year. The texture of leaves and bark and the light they absorb and reflect also are elements. Architectural objects such as paths and walls modify color perception. Neighboring plants greatly affect impressions. Because of these numerous factors influencing color perception, I have used adjectives throughout the plant descriptions that are related to commonplace objects, such as butter-yellow and grassy green. In addition, I have included an appendix giving colors according to the Royal Horticultural Society's Colour Chart, Revised 1966. This chart is arranged by color groups with designated numbers and can be readily referred to if needed. A new edition of the chart, available from the United Kingdom, was released in 1995. The color groups and numbers are exactly the same as the 1966 edition. Even these helpful tools are far from perfect in describing color, a subjective concept given concrete terms.

I hope the reader will find the drawings (including the black and white line drawings, which are drawn to a scale of 1.5 of actual size), photographs, and text of this book stimulating and valuable. I, with my struggle for clarity, am the richer for attempting this project.

# Description
# of Plants

## *Salvia aethiopis* Linnaeus, Plate 1

Native to a large area of central and southern Europe and western Asia, *Salvia aethiopis* is described botanically as being either biennial or perennial. It has become widely naturalized, and in the United States is found particularly in California and Colorado. Roadside banks, rocky slopes, and disturbed fields provide good habitat for this salvia, which has been called tumbleweed. The specific epithet, *aethiopis*, is from the Greek and refers to the sage being from Ethiopia, although surprisingly the botanist Ian Hedge (1974) has found no specimens of the plant collected in a native habitat on the African continent.

A geometrically constructed plant, *Salvia aethiopis* has large, furry, pearl-gray leaves, sometimes 1 ft (30 cm) in length, arranged in a handsome rosette. The leaves are covered with hairs that give them a blanket-like appearance. They look whitish gray and their edges are scalloped, adding another interesting feature. Flowering occurs in early summer. At that time a 1–3 ft (30–90 cm) stem emerges carrying a large rounded candelabra-like inflorescence. Widely branched whorls of falcate-shaped white flowers with a pale yellow lip open more or less at the same time.

*Salvia aethiopis* is a hardy sage known to withstand temperatures to 0° F (−18° C). Propagation is by seed. The culture of *S. aethiopis* includes full sun, fast drainage, and additional water throughout dry periods. Flowering usually continues for two to three weeks, at which time pollination would normally occur and seed be produced. It has been my experience that if this is allowed to happen, the plant soon dies; fulfilling the designation *biennial*. However, if the inflorescence is removed before seed production, the plant will bloom again the next year. When the plant starts to look old and in need of rejuvenation, allow it to go to seed in order to start the process afresh with seedlings. You will probably find seedlings near the old plant in the spring. To be on the safe side, save some seed to be sown the following spring or summer.

In a mild climate, the foliage of *Salvia aethiopis* is handsome throughout the year, recommending it for space in the winter garden. With leaves arranged in symmetrical rosettes, this salvia may be enjoyed to great advantage when elevated to a rocky mound about 2 ft (60 cm) above ground level. If space can be provided, three plants, one at ground level, the second elevated above ground level, and the third wherever it might be tucked in, make an outstanding visual treat throughout the winter and spring. After the blooming period in early summer, the leaves appear tattered and worn and are replaced with new leaves later in the summer. In combination with these salvias, mat-forming plants such as thymes and veronicas cover bare ground without obstructing the view of the salvias' attractive basal leaves.

## *Salvia africana-lutea* Linnaeus, Plate 2

The coast of the Cape of Good Hope in South Africa is the native habitat of *Salvia africana-lutea*. There, within a limited area, it is found growing at close to sea level on coastal sand dunes, arid and rocky banks, and low hills. This plant was known as *Salvia aurea* until the 1990s.

*Salvia africana-lutea* is a shrubby, evergreen plant, with numerous woody stems growing out of the rootstock that reach 3 ft (1 m) or more in height and 3–4 ft (1–1.3 m) in width. Young plants are amply covered with small, gray-green elliptical leaves, but by maturity leaves have become sparse, giving the plant a twiggy appearance. Flowering begins in early spring, with flushes occurring periodically throughout the summer. Flowers appear in whorls and are held erect. The calyx is large, campanulate, and a dark rusty color on the side facing the light and olive-green on the opposite side. During fruiting the calyx persists and is an added attraction for a long time. The flowers, when first emerging from the calyx, are a bright, glowing yellow, but as they develop in size they turn a rusty orange. The first part of the specific epithet, *africana-lutea*, describes the plant's origin, and the second part describes the yellow color of the emerging flowers. The mature rusty orange flowers are 1 in (2.5 cm) or more in length, held within a showy, funnel-like, tan colored calyx that resembles paper with age. The flowers are both attractive and a curiosity. I. C. Hedge (1974) says the flowers at maturity give the impression of being withered. He describes them as golden brown or khaki colored, often with a trace of purple at their base.

Well-draining light soil and full sun are desirable for *Salvia africana-lutea*. Plants need deep watering at least once each month, and a mulch at their base is helpful. Some pruning should be done to keep the plant shapely, but with age, usually about five years or more, a build-up of wood is inevitable. At that point, I recommend a fresh start with a young plant. Propagation is accomplished easily by cuttings.

*Salvia africana-lutea* is generally accepted as hardy to approximately 20° F (−7° C). On one occasion in my garden, a specimen's top growth was completely killed when the temperature fell well below that, but, during the following summer, new growth emerged from the rootstock and within a few years the plant regained its pleasing shrubby habit.

*Salvia africana-lutea* is rarely seen in gardens or nurseries in my home state of California. It is not clear when it was introduced to horticulture, but William Robinson (1933) grew the plant and wrote about it. A famous English gardener and horticultural journalist, Robinson is regarded as the instigator of the herbaceous border, the wild garden, and the alpine rock garden. In his book *The English Flower Garden* he describes 39 salvias for the border.

Because of its foliage and growth habit, *Salvia africana-lutea* combines nicely with many different manzanitas. For example, *Arctostaphylos stanfordiana* subsp. *bakeri* 'Louis Edmunds' at 6 ft (2 m), *A. pajaroensis* at 4 ft (1.3 m), and A. 'Winterglow' at 2 ft (0.6 m) make outstanding companions in a shrubbery border. A dry border of flowering shrubs might include the 3 ft (1 m) tall *Cistus palhinhae*, with its golden centered white flowers, the 4 ft (1.3 m) tall *Eriogonum giganteum* (St. Catherine's lace), which has creamy white clusters of flowers that turn rust-red, and the 4 ft (1.3 m) tall *Phlomis fruticosa*, with its whorls of yellow flowers. All require the same growing conditions and blooming would continue from early spring until frost.

## *Salvia albimaculata* Hedge & Huber-Morath, Plates 3 & 87

The hardy perennial *Salvia albimaculata* was first described by botanists at the Royal Botanic Garden in Edinburgh in 1957, but the plant was not introduced to gardens until the late 1980s. It was then that Jim and Jenny Archibald of Wales, growers and seed collectors par excellence, made a collecting trip to Turkey and returned with seed of

*S. albimaculata* and of a great many other interesting plants. *S. albimaculata* is known to occur naturally in only one area and was found on a steep clay slope over limestone at 4000 ft (1200 m). The location is directly south of Konya in the Taurus Mountains, north of the island of Cyprus. The Archibalds made several trips to this collecting site—first to see the plants in bloom in order to identify them, and subsequently to collect seed.

Under 1 ft (30 cm) in height, *Salvia albimaculata* is about 10–12 in (25–30 cm) wide. Its small, trisected, greenish-gray leaves are under 1 in (2.5 cm) in length and impress one as being both unusual and handsome. They are evergreen—a pronounced gray-green during the cold months, appearing grayer in summer. Striking royal-purple flowers that measure about 1 in (2.5 cm) in length appear in whorls of two to five flowers. Each flower has a prominent white blotch on the lower lip. The epithet *albimaculata* means spotted with white. The white blotch has an outline similar to the royal-blue lower lip and is neatly banded by that color.

Flowering begins in early summer, with many charming inflorescences coming into bloom at the same time. Afterwards, sporadic bloom continues until frost. Because of its mountainous origin, I would expect *Salvia albimaculata* to be hardy to 10° F (−12° C), perhaps even lower. A herbaceous plant that is short and shrubby, this salvia does build wood at its base and tends to be short-lived. In my experience, cuttings must be started about every three or four years. This is the usual method of propagation because seed is rarely found. Flowers and foliage hold well in water and are attractive features in very small bouquets.

Preferring garden loam and good drainage, *Salvia albimaculata* is not a difficult plant to grow. When placed in full sun and given weekly water, its flowers may be enjoyed for an extended period and its foliage year round. A little lime scattered at its roots each spring is beneficial.

A sunny, exposed rock garden is the ideal setting for *Salvia albimaculata*. Its small size makes it a perfect filler among rocks and other plants such as *Dianthus deltoides*, which is a little over 1 ft (30 cm) tall when in flower, or the old and valued *D. gratianopolitanus* (cheddar pink), which is 8 in (20 cm) tall. The spreading *Diascia barberae* from South Africa, 1–1.5 ft (30–45 cm) tall with flowers the color of strawberry ice cream, is another good mixer. The light pink flowered hybrid *Saponaria* 'Max Frei', just under 1 ft (30 cm) in height, is another possible companion. All of these plants require the same culture.

### *Salvia apiana* Jepson, White sage, bee sage, Plate 4

A shrubby and coarsely branched plant, *Salvia apiana* grows 4–5 ft (1.3–1.5 m) tall and about 4 ft (1.3 m) across. Native to California, it occurs from Santa Barbara County south through Baja California, growing on dry, rocky hillsides in exposed conditions.

*Salvia apiana*

Growing at 5000 ft (1500 m) or lower in its native coastal scrub or chaparral habitat, it is not unusual for white sage to cover large areas. On a hot day, its fragrance is often evident long before the plant comes into view. Like lavender, a distant relative, *S. apiana*'s leaves contain aromatic oils and resins. Although some people find the odor of the leaf offensive when it is rubbed, most find the scent released by a hot, dry wind moving through a colony very pleasing and distinctive. Native Americans and others use the dried or fresh leaves for ceremonial purposes. A tea made from the leaves relieves colds or congestion and may also be used as a soapless shampoo. The specific epithet *apiana* pertains to bees and the attraction white sage has for them. Beekeepers have long been aware of this and have kept hives in these chaparral areas.

In spring, several to many flowering stalks 3–4 ft (1–1.3 m) rise above the plant's whitish foliage. Leaves are persistent and remain year round. The stalk is hollow and sometimes a pinkish color, adding interest to the white or pale lavender flowers. The handsome pink-stalked plant is the one to search for. White sage produces viable seed and it is not uncommon to see seedlings at the base of the plant. It is hardy to 20° F (−7° C) or less.

White sage hybridizes freely with other salvia species in the wild; plants at the Santa Barbara Botanic Garden and Rancho Santa Ana Botanic Garden clearly exhibit this tendency. *Salvia apiana* is known to cross with *S. leucophylla* and *S. clevelandii*. Some years ago, a hybrid occurred in the Rancho Santa Ana Botanic Garden that is smaller and more compact than *S. apiana*. The flowering stalk is 3 ft (1 m) high with an inflorescence of lavender-blue flowers in tight whorls similar to those of *S. clevelandii*. It was introduced in 1993 and named *Salvia* 'Vicki Romo' in honor of a young graduate student at Claremont Graduate School who had been in the Garden's doctoral program.

Indeed, *Salvia apiana*, with its tall and stiff habit and conspicuous silver foliage has proved to be a fine plant for sunny and dry areas of the garden and will grow in clay or lighter soil when given good drainage. Good air circulation is also important. When established, this drought tolerant salvia needs no summer water since it is summer dormant with winter growth. After it blooms, prune the tall and coarsely branched flowering stalks in order to encourage compactness.

Good companions are plants that occur naturally in the same habitat, such as the shrubby *Artemisia californica* and *Yucca whipplei*, which has sword-like leaves. This combination features three very different leaf shapes, textures, and shades of gray. A combination featuring flowers might include *Rosmarinus officinalis* 'Tuscan Blue' and *S. apiana* for the back of the border and drifts of *Penstemon heterophyllus* with its electric blue flowers and the rich rose flowered *P. barbatus* at the front. Two perennials that would complement *Salvia apiana* are the purple flowered *Penstemon spectabilis* and the low-growing, shell-pink *Sidalcea malviflora* 'Elsie Heugh'. Another drought tolerant perennial, *Centranthus ruber*, can be added to this combination. Its fluffy flower heads will add many shades of rich rose, pink, and white to the spring flowering picture. *Salvia apiana* is particularly beautiful in moonlight and so is outstanding in a night garden. The botanist, Carl Epling (1938) was referring to this attribute when he called the salvia a snowy shrub.

## *Salvia argentea* Linnaeus, Plate 5

The native habitat of the perennial *Salvia argentea* forms a band across southern Europe from Portugal to Bulgaria. It has no common name at present, but the Latin-based epithet *argentea*, meaning silvery, refers to the color of the leaves and describes the plant admirably.

Here is a plant to be grown and admired for its handsome foliage. Developing a large basal leaf structure that measures 3 ft (1 m) across and 1–2 ft (0.3–0.6 m) high, the leaves persist in all but the coldest climates. At maturity they measure 8–12 in (20–30 cm) in length and 6 in (15 cm) across. They seem woolly, being densely covered with silky hairs on both surfaces of the entire leaf. Do watch for snails and other pests that feast on foliage, because just a little damage would spoil the overall effect of the prominent leaves.

Blooming takes place in spring or summer. At that time, a 2–3 ft (0.6–1 m) tall candelabra of inconspicuous white flowers, tinged pink or yellow, rises above the foliage. The flowering stalk is dramatic during the time of its development. After reaching full bloom the stalk is best removed after a few days of enjoyable observation. This procedure will help lengthen the life of the plant by preventing seed production. Even though it is classified as a perennial, *Salvia argentea* will be short-lived if allowed to produce seed. Eventually, the plant must be allowed to produce a small quantity of seed because this is the quickest and easiest means of propagation. Start new plants every two to three years for continuity in the border. Sow seed in early spring for plants that will bloom the following year.

After flowering, the wonderful woolly leaves lose their silverness and remain pale gray-green throughout the summer. Later, with the return of cool weather, the silver-gray color returns and predominates until the next flowering season.

Full sun, sharp drainage, and friable soil are needed for the culture of this plant, as well as good air circulation. After it is established, a very small amount of lime may be worked around the plant, but fertilizer is not recommended. In my garden I have found this salvia to be drought tolerant with little water necessary in summer. It is a hardy species and will take temperatures of 10° F (−12° C) or less.

Plantswoman and garden writer Beth Chatto (1978) enthusiastically praises *Salvia argentea*, while allowing that it is short-lived. Her Essex garden in England is in an area known for its frosts, winds, and dry summers, yet it has survived there for many years in heavy, cold soil, reseeding itself in dry gravel.

*Salvia argentea* is a bold and strong plant for the front of the border, its leaves providing interest year round. It fits well into a dry bank of low growing rosemary combined with the native California *Eriogonum latifolium*, which has short, gray, evergreen foliage. Or it can be grouped with the taller *E. fasciculatum*, with whitish flowering heads that turn an attractive rusty brown in autumn. All require the same cultural conditions.

## *Salvia arizonica* Gray, Arizona sage, Plate 6

A creeping perennial, *Salvia arizonica* can be found growing in large patches in the shade of boulders or in open forests. Categorized as a groundcover, its native habitat is a fairly widespread area running throughout the rich and moist forests of southern Arizona and the Trans-Pecos mountain area of Texas. It is likely that *S. arizonica* also grows in the wild in New Mexico and northern Mexico, but these locations are not included in its established range at the time of publication. Its frequent occurrence at high elevations of 7000–9500 ft (2100–2900 m) suggests that the plant is very cold tolerant.

*Salvia arizonica*

The trailing stems of Arizona sage have small, deltoid or triangular leaves that are opposite one another and widely spaced. Because of the numerous stems produced from its running rootstock, the overall appearance is one of luxuriant foliage. The length of the stem when in bloom is usually less than 1 ft (30 cm). The leaves are mid-green and glabrous and have a pleasant minty scent when bruised or crushed. Small, indigo-blue flowers with a violet tinge occur in whorls in early summer. If these inflorescences are cut back, the reward is repeated flowerings—as many as three if the growing season is a long one. Water and fertilizer will stimulate reflowering. After deadheading, several applications of a balanced liquid fertilizer applied at half strength will encourage new growth. An interval of a week or 10 days between applications is sufficient.

Well-drained soil enriched with humus is ideal for *Salvia arizonica*. Humus may be applied as mulch each spring before active growth starts. Water is needed every week to 10 days during hot weather.

Arizona sage is easily grown from seed or by division of the creeping rootstocks. Cutting all stems to the ground before applying humus in early spring will ensure fresh foliage for the coming season. This plant deserves wider attention from gardeners. Thriving in the shade of tall herbaceous plants or shrubs such as holly, osmanthus, or viburnum, its graceful green foliage also looks lovely spilling over rocks or walls. *Salvia arizonica* is a graceful and undemanding plant for lightly shaded and woodland gardens.

## *Salvia austriaca* Jacquin, Austrian sage, Plate 7

High and cold altitudes across eastern Europe to Russia provide the native habitat of the hardy herbaceous perennial *Salvia austriaca*. It was described in 1776 by Nicholas Joseph de Jacquin, Professor of Botany at Leyden, The Netherlands. It is not known how long the plant has been in cultivation. The specific epithet, *austriaca*, tells us the origin of the plant and at the same time suggests a convenient common name, Austrian sage.

*Salvia austriaca* develops a basal rosette of leaves that measures 3 ft (1 m) in width. If brushed the leaves release a somewhat fetid odor. Mid-green in color, the individual leaves measure about 1 ft (30 cm) or more in length. The midrib and veins appear indented and give texture to the surface. In a mild climate it is a late spring blooming plant with a repeat bloom in late summer. In colder areas, flowering is in summer. Its flowering stalk will eventually rise 2 ft (60 cm) or more above its foliage. Very pale yellow flowers in whorls of six or more comprise an inflorescence that measures 8–10 in (20–25 cm). These erect and slender blooming stems offer a subtle touch to the flowering border. I have read that the calyx is sometimes violet tinged. Unfortunately, my plants have never exhibited this color. The calyx is small, about 0.25 in (0.6 cm) in width, covered with hairs, and light green in color.

Easy to situate in a garden, Austrian sage needs sun for at least half the day and well-draining soil that has been amended with humus. Weekly watering is required and a light application of all-purpose fertilizer in early spring is beneficial. Seed and, consequently, seedlings occur after the plant is well established. Propagation is by seed or division of the basal rootstock. This delicate looking salvia is long lasting as a cut flower. Austrian sage is hardy to 0° F (−18° C).

Many perennials would make outstanding combinations with Austrian sage in either a spring or early autumn blooming border. For spring blooming at the front of a border, plant mats of *Achillea* 'King Edward', which has flowers of almost the same color as Austrian sage and fern-like gray foliage. For autumn bloom, plant patches of trailing California fuchsia, *Epilobium canum* subsp. *canum* (known previously as *Zauschneria*). California fuchsia's green foliage and red-orange flowers will add sparkle and surprise to the composition. Even though drought tolerant, it will take the extra water that the other plants require. Another combination includes drifts of the garden hybrid *Aster* × *frikartii*, since the aster's clear, violet-blue flowers and yellow-orange discs make fine 2 ft (60 cm) tall companions. 'Monch' and 'Wonder of Staffa' are long blooming cultivars of the aster.

## *Salvia azurea* var. *grandiflora* Bentham, Prairie sage

Described by the botanist George Bentham in 1848, *Salvia azurea* var. *grandiflora* has been popular for a century or more and is the kind of plant that has been frequently handed from gardener to gardener because of its beguiling, almost true blue flowers and ease of propagation. Though there are many old alternatives, I find prairie sage an appropriate common name because it describes the plant's native habitat. Found from Nebraska to Colorado and from Texas to Kentucky, it has become naturalized in the southeast. One of several attributes is its ability to adapt to many climates and edaphic circumstances. Prairie sage is hardy to 10° F (−12° C).

A herbaceous perennial, *Salvia azurea* var. *grandiflora* is an extremely lax plant that is greatly admired for its cerulean blue flowers. Epling (1939) found that in the wild it has several distinct forms. The form commonly distributed by nurseries has linear to lanceolate leaves that are covered with downy hairs, giving them a dusky green appearance. From the base of the plant many stems are produced, some reaching 3 ft (1 m) or more in length. September and October are the usual months for prodigious panicles of wonderful blue flowers to appear. On each inflorescence, many flowers bloom simultaneously. It is the large lower lip of each flower, often 0.5 in (1.3 cm) wide, that creates a pool of color. Propagation is by seed, cuttings, or division of the rootstock. Stems of these salvias make good cut flowers if they are first conditioned by cutting under water.

In 1994 an undesignated selection was distributed by Suncrest Nurseries, Inc., Watsonville, California. Blooming earlier than the typical prairie sage, this selection's erect habit is noteworthy. Its stems are about 2 ft (60 cm) in length and completely upright. Yellow-green leaves are lanceolate in shape and its flowers are pale blue with a whitish splotch on the large lower lip. The plant blooms as early as July and is completely deciduous in winter.

Full sun and friable garden soil are the two necessary cultural requirements for *Salvia azurea* var. *grandiflora*. Because of its sprawling growth habit, an inventive gardener I know grows it next to a wire fence in order to tie it and force its growth upward. I have placed it next to shrubs that provide support and assure an erect plant. Another friend experimented and found that keeping the plant dryer than normal helped in keeping the subsequently shorter stems more erect. In the wild the roots of this plant descend to great depths seeking moisture during periods of drought, but I am told that flowering depends on regular rainfall.

If you have a fence in a sunny location, the fragrant musk rose 'Buff Beauty' could be trained to a space about 5–6 ft (1.5–2 m) in width and about the same in height. The new foliage of the rose is a rich coppery color that later turns green, complementing its rich, chamois-yellow flowers, which bloom repeatedly. Plant prairie sage on both sides of the rose and weave the sage's long stems among its branches. Throughout the summer the rose will give pleasure and in the autumn, in combination with the prairie sage, will provide an intensely colorful display.

### *Salvia blepharophylla* Brandegee, Eyelash leaved sage, Plates 8 & 9

Even though *Salvia blepharophylla* was introduced into cultivation around 1930, it is little known or seen in gardens. In the wild it is found in the Mexican provinces of San Luis Potosi and Tamaulipas, and quite possibly in other locations. The specific epithet, *blepharophylla*, comes from Greek and literally means with leaves fringed like eyelashes. Though it is possible to see a row of tiny hairs on the edge of the leaf with the naked eye, a magnifying glass reveals much better why the plant has the common name eyelash leaved sage.

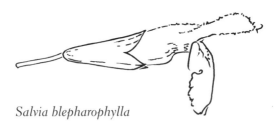

*Salvia blepharophylla*

Under the right conditions, this stoloniferous plant spreads rapidly. Categorized as a creeping procumbent perennial, *Salvia blepharophylla* is practically evergreen in protected places in areas where temperatures seldom go below 20° F (−7° C). When winter temperatures in my garden have dipped below 20° F (−7° C), this plant has managed to come back from its rootstock. The leaves of the clone that grows in my garden are more or less ovate in shape and a rich and glossy grassy green, making the plant attractive enough to be grown for the foliage alone. However, in the wild the shape and texture of the leaves and the hairs on its surface can show variation. From early summer until frost,

S. *blepharophylla* is very seldom seen without 1 in (2.5 cm) long flowers of vibrant signal-red with an orange undertone. The flowers, in loose whorls, are spaced about 1 in (2.5 cm) apart on an inflorescence that elongates to 1 ft (30 cm) or more. The balance between the glossy foliage and the richly colored flowering spike is strikingly beautiful. The height of the plant in full bloom is about 1.5 ft (45 cm) or more. Eventually, it will spread into a patch. Graham Stuart Thomas (1990a) calls the roots "fleshy and questing." Propagation is by division, cuttings, and seed.

Positioned in part shade and in good garden soil enriched with humus, eyelash leaved sage flourishes. Fast-draining soil is necessary, along with weekly watering. Occasional removal of spent flowering stalks removes excess weight from the plant and encourages upright growth and repeat bloom.

In 1992, Yucca Do Nursery in Texas introduced a form of *Salvia blepharophylla* collected in Tamaulipas, Mexico, at 5000 ft (1500 m). Called 'Sweet Numbers', it resembles the plant described above except the hairs on the edge of the leaf can easily be seen without a magnifying glass and the spreading lower lip of each flower is larger (plate 9). The cultivar name honors the remote village Dulces Nombres, in the northern corner of Tamaulipas where this cultivar was found.

Eyelash leaved sage makes a fine companion for plants that have apricot colored flowers. For example, it can be planted as groundcover at the base of roses. The climbing noisette 'Crepuscule', the shrub musk 'Francesca', or the modern upright shrub rose 'Charles Austin' are all enhanced by the salvia's foliage and showy flowers, and the roses, in turn, would protect the salvias with shade.

## *Salvia brandegei* Munz, Plate 10

An evergreen shrub, 3–4 ft (1–1.3 m) or more in height and width in its native habitat, *Salvia brandegei* will rapidly develop into a handsome garden subject. For many years it was thought to occur naturally only on Santa Rosa, one of the islands of the Santa Barbara Channel. However, during the 1960s and 1970s, six large colonies were found in Baja California. In one particular area above Punta Cabras is a hillside overlooking the Pacific Ocean where the vegetation is low and appears level and even. There, *S. brandegei* is one of the main components of the 3 ft (1 m) high coastal sage scrub community. Other plants include *Rhus integrifolia, Artemisia californica, Aesculus parryi,* and *Encelia californica.* The soil is rich brown in color, sandy, and full of disintegrating shells. Wind keeps the plants bushy and low and fog helps with moisture as the rainfall there is both sparse and seasonal. On Santa Rosa Island, *Salvia brandegei* apparently occurs in a typical coastal sage formation with *Artemisia californica.* On the mainland, the typical sage formation is dominated by *Salvia mellifera* and *S. munzii.*

In the garden, *Salvia brandegei* will reach 4–5 ft (1.3–1.5 m) in height and 5–7 ft (1.5–2.3 m) in width. Its dark green leaves are linear, the longest measuring about 3–4 in (7–10 cm) in length and barely 0.5 in (1.3 cm) in width. They are particularly beautiful because of the rough and varnished texture of the surface and the scalloping along the edge of the entire leaf. The underside appears felt-like, with white hairs. When flowering takes place in early spring, the leaves cover the plant fully, but during the hot summer the shrub looks more open and sparsely clothed. The flowers are pale lavender and about 0.5 in (1.3 cm) in length, held in widely-spaced, tight whorls. In spite of their small size, the flowers are showy since the two lips are opened wide. The calyces are violet-gray and very ornamental. The flowering stems hold well and make nice cut flowers. The foliage also lasts well in arrangements.

This is a shrub for exposed and sunny areas. Evidently deer never browse on it. Good drainage is a necessity and after the plant is established no additional water is needed. If it is watered, this drought tolerant shrub will produce excessive branches and foliage. A good time to remove a few branches to keep the shrub shapely is when it blooms in the spring. It is hardy to 20° F (−7° C) or less for short periods. Propagation is by seed or cuttings.

In a dry Mediterranean garden, *Salvia brandegei* would complement the gray foliage of lavender, stachys, and artemisia. All require the same bright exposure and other cultural conditions. Another combination consists of three California sages with different foliage, *S. brandegei, S. apiana,* and *S. spathacea.* The dark green foliage of *S. brandegei* makes a strong contrast interspersed with *S. apiana*'s gray foliage. Both reach about the same height. At their base, *S. spathacea* can be used as a groundcover. All have evergreen leaves, and the magenta to rose flowering spikes of *S. spathacea* are enhanced by the foliage of the other two sages.

## *Salvia buchananii* Hedge, Buchanan's sage, Plate 11

*Salvia buchananii* is not known in the wild but is probably of Mexican origin. Seed from a garden plant in Mexico City was taken to Britain and grown in a greenhouse by Sir Charles Buchanan. He also grew it in his Leicestershire garden during the summer. From this source, Professor Ian Hedge of the Royal Botanic Garden in Edinburgh was able to describe the plant in 1963 and name it in Buchanan's honor.

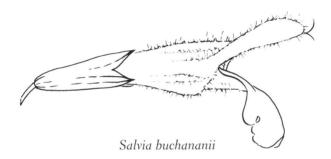

*Salvia buchananii*

Occasionally called Buchanan's fuchsia sage, this herbaceous perennial grows 1–2 ft (30–60 cm) in height and 1 ft (30 cm) or more across. Glossy, rich green foliage is widely spaced along the stem, with young leaves emerging from the leaf axils. The ovate-lanceolate leaves vary in size; the larger ones are about 2 in (5 cm) in length and 0.75 in (2 cm) wide. In a mild climate, plants will produce a few flowers year round with heavy blooming occurring in summer and autumn. Rather hairy, rich magenta flowers about 2 in (5 cm) long adorn the plant. Arranged in verticels of three to six flowers, only one or two come into bloom at a given time. Many lax stems arise from the base of the salvia. Propagation is by cuttings. Even though I have grown this plant for many years it has never set seed. I suspect a specific pollinator is needed.

Although suited for only the mildest climates, on occasion *Salvia buchananii* has overwintered in my garden. Because it strikes roots rapidly from cuttings it is easily housed indoors as a precaution against light frost.

Some protective shade, good sandy loam, and a mulch of compost are needed along with deep watering every week. During hot spells more water will be required. Remove spent inflorescences and pinch back lax growth in order to encourage more flowers and a shapely plant.

This salvia is eminently well suited to container culture. It performs well in the garden too, when given the safeguard of other plants. Stiff and upright-growing perennials such as *Penstemon* 'Hidcote Pink', 'Apple Blossom', or the dark purple flowered 'Midnight' would encourage upward growth and also give protection from the sun. In a south-facing border, I have three of these salvias planted on the north side of the 8 ft (2.5 m) tall evergreen *Arbutus unedo* 'Compacta'. On either side of the salvias is *Helichrysum splendidum*, the marvelous, gray foliaged, shrub-like perennial from South Africa. It was a pleasant discovery to find that these gray leaves are an excellent contrast to the glossy green ones of *Salvia buchananii*. These two appealing plants make a wonderful feature in any garden.

## *Salvia cacaliaefolia* Bentham, Plate 12

In moist or dry mountains in the province of Chiapas, Mexico, and in several similar locations in Guatemala and Honduras, colonies of *Salvia cacaliaefolia* can be found frequently. Growing at elevations of 5000–8000 ft (1500–2500 m), this perennial herb prefers the high shade and protection of pine or oak forests. The specific epithet, *cacaliaefolia*, means with foliage like *Cacalia*, a *Senecio*-like genus.

*Salvia cacaliaefolia*

Recognized as a fine garden plant by William Robinson (1933), it has been favored in British gardens for many years. Since the late 1980s, it has been found on many nursery lists and catalogs in Britain, France, and the United States. It is most likely that Strybing Arboretum and Huntington Botanical Gardens are responsible for its introduction in the 1970s to California growers and gardeners.

Coming into bloom in mid-summer, *Salvia cacaliaefolia* makes racemes of delightful gentian-blue flowers until late autumn. Gardens located in mild climates are favored with flowering for eight to 10 months. The flowers are short, about 0.5 in (1.3 cm) in length, but plentiful—many reaching full bloom at the same time. The green calyx is tiny and about the same color as the leaves. Deltoid leaves, shaped like an arrowhead, cover this herbaceous perennial amply. Rich grass-green in color, they are covered with gland-tipped hairs. Many stems arise from the creeping, fleshy rootstock, which soon grows into a patch of plants. These roots with stems can be readily divided, assuring easy propagation. In September or October, seed has been found by watchful gardeners. *S. cacaliaefolia* has proved to be hardy to 20° F (−7° C) if its crown is protected. It can be tried in a colder zone using conifer boughs as a safeguard. Robinson apparently grew it outdoors.

A border with some high shade, good drainage, and friable soil will help this salvia flourish. Weekly water is necessary, along with the removal of spent inflorescences. After danger of a late frost is over, cut the stems almost to the ground in order to have a shapely patch of plants. A dressing of compost in mid-spring assures an easy root-run. Fertilizer does not seem to be necessary, but occasionally the leaves of my plants turn slightly yellow, indicating an iron deficiency. This can be treated with applications of chelated iron.

This is a plant that would add summer and autumn color to a collection of spring blooming viburnums or rhododendrons, whose green foliage would make a fine background for the salvia's gentian-blue flowers. All prefer high shade, soil with humus, and regular water. Quite by chance, I planted a group in front of the deciduous *Viburnum opulus* 'Aureum'. The viburnum's bright yellow leaves make a handsome contrast to the salvia's rich blue flowers. The 3–4 ft (1–1.3 m) tall evergreen *Lonicera nitida* 'Baggesen's Gold', with its yellow summer leaves that turn yellow-green in winter, also makes a highly effective companion.

## *Salvia canariensis* Linnaeus, Canary Island sage, Plate 13

From the Canary Islands, with their mild and dry climate, comes
*Salvia canariensis*. It is an erect and ample shrub with foliage that not
only persists but looks attractive throughout the winter months in benign
climates. Brief periods of temperatures falling to 15° F (−10° C) will kill
it to the ground, but it will generally come back from its rootstock the
following spring. Even though it seeds itself readily in the garden, it has
not become naturalized in temperate California due to its need for
summer water.

Canary Island sage will reach 6–7 ft (2 m) in height and 5 ft (1.5 m)
across in a growing season. It can be held to a smaller size by infrequent
watering. Its stems are densely covered with long white hairs and the triangular, hastate leaves are a pale green with numerous long white hairs
on the underside. The tips of the hairs have aromatic oil glands.
Blooming begins in summer and continues until the days are noticeably
shorter and cool. Fine panicles of purplish violet flowers with purple-red
tipped calyces adorn the shrub throughout this lengthy period. In its
native habitat, plants show variation in the color of these panicles. They
range from a pale purple to a strong and deep purplish magenta. When
conditioned by cutting stems under water, they make long lasting and
good-looking cut flowers that are prized by flower arrangers. Conditioned
branches of foliage are also useful to arrangers.

Before the new season of growth begins, usually in late February, it
is necessary to cut the main stems to 1 ft (30 cm) or less above the
ground. This will encourage a more shapely shrub during the long growing season to come. Full sun, good drainage, and water every two to three
weeks will promote moderate growth. Humid or damp air can cause
fungal problems and good air circulation is vital. Propagation is by seed,
or by cuttings taken from spring through autumn. Seedlings are usually
found at the base of the mature plant. They are large and easy to remove
or pot up for a friend.

A large shrub rose, such as the deep red-violet flowering *Rosa* 'Mons.
Tillier' or the pale pink, almost single flowered 'Sparrieshoop', would
make impressive companions. Because of its size, *Salvia canariensis* can
be positioned in a hot and dry sunny border to give shade and protection

to smaller herbaceous or shrubby plants. Planted outside my fenced garden, it remains untouched by a large deer population and also gives cover to many species of birds and small animals.

### *Salvia carduacea* Bentham, Thistle sage, Plates 14 & 88

The best word for *Salvia carduacea* is spectacular, whether it is being seen for the first or the hundredth time. A California native, this annual has a distribution from Contra Costa County south through the central valley and coast ranges and on through the southern deserts into northern Baja. Growing in sun-swept places that are sandy and gravelly, thistle sage is found at elevations below 4500 ft (1400 m). Native grasses along with annual wild flowers are its usual companions.

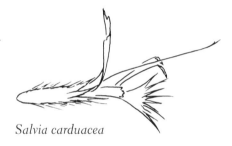

*Salvia carduacea*

Thistle sage responds dramatically to its environment. With rain and other moisture, plants can reach 3 ft (1 m) in height. In an arid setting plants are dwarfed and may only be 6 in (15 cm) tall. Spring blooming, the whole plant is woolly white with basal leaves that resemble a thistle's, being toothed and long-spined. The flowers appear in whorls held in congested calyces that are woolly and spiny. Flower color varies little and is usually a lively lavender electrified by bright orange anthers. Epling (1939) is almost lyrical in his description, calling the flower exquisite in color and form, with pungent foliage similar to *Citronella* (it resembles *Salvia greatae*, another California native, in that regard). He concludes by saying thistle sage flowers soon after the winter rains and, along with that group of plants known as "winter annuals," soon disappears.

Thistle sage can successfully be brought into the garden. On many occasions I have sown seed directly into beds but seldom has germination been achieved. Only once have I had good luck, when self-sown seedlings appeared in the garden in the spring of 1982. A surer method is to sow seeds in a container in a greenhouse then to transplant seedlings into individual containers before eventually moving them into the garden. By following these steps, the transplanted seedlings adjust rapidly.

Full sun and well-drained, gritty soil are practically the only requirements of thistle sage. It is necessary to water plants until they become established, after that, watering increases the size of the plants. In the desert large hover moths help with pollination. These moths are as large as small hummingbirds and their activity is similar. In a garden setting, hummingbirds probably help with pollination, as do butterflies and moths.

A rocky, dry hillside is well suited for the drought tolerant thistle sage. It looks natural if grown in front of black sage, *Salvia mellifera*. The dusky green foliage of black sage is a perfect foil for the almost completely white thistle sage. A combination that occurs in the wild is thistle sage and *Stipa speciosa*, *S. pulchra*, or *S. cernua*. These grasses are California natives and prefer the same dry and sunny culture. *Yucca whipplei* is another native companion whose stiff and pointed leaves would add stature to the composition. The 2 ft (60 cm) tall Mexican native *Beschorneria yuccoides*, with its rosettes of soft and flexible apple-green leaves, is another easy candidate for companion planting.

## *Salvia cedrosensis* Greene, Plate 15

*Salvia cedrosensis* is an evergreen, fruticose plant. Its native habitat is restricted to the Vizcaino Peninsula, situated midway along the western coast of Baja, and the nearby Cedros Island. It occurs in small canyons and dry river beds that have rocky and gravelly soil. *Encelia californica*, *Hyptis emoryi*, *Solanum hindsianum*, and *Cercidium microphyllum* are sometimes present in small numbers and give protection to the salvias. The canyon walls in these washes also shade and protect the salvias. These natural habitats are close to sea level and most years experience summer fog, but winter rains are erratic and variable. Measurable rainfall can be less than 0.5 in (1.3 cm) in a year, or deluges can occur, drenching the area repeatedly.

A charming, herb-like plant, in cultivation *Salvia cedrosensis* usually reaches 1 ft (30 cm) in height and width, but in the wild it can be twice that size. Small, felted leaves less than 1 in (2.5 cm) long are almost white in appearance when first emerging. At maturity they are pearly gray and reflect the sun's rays, as do the stems and calyces. All parts of the plant except the spreading lower lip of the corolla are covered with fine hairs. The flowers are a lively violet-blue, but in bright sunlight call little attention to themselves. The calyx is pearl gray with a light dusting of violet around the pointed edges. The two verticils hold three to six flowers each with only one or two flowers on the entire inflorescence coming into bloom simultaneously. In my garden there is a long period of meager but alluring bloom throughout the summer, with a few flowers occurring in autumn. Over time, *S. cedrosensis* builds wood at its base.

*Salvia cedrosensis* looks as though it is a rather delicate plant, but in reality it is able to withstand flaming sunlight and searing temperatures as well as battering rains and wind. It thrives in full sun when planted in gritty soil on the south side of a rocky mound. The rocks give off reflected heat and supply some small protection from winds. Water the plant regularly until well established, after which only occasional water is necessary. I have not grown the plant long enough to determine its hardiness, but it has survived temperatures in the low 30°s F (around −1° C). Propagation is by seed or cuttings.

A plant that is rarely seen or grown, *Salvia cedrosensis* is proving to be a reliable rock garden specimen and I am hopeful that it will start to enjoy a reputation that will ensure its distribution among gardeners. Look for specimens at Strybing Arboretum, Rancho Santa Ana Botanic Garden, and the University of California Botanical Garden, Berkeley.

**Salvia chamaedryoides** Cavanilles, Germander sage,
Plates 16 & 57

From high and somewhat dry altitudes comes *Salvia chamaedryoides*, an evergreen perennial from Mexico. It occurs at 7000–9000 ft (2100–2800 m), primarily in desert-like habitats throughout the Sierra

Madre Oriental. The specific name, *chamaedryoides*, literally means dwarf-like, and refers to the plant's habit. In a garden situation, germander sage appears dwarf-like only in its winter dormancy. The common name, germander sage, refers to the common name of *Teucrium chamaedrys*, wall germander. The plants share the character of running rootstock.

*Salvia chamaedryoides*

With many ascending stems, germander sage reaches 2 ft (60 cm) in height when in bloom and spreads freely from an underground rootstock. The small, gray, evergreen foliage gives year-round pleasure. Small, almost true-blue flowers appear sporadically during warm spells throughout the growing season, with full bloom occurring in early summer and again in autumn when nights are cool. The plant is hardy to approximately 10° F (−12° C). Propagation is by seed, cuttings, and division. Division is easily accomplished, particularly in early autumn, because of the plant's running rootstock.

Full sun and loamy, quick-draining soil are prerequisites for growing *Salvia chamaedryoides*. Prune all spent inflorescences two or three times during the growing season in order for the plant to produce more flowers. No fertilizer is needed. This is a drought tolerant plant, but after pruning the inflorescences you may help induce further flowering by watering once every week or two.

In the 1980s growers from the United States discovered a whole array of plants in neighboring Mexico that make fascinating additions to our gardens. At about that time, *Salvia chamaedryoides* was introduced to horticulture in the United States, though it had been known and grown in European horticulture since the early 1800s.

Two English gardeners, Harold and Joan Bawden (1970), wrote of their enjoyment in growing the lucid blue flowered germander sage. This would not seem to be a plant for long damp English winters, but clearly the Bawdens were delighted with it.

A compact selection called 'Desert Green', with silver-green foliage, was introduced in 1990 by nurseryman Pat McNeal of Austin, Texas. Similar to the species in growth, habit, and cultural requirements, *Salvia chamaedryoides* 'Desert Green' has soft colored, apple-green leaves of a different texture and color than the typical species. Blooming best in spring and autumn when the weather is cool, this selection is noteworthy for its uncommon and attractive foliage. In gardens along the French Riviera the apple-green leaved form of *S. chamaedryoides* is frequently seen, whereas in the United States the gray leaved form is more commonly planted.

Sparkling and versatile, *Salvia chamaedryoides* has no attraction for browsing deer, and is extremely attractive planted in groups with gray-green ballotas and deep green rosemary plants. Another combination for a sunny site is the gray foliaged germander sage and the 1 ft (30 cm) tall *Artemisia schmidtiana* 'Silver Mound', which forms a many stemmed, compact mound each year. The gray to light green foliaged creeping perennial *Silene maritima*, with large white flowers, ties the gray foliaged combination together. All three plants require the same culture.

## *Salvia chamelaeagnea* Bergius, Plate 17

From the Cape of Good Hope in South Africa comes *Salvia chamelaeagnea*, a heavily flowering, shrubby sage. Its distribution is apparently limited to the western side of the Cape and the species exhibits little variation. It is commonly found in sandy soil in open fields and stream beds and on roadsides, and appears to be adaptable to many situations.

After several years in the garden, *Salvia chamelaeagnea* will build slowly to about 4 ft (1.3 m). Given time and attention, it will attain 5–6 ft (1.5–2 m) in height and 4 ft (1.3 m) or more in width. Its habit is to send many stems from the rootstock. These may be divided from the plant with care. Propagation is also by seed and cuttings.

Mid-summer is the usual time for this freely flowering salvia to start blooming. Clusters of lightly colored violet-blue flowers develop throughout summer into autumn. The inflorescences are crowded because of much branching at the top of each stem. This characteristic gives the plant an untidy look when the numerous calyces turn brown while holding the maturing seed. The flowers are falcate (shaped like a scythe) and the hood is a light violet-blue. The lower lip is paler and the throat is white. Overall, the flower is about 0.75 in (2 cm) in length. The leaves are small, more or less the same length as the flower. Egg-shaped, they are mid-green and give substance to the plant. When brushed they release a light, not unpleasant, medicinal odor.

Cultural conditions include full sun, good drainage, soil prepared with grit and humus, and weekly water in summer. My experience with the plant's hardiness is limited, but it regularly withstands temperatures of 25° F (−4° C) in my garden. I advise taking cuttings for the greenhouse in late August to be on the safe side. Shaping the plant in late winter will help control new growth. In fact, during the entire growing season it is advisable to remove growth when the plant begins to look scruffy.

Described in 1767, *Salvia chamelaeagnea* was given a Latin name that literally means dwarf olive, though it is used to mean shrublike. No reference exists to show that it has ever been introduced to horticulture in South Africa, Britain, or the United States, but it has been introduced and distributed by the nursery that holds the National Collection of Salvias in France, Pépinière de la Foux. In addition, in the spring of 1991, Western Hills Nursery in Occidental, California, a source for many unusual plants, distributed *S. chamelaeagnea*, and the salvia may now be found on several seed and nursery lists.

The worthwhile *Salvia chamelaeagnea* is adaptable to many different cultural situations, an outstanding characteristic. In a herbaceous border it would give height, and its handsome dark green foliage would anchor flowering perennials such as penstemons, yarrows, feverfew, asters, veronicas, geraniums, and saponarias. In a bed with annuals it would serve the same function very well indeed. Practicing gardeners are constantly on the lookout for a plant of medium size that has substantial green leaves to be the mainstay of a border of flowering plants, and this is a prime candidate. Because of its size and desirable leaf color, it will enhance innumerable spots in the garden.

## *Salvia chiapensis* Fernald, Chiapas sage, Plate 18

To the best of my knowledge, *Salvia chiapensis* has only been collected in the wild near San Cristobal, in the province of Chiapas, Mexico. There it grows at elevations of 7000–9500 ft (2100–2900 m) in moist habitats called cloud forests. On a study and collecting trip in 1981, a group from the University of California Botanical Garden, Berkeley, visited this area and returned with seeds and cuttings for the Mesoamerican section of the Garden. Chiapas sage was probably introduced to horticulture from the Berkeley Botanical Garden sometime after that trip.

A tender, herbaceous perennial, Chiapas sage grows about 1.5–2 ft (45–60 cm) in height and the same in width. Several stems rise out of the plant's rootstock. Ivy green, glossy and deeply veined leaves are widely spaced along the stems. The largest measures about 3 in (8 cm) in length and 1.5 in (4 cm) in width, giving the plant a lightly clothed look. They are elliptic in shape (broadest at the middle, the ends rather equal) and appear sleek and hairless on both surfaces. The calyx is pea-green and 0.5 in (1.3 cm) long. Three to six flowers in whorls are widely spaced along the inflorescence. They are a bright fuchsia color, about 0.75 in (2 cm) in length, and covered with hairs. This is an attractive, upright, and airy looking salvia.

Only in frost-free zones can *Salvia chiapensis* survive in the ground year round. Because it cannot tolerate low temperatures, it should be kept in a container in order to overwinter indoors, or cuttings should be taken to ensure plants for the coming spring. Preferring good sandy loam with fast drainage and dressings of rich compost, it needs frequent deep watering, including moisture on its leaves to imitate its cloud forest habitat. Half-strength solutions of a liquid fertilizer are helpful and may be applied occasionally throughout the growing season.

Blooming commences in the summer, and if the salvia is brought into a light-filled greenhouse in the autumn, flowering will continue throughout the winter. It is a tireless bloomer. Before it is moved into the garden in late spring, cut the foliage back hard to encourage a rest period before fresh growth begins. Propagation is easily accomplished by cuttings and seed. Seedlings frequently appear in gardens that have no frost. It has generously seeded itself in the Mesoamerican section of the Botanical Garden in Berkeley.

Chiapas sage makes an attractive hanging basket, though it requires generous amounts of water. I frequently plant it in a two-gallon, black plastic nursery container and sink it in a bed in the garden. At a moment's notice, it can be retrieved and made safe in the greenhouse. It is very handsome in a large container surrounded by the 6 in (15 cm) tall *Geranium dalmaticum*, which has dainty pink flowers that rise just over its foliage, or with the 2 in (5 cm) tall *Campanula rotundifolia*, which sends up delightful 6 in (15 cm) stems of violet bellflowers in summer and autumn. For the salvia connoisseur, the blue flowered *Salvia sinaloensis*, with its graceful, plum-purple stems, makes a fine companion.

## *Salvia clevelandii* (Gray) Greene, Blue sage, Plates 19 & 20

A handsome, rounded shrub, *Salvia clevelandii* is known and enjoyed for its fragrant foliage, which is reminiscent of rose potpourri, and its sparkling, violet-blue flowers. Native to dry chaparral and coastal sage scrub plant communities, it is found below 3000 ft (900 m) in southern California and northern Baja California. It was named in 1874 by Asa Gray in honor of the plant collector Daniel Cleveland.

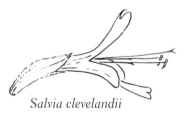

*Salvia clevelandii*

Developing a woody base in time, *Salvia clevelandii* is evergreen and grows in a pleasing shape to 3–5 ft (1–1.5 m) in height and width. Its obovate, rugose leaves are less than 1 in (2.5 cm) in length, are an ashy green color, and amply cover the plant. After other California native sage species have bloomed and passed their prime, *S. clevelandii* comes into prominence. May or June is the usual time for a three to four week flowering period to begin. Luxuriously flowering spikes about 1 ft (0.3 m) in length, with many whorls of amethyst flowers are held upright. Occasionally, inflorescences are short, with only one whorl of flowers.

Flowering stems hold well as cut flowers if conditioned by cutting under water. After the flowers drop, the whorls of tightly packed calyces dry and are quite attractive in the garden or in dried arrangements. A sweet and pleasant odor is released when the calyces are dampened or touched.

In cultivation since the 1940s, *Salvia clevelandii* and its cultivars and hybrids are not widely known to gardeners outside California, but of the native California salvias they are the most popular. Preferring a climate with dry summers and winter rains, specimens have proved susceptible to root rot and fungal problems in humid areas. Because of the plant's summer dormancy, ideal growing conditions include fast drainage, full sun, good air circulation, and very little additional water after the plant is established. Hardy to 20° F (−7° C), *S. clevelandii* is short-lived and needs replacing every five to 10 years. Although its seed is viable, the usual method of propagation is by cuttings taken in spring before flowering and before new wood has formed.

*Salvia clevelandii* 'Winnifred Gilman' (plate 20) is a delightful selection that is both compact and colorful. Unfortunately, records do not reveal the name of the collector or the collection site of this plant. It was distributed by Strybing Arboretum in 1964 at an annual plant sale under its cultivar name to honor one of their volunteer propagators. In 1989 in the Berkeley, California, garden of Jenny Fleming, a mature plant of *S. clevelandii* 'Winnifred Gilman' (plate 20) came to the attention of Sherrie Althouse and Philip Van Soelen of California Flora Nursery, which is located near Santa Rosa, California. Cuttings were taken and since 1990 plants of this desirable clone have been distributed from California Flora Nursery and, subsequently, many nurseries.

A 3 ft (1 m) tall, evergreen plant with flower stems and calyces of dark ruby red, *Salvia clevelandii* 'Winnifred Gilman' has intense violet-blue flowers. Upright in growth, it makes an outstanding filler in a dry border.

In the 1950s at Rancho Santa Ana Botanic Garden, a number of *Salvia clevelandii* plants collected from the wild were placed in the garden. Much later on, in 1992, a seedling in the group raised comment because of its unusual random flower color. One flower might be bluish lavender, the next a cool white. Or there might be two or three flowers of one color before another color was repeated—there were even bi-colored flowers. The plant is thought to be a true *S. clevelandii*, but one that shows genetic instability through random flower color. After being tested for its ability to adapt to garden conditions, it was introduced in 1994 as *S. clevelandii* 'Betsy Clebsch'. I am honored the plant has been named for me and given cultivar status. It is particularly well suited to the small garden because it reaches less than 3 ft (1 m) in height and width.

Five hybrids of *Salvia clevelandii* are so similar in overall appearance and performance that it takes a very discerning eye to distinguish one from the other with assurance. 'Allen Chickering' is a hybrid that occurred at Rancho Santa Ana Botanic Garden. The original selection was lost prior to propagation and consequently a second generation seedling was selected and named, then introduced in 1949. 'Aromas' occurred in the garden of Ken Taylor, a native plant nurseryman, and was introduced by Saratoga Horticultural Foundation in 1981–82. 'Pozo Blue' (plate 19) occurred as a chance seedling in the Las Pilitas Nursery of Bert Wilson in Santa Margarita, California. Wilson introduced the plant in 1989. 'Santa Cruz Dark' is a selection made by Ginny Hunt and introduced by Western Hills Nursery in 1989. 'Whirly Blue' is a selection made by William Nolan, named and recommended by the Saratoga Horticultural Foundation in 1990.

In the spring of 1996 near the Pacific Ocean in northern Baja Calfornia I saw *Salvia clevelandii* in one of its native habitats for the first time. One of the dominant shrubs in a limited area, the plant was 3 ft (1 m) tall and as wide, with graceful stems that swept the ground. Several plants exhibited prostrate growth that hugged the ground, making them prime candidates for cultivars. In this location, *S. clevelandii* grew in colonies or with ambrosia, artemisia, and agave as companions.

In a climate with more or less dry summers, *Salvia clevelandii* and its cultivars and hybrids can be the backbone of a difficult garden site. Imagine a hillside with a number of these salvias interplanted with the 2 ft (0.6 m) tall *Yucca whipplei* with its rosettes of rigid, gray-green leaves, and *Y. rostrata*, which has undulating, bluish foliage. Once established, this combination is drought tolerant and can withstand strong winds and predation by deer.

## *Salvia coahuilensis* Fernald, Plate 21

In the wild, *Salvia coahuilensis* is found in Mexico in the Sierra Madre Oriental in the province of Coahuila, west of Saltillo. Apparently, this sage's limited location is restricted to a mountainous region in the southern part of the province.

Classified as a perennial herb, *Salvia coahuilensis* is a graceful, low-growing, evergreen shrub. Under 2.5 ft (75 cm) in height and width, the plant builds many slender woody branches from its base. A liberal and relentless bloomer, the small, 1 in (2.5 cm) long, beet-purple flowers of *S. coahuilensis* grace the garden from early summer though autumn. Linear, olive-green leaves, usually 1 in (2.5 cm) long, are so narrow and widely spaced that the plant looks sparsely clothed. Many different insects and hummingbirds work the flowers for nectar, and pollination is achieved through this activity. *S. coahuilensis* produces viable seed, and hybrid seedlings are frequently found near the plant. Known to hybridize freely with a number of other salvia species, propagation by cuttings or division of the rootstock is advisable to avoid the risk of cross-pollination.

Fast drainage, friable soil, and full sun are cultural conditions that enable *Salvia coahuilensis* to flower from June until frost. Additional water is needed on a weekly basis. The heavy blooming periods are early summer and autumn when days are hot and nights cool. In my garden the plant has a few flowers practically year round, proclaiming its propensity to stay in bloom. In late winter, plants should be cut back to active growing nodes 6–8 in (15–20 cm) above the ground. Hard pruning will stimulate the growth of new stems that will break into flower in early summer. It is hardy to 20° F (−7° C) or lower, reflecting its native mountainous habitat.

Described by the American botanist M. L. Fernald in 1900, *Salvia coahuilensis* remained unknown to gardeners until the late 1980s. I find no mention of the salvia in catalogs or lists until that time. It is rarely seen in nurseries or gardens in spite of its adaptability and long flowering period.

Placed on a sunny bank beside a drift of the 6–8 in (15–20 cm) tall, blue-silver grass *Festuca cinerea* 'Blausilber', the impact of the small but colorful beet-purple flowers of *Salvia coahuilensis* is intensified. Add several compact lavenders for their grayish foliage, such as the 1 ft (30 cm) tall *Lavandula angustifolia* 'Loddon Blue' with its 6 in (15 cm) spikes of rich purple flowers. Try arranging these three plants of dissimilar but attractive foliage and flowers in drifts of threes or sixes; each plant's unique and individual characteristics will contribute to the value of the group.

## *Salvia coccinea* Jussieu ex Murray, Tropical sage, Plates 22 & 23

Widely distributed throughout tropical South America, *Salvia coccinea* is commonly called tropical sage. Due to its adaptability, it has spread far and wide in the subtropical regions of both North and South America. Once thought to have its origins in Brazil, *S. coccinea*'s diploid chromosome count suggests that it in fact comes from Mexico. A self-sowing, reliable, and handsome annual (occasionally perennial) it has been carried and commended all over the world.

*Salvia coccinea*

*Salvia coccinea* was first described and named in 1778. Carl Epling (1939) found the species had been widely introduced or naturalized in subtropical regions of both hemispheres and was ubiquitous in all warm parts of the Americas. It has been known and grown since the late 18th century.

Depending on seed selection and cultural conditions, tropical sage usually grows to 3 ft (1 m). Heights can vary from 2 to 4 ft (0.6 to 1.3 m). Without looking dense, tropical sage has many branches and spreads about 2.5 ft (0.8 m) in width. Leaves are hairy, pea green, and graduated in size along the stems. Widely spaced, the largest leaves measure 3 in (8 cm) in length and 2 in (5 cm) in width and are primarily deltoid in shape. Scalloped at the edge, they clothe the plant lightly. *Coccinea* comes from the Latin for scarlet and refers to the typical flower color for this species. However, flowers come in many shades—orange-red, red, scarlet, pink, salmon, and white—including bicolors, when the upper lip differs from the lower lip. Flower size also varies. 'Lactea' is a particularly nice white flowering form; 'Brenthurst' (plate 23) is a fine pink form. These will come true from the seed they produce if cross-pollination with other forms of *Salvia coccinea* does not occur.

Propagation is by seed or cuttings. Seed sown in early spring will produce blooming plants by August. All color forms of tropical sage make fine cut flowers. Be sure to condition each stem by cutting it under water to assure long life in a bouquet.

Cultural requirements include full sun, good garden soil enriched with humus and grit, and weekly watering. It is a good idea to remove inflorescences that have been pollinated and are making seed. This kind of pruning, along with using stems for cut flowers, encourages more flower production. Plants will bloom until arrested by cold weather or killed by frost. In very mild climates, *Salvia coccinea* can be perennial. In such circumstances, severe pruning in spring, before new growth begins, along with applications of fertilizer, will encourage heavy blooming.

Easy to grow, tropical sage is a plant that adds sparkle to a herbaceous border in all climate zones. Three or more plants grouped with late blooming annuals or perennials make a fine combination. In my own garden, tropical sage seeds itself year after year in front of climbing roses and evergreen shrubs. The flowers are all colors, including the white 'Lactea', which I find to be an exceptionally good mixer.

## *Salvia columbariae* Bentham, Chia, Plate 24

Commonly called chia in Mexico and some central American countries, *Salvia columbariae* is an annual that comes into bloom in late spring or early summer. It has a wide distribution in California through coastal and inner coastal ranges from Mendocino County south throughout southern California. It is also found in Utah, Arizona, and Baja California. In the wild, it is reported to hybridize with *S. mellifera*, a 3 ft (1 m) tall evergreen shrub.

Water and exposure greatly influence the size of chia. Plentiful amounts of moisture will produce a basal clump of wrinkled green leaves with a grayish cast that measures 2 ft (60 cm) across. A clump less than 1 ft (30 cm) in width is more usual. Individual gray-green leaves are deeply divided and approximately 4–6 in (10–15 cm) in length. Their wrinkled texture makes them singularly handsome. Flowering stalks rise about 1 ft (30 cm) over the foliage, and numerous tight whorls of clear amethyst-blue flowers are spaced about 1 in (2.5 cm) apart along the stalk. The purplish calyx and bracts add to the plant's allure. With little or no moisture the flowering stalk and leaves are reduced in size and become tiny miniatures of the full-grown plant. In desert or dry habitats, plants are frequently less than 2 in (5 cm) tall.

The specific epithet, *columbariae*, means pertaining to a dovecote or niches. I am unsure how to relate this meaning to the plant, unless the structure of the inflorescence perhaps reminds one of a dovecote. Apparently three species of salvia are referred to as chia by native Americans and rural Mexicans; *hispanica*, *polystachya*, and *columbariae*. All three have seed that is exceptionally high in food value and was sown as a crop and regularly cultivated along with corn in ancient Mexico. Chia formed part of the diet of native Americans in the western states before the country was occupied by Europeans. The seeds are very nutritious, are soothing to the stomach, and have thirst-quenching properties. At burial sites on Santa Rosa Island, off the coast of California south of Santa Barbara, *Salvia columbariae* seeds found in pottery jars have been carbon-dated to over 600 years of age.

Mary Elizabeth Parsons (1921), an early California botanist, wrote of her warm appreciation of the California flora as it gradually dries and turns warm shades of beige and gold in the late spring and early summer. At that time, she noted, chia may be found literally covering hillsides with its dried stems and heads held erect. Later, its abundant small gray seed will cover the hillsides too. For centuries these seed have had economic importance to the aborigines and their descendants.

Once established, this showy annual self-sows and will produce a colony each spring. Try sowing seed in an area that has good drainage and little or no summer irrigation. Protection of seed from foraging birds, mice, and ants is essential. It is reported that seeds of varying color have evolved in order to match the color of the soil and thus avoid predation. Chia and California poppies among manzanitas or other drought tolerant plants will provide a visual springtime treat. Drifts of *Salvia columbariae* would mingle nicely with drought tolerant Mediterranean plants such as rosemary and lavender.

## *Salvia confertiflora* Pohl, Plate 25

Native to Brazil, *Salvia confertiflora* has been grown in gardens in the United States since the 1960s, and more than likely even earlier in both Britain and France. Only since the late 1980s has it become an ornamental in California gardens. Perhaps its large size is the reason that it is rarely seen in nurseries or listed in catalogs.

*Salvia confertiflora*

An autumn blooming plant, *Salvia confertiflora* is a herbaceous perennial that will easily reach 4–6 ft (1.3–2 m) in both height and width in a season. By the time it blooms its stems and branches are heavily weighted with leaves and inflorescences. Consequently, it needs the support of a stake or another shrub. This voluminous growth also necessitates protection from winds. The largest leaves are about 7 in (18 cm) long and 3.5 in (9 cm) wide, dark green with a yellowish undertone. The surface is quite rugose and the edge of the leaf is serrated. The petiole and stem of the new leaves are covered with velvety, red-brown hairs.

The leaves give a strong pattern to the entire plant. As the season progresses, *Salvia confertiflora* grows and develops with age. Inflorescences lengthen to at least 1 ft (30 cm); an inflorescence that is 2 ft (60 cm) in length is not at all unusual. The inflorescences are spike-like and covered with hairs that give the impression of red-brown velvet. The stems of both the inflorescence and the calyx are velvety red-brown. The flowers are small, less than 0.5 in (1.3 cm) in length, and orange-red. The specific epithet, *confertiflora*, literally and accurately means crowded with flowers.

Full sun and sharp drainage encourage the complete development of this late blooming perennial. Deep weekly watering is also needed. The blooming period is from early September until frost. In the mild San Francisco Bay area, *Salvia confertiflora* will winter over in the garden most years, but to be on the safe side cuttings should be made in August or September and kept in the greenhouse. If temperatures fall below 25° F (−4° C) this salvia may succumb to the cold or be severely damaged. Propagation is by cuttings.

Areas of high humidity in Texas and the Gulf of Mexico provide a different habitat for *Salvia confertiflora*. There the plant is shade loving, blooms in spring and autumn, and is reported to survive temperatures to 10° F (−12° C).

In late winter or early spring, *Salvia confertiflora* should be heavily pruned so that a well-proportioned plant can develop. Because of my mild climate and long growing season, I remove woody stems and leave only a few stems showing buds that will break near the base of the plant.

*Salvia confertiflora* needs the support and protection of other plants. In the back of a border next to the dark green foliage of *Osmanthus fragrans* or its cultivar 'San Jose', it will be screened from wind and the color of its cinnabar inflorescences will be heightened. It can also be grown with the 6 ft (2 m) tall, butter-yellow *Salvia madrensis*, which is upright in habit. These two salvias bloom simultaneously, each adding to the other's beauty. Another possibility for a focal point in a large border is to place *S. confertiflora* among clumps of *Panicum virgatum*, a 5 ft (1.5 m) tall grass that reaches maturity in autumn when it blooms. Soon afterward it turns the color of ripe, golden wheat and is a fine companion to the salvia through all stages of development.

## *Salvia coulteri* Fernald, Coulter's sage, Plate 26

Even though *Salvia coulteri* has been found in five provinces in Mexico (Nuevo Leon, Zacatecas, Tamaulipas, Durango, and Hidalgo), it is not a common plant. It grows on dry, hot, rocky mountainsides, sometimes near oak, ash, rhus, and acacia. Collected in Mexico by John Merle Coulter, the plant was described by the botanist M. L. Fernald in 1900 and named in honor of the collector. In June of 1991 it was collected in Nuevo Leon at 4000 ft (1200 m) by John Fairey and Carl Schoenfeld and was introduced to horticulture through their Yucca Do Nursery, located in Texas.

A much branched shrub, *Salvia coulteri* is about 2.5 ft (0.8 m) high and 3 ft (1 m) wide and has a graceful appearance. Its woody stems are slender and covered with very short white hairs. Hairs also cover the lanceolate leaves, which are rounded at the tip. The top of the leaf is pale olive-green and the underside looks whitish. The leaves are widely spaced along the wiry stems, revealing the structure of the plant.

By September *Salvia coulteri* has produced many inflorescences, and flowering continues until frost. Tight whorls of flowers are jammed together on a flowering stem at the side and top of each branch. These electric lavender-blue flowers are small, measuring less than 0.5 in (1.3 cm), but the vivid color makes this plant seem to bloom as profusely as one with larger flowers. A curious characteristic of *S. coulteri* is the way the calyces are all turned to one side of the flowering stem. Even though they appear in whorls, they sweep to one side. Only about 0.25 in (0.6 cm) long, they persist long after the flowers they hold have bloomed and dropped. If you stroke these dried calyces, they release a pleasant, somewhat mint-like odor.

Full sun and fast drainage are needed for *Salvia coulteri*. In areas with hot summer temperatures, light shade is mandatory. I find deep watering once every week or two is beneficial. In time, the plant will require some pruning in order to keep its shapeliness. Small branches of flowers hold well in arrangements if woody stems are conditioned by cutting them under water. Enjoying the flowers indoors is a way of keeping the plant trimmed and well proportioned.

I have not grown *Salvia coulteri* long enough to test its hardiness, but judging from its collection site, I believe it to be hardy to 20° F (−7° C). Propagation is by seed or cuttings.

Well-suited to a sunny hillside, *Salvia coulteri* would add grace and color to a border of Mediterranean and California native plants. A slope where flowers could be enjoyed from early spring through autumn might include *Rosmarinus* 'Ken Taylor' and *Ceanothus gloriosus* var. *porrectus* for dark green foliage and early flowering; for early summer blooming and contrasting foliage, add the gray foliaged herbaceous *Ballota acetabulosa*; then the late summer blooming of *Eriogonum arborescens* would lead into the flowering period of *Salvia coulteri*. All of these plants require the same cultural conditions and very little attention. Their foliage would look handsome year round.

## *Salvia cyanescens* Boissier & Balansa

A herbaceous perennial that is endemic to Iran and Turkey, *Salvia cyanescens* was introduced to horticulture in 1959. Even though it readily produces viable seed and is easy to propagate, gardeners and nurseries have been slow to learn about it. In its native habitat it interbreeds freely with *S. candidissima* and would seemingly be a good candidate for hybridizing.

Developing a small, 1 ft (30 cm) clump of gray-green leaves that are ovate in outline, *Salvia cyanescens* is evergreen in a mild climate and tends to look good year round in the garden. Covered with hairs, the leaves are about 2 in (5 cm) long by 1 in (2.5 cm) wide, and make a mounding and handsome plant. Although its pale gray-green foliage appears soft and frail, *S. cyanescens* is a hardy and tough plant. During the hot days of summer, as with many gray foliaged plants, its leaves become whiter and appear silvery. This may be a mechanism for protecting the leaf surface from excess heat by reflection of light and may also prevent water loss by evaporation.

If warm weather prevails, blooming periods are summer and late autumn. Flowers are small, barely 1 in (2.5 cm) in length, and a rather delicate purple-violet color. The inflorescence is candelabra-like and about 1 ft (30 cm) tall. This description sounds spectacular but, in fact, very few flowers are in bloom simultaneously and they are so small that it is easy to walk by the plant and miss the flowering completely. The specific epithet, *cyanescens*, means bluish or becoming blue—a name that is far from precise in this instance.

Good drainage, full sun, and ordinary garden soil with only occasional water are *Salvia cyanescens*' main requirements. In its native habitat it is found growing on limestone and igneous rock slopes as well as shale banks and dry, rocky streambeds. Hardy to 0° F (−18° C), it is considered drought tolerant. Propagation is by seed or cuttings.

The handsome foliage of *Salvia cyanescens* is enhanced by the dark green and narrow foliage of the prostrate rosemaries. *Origanum rotundifolium*, *Santolina virens*, and *Teucrium chamaedrys* are other suitable companions when arranged on a sunny, rocky bank. All require the same culture. Another grouping for an area set aside for sun loving annual wildflowers is California poppy (*Eschscholzia californica*) along with chia (*Salvia columbariae*) between drifts of *Salvia cyanescens*. This grouping results in a delightful spring into summer floriferous display.

## *Salvia darcyi* Compton, Plate 27

The native habitat of *Salvia darcyi* is a very limited area at an altitude of 9000 ft (2800 m) in the eastern range of the Mexican Sierra Madre Oriental. Found in the wild in 1988 by John Fairey and Carl Schoenfeld of Yucca Do Nursery in Texas, *S. darcyi* has been offered by several nurseries under various names. In the autumn of 1991 Fairey and Schoenfeld accompanied a party of plant professionals from Great Britain to northeastern Mexico. The party included botanist James Compton. On this trip, Compton was shown this handsome salvia. He collected and subsequently described it, naming it *S. darcyi* in honor of a fellow British botanist, William D'Arcy, who had accompanied him on this particular trip.

A perennial herb that reaches 3 ft (1 m) in height in the wild but usually less than that in cultivation, *Salvia darcyi* dies back to its rootstock in winter. The roots are stoloniferous and with time will produce new

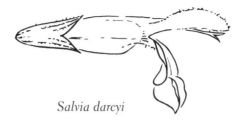

*Salvia darcyi*

plants from the shoots. I was fortunate enough to see the native habitat of *S. darcyi* in Nuevo Leon Province in late spring, when large numbers of the plant could easily be seen emerging from rich loam among limestone rocks in a wide, dry stream bed. Sycamore trees (*Platanus mexicana*) dotted the valley.

In the garden, *Salvia darcyi* rapidly develops branching top growth, and by early summer its blooming period begins. Pastel green, deltoid leaves cover the plant amply, making a perfect foil for the 1.5 in (4 cm) long, coral-red flowers. Inflorescences are 6–12 in (15–30 cm) in length and sometimes elongate to 2 ft (60 cm). *S. darcyi* generates many widely spaced whorls of flowers until short days and cool nights slow or stop the display. This salvia's high mountain habitat is reflected in its hardiness to 20° F (−7° C), possibly lower.

Easy to care for, *Salvia darcyi* requires three-quarters to a full day of sun, fast drainage, friable soil, and deep watering at least once a week. A light dressing of lime on the root surface in early spring is helpful. Snails and slugs are attracted to new growth. Propagation is by cuttings, but after the plant is well established, rooted shoots can be removed by teasing and potted for gardening friends.

Gardeners who are interested in working with color will find *Salvia darcyi* an unprecedented plant. When positioned near orange-red or magenta-red flowers or leaves, this plant has the capacity to blend with whichever red group is near. I urge gardeners to experiment with its color in different combinations.

A grouping of plants for a long blooming, sunny summer border includes in the background the 3 ft (1 m) tall and wide *Phygelius* 'Salmon Leap', with its dark green, glossy, evergreen foliage and pale orange-red flowers. In the midground, incorporate several *Salvia darcyi* plants with the 2–3 ft (0.6–0.9 m) burnt-orange flowered *Agastache* 'Apricot Sunrise'. The front of the border can be cooled with a few clumps of *Festuca amethystina* 'April Gruen' or *Briza media*, the perennial quaking grass. Both grasses are about 1 ft (30 cm) in height and width. Chosen primarily for size and color of foliage and flowers, each of these plants requires the same cultural conditions.

## *Salvia discolor* Kunth, Andean sage, Plate 89

*Salvia discolor* is only known to occur naturally in a small geographical location in Peru, and is equally rare in horticulture. It is not known precisely when this plant was introduced to horticulture, but William Robinson (1933) wrote of its charm and merits. Its growing habit is scandent—meaning that the plant climbs without the aid of tendrils. With only speculative information about *S. discolor*'s precise native habitat, the following cultural information is inevitably limited.

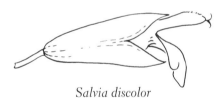

*Salvia discolor*

*Salvia discolor* is a herbaceous perennial with many wiry white stems arising from the base. It tends to bloom during warm or hot spells throughout the summer and autumn. When situated in a frost-free garden where temperatures do not fall below 32° F (0° C), it builds a strong root system that allows top growth to elongate and extend to about 3 ft (1 m). In areas without the necessary long, warm growing period, pot the plant and move it into the greenhouse or take cuttings in September. Andean sage tends to stay in bloom for a long period if wintered in a greenhouse.

Along the Riviera in both France and Italy, *Salvia discolor* is frequently grown as an ornamental specimen plant. In that warm and benign climate, it is not unusual to see a plant reach 3 ft (1 m) in height and width. Its habit is more upright there than in California.

Support is needed for the thin stems of Andean sage if the inflorescences are to be distinguished and seen. Mistletoe-green leaves of graduated sizes, the largest 4 in (10 cm) in length by 1.5 in (4 cm) across, are spaced in pairs about 1–2 in (2.5–5 cm) apart. The back of the leaf is covered with white hairs and veins and is quite noticeable due to the sparse leaf arrangement. The inflorescence usually extends to 1 ft (30 cm) or more. Exceedingly dark purple flowers, saturated with color and less than 1 in (2.5 cm) long, are held in a beautiful, pistachio-green, two-lipped calyx. In certain lights the flowers appear to be black. The colors of the plant are subtle and harmonious. The stem of the inflorescence looks shiny and is covered with glands that make it sticky to the touch. Often little insects are found stuck to it, prompting a gardening friend to remark, "It's its own flypaper." I do not know the reason for this stickiness, but it may have something to do with detracting predators in the plant's home territory.

The specific epithet, *discolor*, means of two different colors. In the case of this salvia the epithet applies both to the green and white leaf surfaces and to the purple flower in its pale green calyx.

Friable garden soil lightened with humus and deep weekly watering are recommended for *Salvia discolor*. No more than a half day of sun is needed, and occasional light applications of liquid fertilizer are beneficial. Staking is almost a necessity due to the scandent growth habit. *Salvia discolor* is a collector's plant and does well in a container. Because of its wiry appearance, it can be most easily seen without the foliage of other plants surrounding it. Some form of staking is helpful, such as thin, light bamboo. If kept in a container, *S. discolor* can be easily moved from the greenhouse into the garden for the summer and placed in filtered light. If grown in the garden, elevate the plant in order for the viewer to look directly into it. Because of the long arching stems it is a difficult plant to place in a border.

1 The conspicuously felted leaves of the biennial *Salvia aethiopis* draw attention to the plant throughout the winter. (Christine Andrews)

2 The early spring flowering *Salvia africana-lutea* has a shrub-like habit. (Don Mahoney)

3 *Salvia albimaculata*, a Turkish endemic that grows on limestone. (Robert Kourik)

4 The handsome gray-white leaves of *Salvia apiana*, a California native, embellish the garden throughout the year. (Bart O'Brien)

5 Dramatic basal leaves of *Salvia argentea*. (Ed Carman)

6 *Salvia arizonica* repeats bloom in summer and autumn. (Ginny Hunt)

7 Stems of *Salvia austriaca*'s soft yellow flowers are prized by flower arrangers. (Christine Andrews)

8 The richly colored *Salvia blepharophylla* in part shade. (Robert Kourik)

9 The shade loving *Salvia blepharophylla* 'Sweet Numbers', with its wide, intensely colored lower lip. (Christine Andrews)

11 The magenta flowered *Salvia buchananii* and gray foliaged *Helichrysum splendidum*, along with the day flowering evening primrose *Oenothera speciosa*. (Robert Kourik)

10 *Salvia brandegei* has linear, evergreen leaves of unusual beauty. (Robert Kourik)

12 Blooming from summer through autumn, *Salvia cacaliaefolia* has almost true-blue flowers. (Christine Andrews)

13 *Salvia canariensis* at Strybing Arboretum. (Christine Andrews)

14 In a spring display on the Carrizo Plains in California, *Salvia carduacea* is seen in a mass of poppies and *Coreopsis bigelovii*. (Bart O'Brien)

15 *Salvia cedrosensis* shown in its native habitat on the Vizcaino Peninsula, Baja California Sur. (Bart O'Brien)

16 The sparkling blue flowered *Salvia chamaedryoides* in the author's garden with *Salvia microphylla* (Graham's sage) in the background. (Robert Kourik)

17 *Salvia chamelaeagnea* blooms from late summer through autumn. (Christine Andrews)

18 The shiny, deeply veined leaves of *Salvia chiapensis* add to the beauty of the plant. (Ginny Hunt)

19 *Salvia clevelandii* 'Pozo Blue' in the author's garden. The green leaved *Euphorbia* × *martinii* is in the foreground. (Robert Kourik)

20 In a good year, *Salvia clevelandii* 'Winnifred Gilman' is laden with flowers. (Christine Andrews)

21 This Strybing Arboretum border of plants native to Mexico includes *Salvia coahuilensis* and *Calylophus hartwegii*, a member of the evening primrose family. (Christine Andrews)

22 At Thomas Jefferson's Monticello, *Salvia coccinea* blooms well into October and even November. (Carol Ottesen)

23 The summer flowering *Salvia coccinea* 'Brenthurst'. (Ginny Hunt)

24 Spring blooming wildflowers in Antelope Valley, California, including California poppies and *Salvia columbariae*. (Bart O'Brien)

25 The rich, velvety flowers of *Salvia confertiflora*. (Christine Andrews)

26 *Salvia coulteri* on a shrub-covered hillside in the province of Nuevo Leon, Mexico. (Carl Schoenfeld)

27 The coral-red flowered *Salvia darcyi* with *Vigueria*, a shrub-like sunflower. (Ginny Hunt)

28 The winter-flowering *Salvia disjuncta* is well suited for a mild climate. (Don Mahoney)

29 *Salvia dombeyi* has probably the
longest flower of any salvia, usually
measuring a good 3 in (8 cm) in
length. (Christine Andrews)

30 Large, crisp leaves and pink flowers adorn
*Salvia eigii* for a three or even four month period.
(Christine Andrews)

32 The distinctive beelines that guide insects to nectar are prominent on *Salvia forskaohlei*. This clone has particularly richly colored flowers. (Christine Andrews)

31 The repeat blooming *Salvia elegans* 'Honey Melon' with the variegated *Salvia officinalis* 'Icterina'. (Robert Kourik)

33 *Salvia fruticosa* has a prolonged flowering period in early spring, and handsome gray-green foliage year round. (Christine Andrews)

34 Throughout the winter and well into spring *Salvia gesneraeflora* 'Tequila' will repeat bloom. (Ed Carman)

35 Well-suited for a shady area, *Salvia greggii* 'Cherry Red' is an excellent cultivar. (Robert Kourik)

36 *Salvia guaranitica* is unparalleled in its ability to repeat bloom over a long period throughout summer and autumn. (Robert Kourik)

37 'Argentina Skies' is a pale blue selection of *Salvia guaranitica*, shown here with Queen Anne's Lace and, on the right, *Rosa* 'La Marne'. (Robert Kourik)

38 The dusky violet flowers of *Salvia hians*. (Robert Kourik)

39 The long blooming *Salvia hirtella*. (Ginny Hunt)

40 *Salvia holwayi* is a useful winter blooming plant. (Christine Andrews)

41 *Salvia* 'Indigo Spires' is a long blooming and reliable border plant. *Stipa ramosissima* can be seen on the right. (Ginny Hunt)

42 With handsome divided leaves, *Salvia interrupta* blooms throughout the summer and will continue to throw flowering stalks in a mild autumn. (David Madison)

43 The rich and deeply colored flowers of *Salvia involucrata* 'El Cielo' in autumn. (Christine Andrews)

44 'Mulberry Jam' is a hybrid of *Salvia involucrata* that has an upright habit and is in continuous bloom from summer to frost. (Christine Andrews)

45 Naturally occurring selections of the newly described *Salvia × jamensis* collected from the wild. In the foreground is the pale yellow 'Cienega de Oro', with the peach and yellow 'Sierra San Antonio' in the background. (Robert Kourik)

46 The small, upside-down flowers of *Salvia jurisicii* are easily seen on a white flowered form. (Robert Kourik)

47 A tall shrub with handsome foliage and form, *Salvia karwinskii* blooms prodigiously in winter. (Christine Andrews)

48 *Salvia leucantha* 'Midnight', a purple flowered form of the species. (Ginny Hunt)

49 In the background is 'Bee's Bliss', a beautiful hybrid of *Salvia leucophylla* with an attractive spreading habit. In the foreground is a graceful, low growing coastal form of the same species. (Christine Andrews)

50 The lustrous magenta flowers of the autumn into winter blooming *Salvia littae*. (Don Mahoney)

51 *Salvia lycioides* blooms in spring and again in autumn and is well suited for a rock garden. (Ginny Hunt)

52 A ripe peach colored clone of *Salvia macellaria*. (Christine Andrews)

53 The rich butter yellow flowers of *Salvia madrensis* are enhanced here by the fire engine–red flowers of *Salvia fulgens*. (Ginny Hunt)

54 *Salvia mellifera* blooming in May on the south-facing slope of Mount Baldy, southern California. (Betsy Clebsch)

55 A graceful, shrub-like garden plant with a pleasing scent, *Salvia melissodora* attracts insects and hummingbirds. (Ginny Hunt)

56 The large flowered 'Lollie Jackson' is a
4 ft (1.3 m) tall selection of *Salvia mexicana*.
(Christine Andrews)

57 The shrubby *Salvia microphylla* (Graham's sage) is dazzling all summer. To the
right is S. *chamaedryoides*. (Christine Andrews)

58 *Salvia microphylla* var. *neurepia* is never without flowers from early summer through autumn. (Christine Andrews)

59 'Red Velvet' is a lustrous, red flowered selection of *Salvia microphylla*. (Don Mahoney)

60 The small and colorful *Salvia muelleri* alongside *Origanum dictamnus*. (Robert Kourik)

61 *Salvia nubicola* is a fine filler for a summer border. Here is it seen nestled between an *Agastache* and *Tanacetum parthenium* (feverfew). (Robert Kourik)

62 The lavender blooms of *Salvia officinalis* along with the white and rose valerian, *Centranthus ruber*. In the midground are the iris-like leaves of *Sisyrinchium striatum*, with the yellow flowering *Euphorbia characias* subsp. *wulfenii* behind. (Robert Kourik)

63 The bright yellow, variegated foliage of *Salvia officinalis* 'Icterina' is seen here above the golden foliage of *Origanum vulgare* 'Aureum'. (Mark Kane)

64 Foliage that is rich purple year-round makes *Salvia officinalis* 'Purpurascens' a notable garden companion. (Christine Andrews)

65 Considered a weed in its native Mexico, *Salvia polystachya* is a charming addition to an autumn border. (Christine Andrews)

66 *Salvia pratensis* grows rapidly and blooms in early spring. (Christine Andrews)

67 Autumn blooming *Salvia puberula*, with large inflated flowers. (Christine Andrews)

68 The aptly named *Salvia* 'Purple Majesty'. (Christine Andrews)

69 The flowers of *Salvia purpurea* are truly lavender-violet, a color rarely seen in winter. On the right is the long needled *Pinus oaxacana*. (Don Mahoney)

70 The pink flowering Turkish endemic *Salvia recognita*, with the foliage of *S. sclarea* evident in the foreground and the taller foliage of *S. guarantica* behind it on the left. (Betsy Clebsch)

71 *Salvia regla* sited on the southeast side of the house where it is protected from winds and sun during the hottest part of the day. (Christine Andrews)

72 Naturally occurring in a limestone habitat in the province of Tamaulipas, Mexico, *Salvia roemeriana* is a natural rock garden plant. (Carl Schoenfeld)

73 Revered for centuries for its healing powers and beauty, *Salvia sclarea* is a striking plant in the summer border. Companions here are *Convolvulus mauritanicus* in front, *Salvia* 'Indigo Spires' to the left, and *S. recognita* to the right. (Betsy Clebsch)

75 *Salvia semiatrata*: note the very dark violet blotch on the flower's lower lip. (Robert Kourik)

74 The impressive *Salvia sclarea* 'Turkestanica'. (Robert Kourik)

76 *Salvia sinaloensis*, a densely compact and clumping plant. (Christine Andrews)

77 The summer blooming *Salvia somalensis*. (Ginny Hunt)

78 *Salvia sonomensis* at peak bloom in East Bay Regional Parks Botanic Garden, Oakland, California. (Bart O'Brien)

79 The splendid California native *Salvia spathacea* with California poppies in the foreground. (Robert Kourik)

80 *Salvia splendens* 'Van Houttei' adds drama to the autumn garden. (Ginny Hunt)

82 The dainty pink flowers of *Salvia taraxacifolia*. (Robert Kourik)

81 The dark purple spikes of *Salvia sylvestris* 'East Friesland' in the foreground along with *Penstemon* 'Huntington Pink'. Behind is a purple hybrid penstemon. (Christine Andrews)

83 *Salvia thymoides*, here seen at Strybing Arboretum. (Christine Andrews)

84 A mound of foliage supports *Salvia transsylvanica* in the center of this photo. Directly behind is the tall *Anigozanthos flavidus*, with the yellow flowered *Salvia × jamensis* 'Cienega de Oro' to the left and an unidentified verbascum on the right. (Ginny Hunt)

85 The light and airy *Salvia uliginosa* interplanted with *S. dumetorum*. (Christine Andrews)

86 *Salvia verticillata* 'Purple Rain' blooms without interruption in the summer and autumn. (Robert Kourik)

87 *Salvia viridis* shown with *Salvia albimaculata* in the foreground and the outstanding gray foliaged *Brachyglottis* 'Sunshine' in the background. (Christine Andrews)

88 *Salvia carduacea*

89 *Salvia discolor*

90 *Salvia interrupta*

91 *Salvia macellaria*

92 *Salvia mexicana* 'Limelight'

93 *Salvia nubicola*

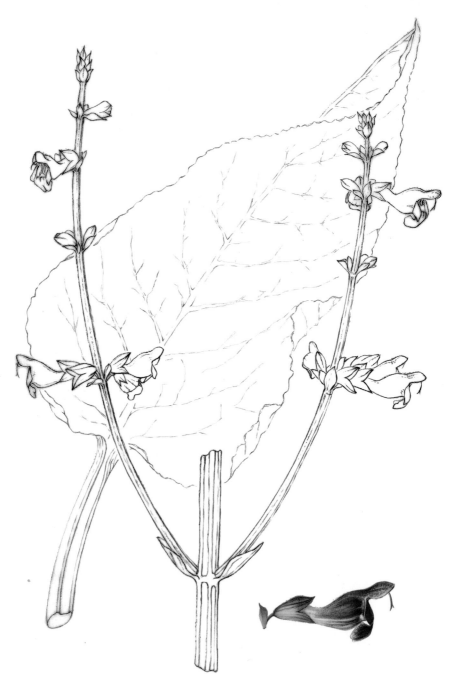

94 *Salvia przewalskii*

95 *Salvia recognita*

96 *Salvia regla*

## *Salvia disjuncta* Fernald, Plate 28

A late blooming, shrub-like plant, *Salvia disjuncta* is a herbaceous perennial with a woody base. It is native to the Mexican provinces Oaxaca and Chiapas, and its distribution extends into Guatemala. It is found at high elevations between 7500–11,000 ft (2300–3400 m) where the warm and moist mountainous habitat receives some summer rain. Collected in the wild by botanists from Strybing Arboretum in the late 1980s, this salvia became available to nurseries and gardeners in 1993 through Arboretum plant sales.

Coming into full bloom in late October, *Salvia disjuncta* consistently continues to flower lightly throughout the winter in a mild climate. The species appears in two forms, one with green or pale tan stems and mid-green leaves, the other with raisin colored stems and mature leaves that are purplish green. Both are shrubby in habit reaching 3–4 ft (1–1.3 m) in height and width with many thin stems emerging from the base of the plant. The stems are lightly covered with short, straight hairs, which are particularly conspicuous when they catch the dew. The few signal-red flowers, 1 in (2.5 cm) or more in length, are held in widely spaced whorls, and their bright color and size blend harmoniously with the deltoid-shaped leaves. Frequently, this salvia has but one pair of flowers in bloom at the end of a branch, making a graceful and delightful display. Stems last well as cut flowers when conditioned by cutting them under water.

*Salvia disjuncta* needs at least a half day of sunlight throughout summer and winter. Regular water and friable garden soil that drains well are also necessary. In a mild climate, the rootstock of a well-established *S. disjuncta* tends to run a limited amount. Unfortunately, it is not cold tolerant and I have lost plants at 30° F (−1° C). However, it roots easily from cuttings and by that method can be wintered in a greenhouse. Propagation by cuttings assures selection of the correct form, though seed germinates readily and it is likely that seedlings will resemble the parent. If plants have wintered over in the garden, in early spring cut them within a few inches of the ground, above active buds, in order to have a plant of medium size and pleasing proportions by autumn. Occasional light applications of a complete fertilizer will speed growth.

An attractive plant for the border because of its medium size and strong, dark leaf color, *Salvia disjuncta* combines beautifully with the autumn blooming *Ceratostigma griffithii*. A small shrub, usually 2 ft (60 cm) in height, with heavenly blue flowers, *C. griffithii*'s leaves turn red when the days shorten. *Ajuga reptans* 'Jungle Beauty' makes an admirable dark green groundcover. Spikes of indigo-blue flowers, 6–8 in (15–20 cm) tall, appear in spring above handsome evergreen foliage. All plants require deep weekly watering during the active growing period.

## *Salvia dolomitica* Codd

A handsome, gray leaved shrub, *Salvia dolomitica* is found at elevations of 3000–5000 ft (900–1500 m) in the northeast province of Transvaal in South Africa. As its name implies, it grows in dolomite, a rocky soil containing high concentrations of the mineral calcium magnesium carbonate.

Generously covered with leaves, *Salvia dolomitica* usually reaches 3 ft (1 m) in height and width in a garden. In the wild, it can reach twice those dimensions. Elliptic, gray-green leaves held in an upright position are prominently veined on the underside. Blooming in early summer, the inflorescence is short and verticils are two flowered. The calyx is pea-green and covered with oil globules that smell lemony. The two-lipped calyx has distinct lobes, three on the top lip and two on the bottom. The flowers are pale lilac with a wide cream streak extending into the throat. Though not showy, the inflorescence has many interesting features when observed closely. *S. dolomitica* has never produced seed in my garden, though seeds germinate readily. Cuttings are a reliable means of propagation.

Sited where it receives at the very least a half day of sunlight in a gravelly soil that drains rapidly, *Salvia dolomitica* will thrive. Occasionally, some summer irrigation is needed in order for the root-run not to become dry. I have found that less than a handful of crushed oystershells sprinkled around the base of the plant in early spring is beneficial. The plant has proved hardy to around 25° F (−4° C), and because of the high elevation of its natural habitat it may well withstand colder temperatures.

A foliage border featuring plants from areas of dry summers and wet winters can be built around salvias native to the Mediterranean, South Africa, and California. I call this a "Geography Bed" because it demonstrates the similar growing conditions of plants separated in their native habitats by thousands of miles. For a dark green background, *Salvia brandegei* and *S. mellifera* from the California chaparral make a screen 5 ft (1.5 m) high. In the midground, group several plants of the gray-green leaved *S. dolomitica* and the mid-green leaved *S. chamelaeagnea* from South Africa. In a foreground of low-growing Mediterranean natives, feature drifts of the spreading, mid-green leaved *S. officinalis* 'Berggarten' and the biennial *S. aethiopis* for its ornamental leaves and large inflorescence. All plants require more or less the same culture and little time or trouble.

## *Salvia dombeyi* Epling, Plate 29

The native habitat of the spectacularly flowered *Salvia dombeyi* is Peru and Bolivia. An extremely tender plant, this sage is found at altitudes of 9800 ft (3000 m) in the wild. Robert Ornduff, while director of University of California Botanical Garden, Berkeley, observed *S. dombeyi* growing as a vine to a height of two stories in the courtyard of the Museum of Archeology at the University of Cusco, Peru. Named in honor of the French botanist Joseph Dombey, this salvia is popular with gardeners in both Peru and Bolivia.

With a woody base and several to many stems, *Salvia dombeyi* is scandent and needs support in order to elongate and flower successfully. In cultivation with ideal conditions it might climb 9–20 ft (3–8 m). Exceedingly sensitive to cold temperatures, I have lost this salvia on several occasions when temperatures dipped to the low 30°s F (around −1° C) for short periods of time. However, Strybing Arboretum in San Francisco has mature plants growing outdoors in a benign climate on and above a 12 ft (4 m) fence. Tall conifers give excellent protection from cold air and wind.

Heart-shaped leaves that are graduated in size lightly cover the actively growing portion of *Salvia dombeyi*. The dark green leaves have a long petiole covered with short, distinct hairs that sparkle in dew or fog. Late summer and autumn is the usual time for the uncommonly long and beautiful flowers to appear. The 1.5 in (4 cm) currant-red calyx holds a 3.5 in (9 cm) long scarlet corolla, providing a dazzling display. Only a few flowers mature at the same time, so the inflorescence is in bloom for a long period.

Place *Salvia dombeyi* where it will receive support from other plants and a half day of sun. Good garden loam with fast drainage is desirable along with applications of half-strength liquid fertilizer twice each month throughout the active growing season. A mulch over the root area will conserve moisture and condition the soil. If temperatures drop below freezing, pot the salvia to be kept in the greenhouse for the winter or take cuttings in early autumn. Propagation is by cuttings.

Grown and cared for in greenhouses in this country and abroad, *Salvia dombeyi* is worth this extra effort by the gardener who lives in all but the warmest areas.

## *Salvia dominica* Linnaeus

A strong-smelling and much branched shrub that tends to be ever-green in a mild climate, *Salvia dominica* is found throughout the eastern Mediterranean region. It is particularly abundant in Israel, Lebanon, and Syria, and in its native habitat is a dominant species commonly found in association with *Ballota undulata*. Horticulturally, it has never been a well-known or popular sage. However, in Israel, where Nogah Hareuveni (1980) has interpreted Jewish tradition as reflected in plants, the branched inflorescence of the fragrant S. *dominica* is one of several salvias thought to have inspired the design of the menorah, or seven-branched candelabra.

Linnaeus, in describing *Salvia dominica*, believed it to be from the West Indies and gave it the specific epithet *dominica* to commemorate the island of Dominica. The literal meaning is "belonging to the Lord." A student of Linnaeus, Martin Hendriksen Vahl, also described this salvia and gave it the specific name *graveolens*. According to the botanical rules of nomenclature, the earlier name stands. Incidentally, *graveo-*

*lens* means heavily scented and refers to the fragrant glands on the hairs covering the leaf, making it a more relevant epithet than the misleading *dominica*.

Reaching about 3 ft (1 m) in both height and width, *Salvia dominica* adapts well to garden situations. It tolerates overhead watering if quick drainage follows. The chalky hills of its native surroundings receive only infrequent water. In my garden it has proved hardy when temperatures have fallen to the low teens (around −11° C). The hastate (arrowhead-shaped) leaves are gray-green and fuzzy, being covered with the previously mentioned aromatic hairs. The plant blooms in spring or early summer and produces pale, yellowish white flowers in delicate and airy whorls. The inflorescences hold well as cut flowers. In a short time this salvia will build wood at its base and should be replaced every three to four years. This can be smoothly managed because propagation is easily accomplished by layering, cuttings, or seed.

*Salvia dominica* is considered drought tolerant and can be planted with a rosemary such as 'Collingwood Ingram' on a bank receiving full sun, where the differences in the plants' shape and foliage color make a pleasant display. This sage also looks handsome planted among herbaceous perennials such as penstemons, agastaches, and the gray leaved, sterile *Nepeta × faassenii*. *Salvia dominica*'s woolly leaves contrast nicely with the perennials' foliage and heighten the effect of their colorful flowers.

### *Salvia dorisiana* Standley, Fruit-scented sage, peach sage

From Honduras comes *Salvia dorisiana*, a tender perennial that is sometimes called fruit-scented or peach sage. This sage apparently commemorates Doris, daughter of Oceanus, wife of Nereus, and mother of 50 sea nymphs. In its warm native habitat it reaches 3–4 ft (1–1.3 m) in height and is heavily branched. Widely known and grown for the lovely fruity scent that is released when its leaves are brushed, fruit-scented sage is also admired for the large, hot-pink flowers it produces in winter.

First named and described in 1950, *Salvia dorisiana* has become a popular greenhouse plant. It requires a warm climate year round, but I

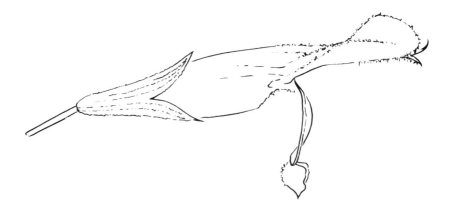

*Salvia dorisiana*

have found it to withstand temperatures as low as the high 20°s F (around −2° C) in my garden for short periods of time. Cold air will cut the top of the plant down, but with the return of reliably warm weather, new growth will break from its base. Frosty and cold spells coincide with this sage's December to March blooming period and, consequently, it must be kept indoors in all but the warmest areas to encourage flowering. To enjoy its flowers, I keep pots of the sage in the greenhouse in winter, then move them into the garden, to a spot with filtered light, for the long summer.

Large magenta-pink flowers sometimes reach 2 in (5 cm) in length and are held in a lime-green calyx that can reach 0.75 in (2 cm) in length. The color of the calyx is repeated in the hairy, ovate leaves. Practically the entire plant is covered with hairs that have glands that release a delightful pineapple-grapefruit scent when stroked.

A half day of sunlight, friable soil enriched with humus, frequent water, and light applications of a balanced fertilizer are needed to keep fruit-scented sage in good condition. Because of its frequent spurts of growth and its branching habit, periodic pruning is required. The flowering shoots are most attractive to hummingbirds and make nice, long-lasting cut flowers. Propagation is by seed or cuttings.

*Salvia dorisiana* is an excellent choice for a container garden. Because of its attractive and heavy foliage, it furnishes a quiet background for plants that flower for long periods. Ivy geraniums and impatiens come quickly to mind for companions. The trailing foliage of variegated ivy, such as *Hedera helix* 'Helena' or one of the many other ivy cultivars, might be used to soften the edge of the container. All require similar growing conditions.

## *Salvia eigii* Zohary, Plate 30

Blooming in late winter and early spring, the herbaceous perennial *Salvia eigii* has only recently come to the attention of gardeners. It has never been formally introduced, but since the early 1980s its seed has been passed from one gardener to another in the San Francisco Bay area. In its native habitat, in the Eastern Mediterranean, it is rather rare— being found in fallow fields on alluvial soils. Botanists believe it endemic to that particular region.

Fresh growth begins in winter as *Salvia eigii* builds a large clump of basal leaves that measures over 1 ft (30 cm) in height and 2 ft (60 cm) in width. The dark green leaves are ovate in outline and the largest measures 1 ft (30 cm) in length and 8 in (20 cm) in width. The flowering stalk is 3 ft (1 m) in height and supports many 8–12 in (20–30 cm) inflorescences. The 1 in (2.5 cm) flowers appear in whorls and generously fill the inflorescence. The upper lip of the flower is cyclamen-purple, and the lower lip is a pale pink with ruby beelines into the throat. The beelines guide the insect or hummingbird to the nectar and pollen within the flower. A prominent ruby calyx, which is distinctly veined and hairy, adds to the beauty of the flower. Many flowers open simultaneously, making this salvia a good candidate for a bouquet, especially since the cut flowers last well.

Full sun, good garden soil enriched with humus, and sharp drainage are needed for *Salvia eigii* to flourish. Regular, deep watering every week or two is necessary throughout the summer, depending on temperatures. Propagation is by seed. One plant will produce an abundant supply and it is not unusual to find seedlings around the base. Hardy to 10° F (−12° C), *Salvia eigii*, with the protection of conifer boughs, would probably survive even lower temperatures. In a mild climate it tends to have evergreen leaves and its blooming period is three to four months long beginning in late winter and continuing through spring. In my garden, plants tend to throw inflorescences throughout the warm months.

Named for the botanist Alexander Eig, *Salvia eigii* is a fine addition for an informal cottage garden. Its shape would provide a good contrast to hollyhocks, foxgloves, larkspurs, and delphiniums, and its lengthy blooming period would probably overlap with these plants'—particularly in a cold climate. On a large scale, a combination of early spring blooming plants might include a drift of *S. eigii*, with its pale pink and ruby colors, under the flowering cherry *Prunus* 'Shirotae' (Mt. Fuji), which has semidouble flowers that are pink in bud and white when fully open, aging to purplish pink. *Lychnis flos-jovis*, an airy looking, well-branched perennial that is 2 ft (60 cm) tall with pink or white flowers, would complete the picture.

### *Salvia elegans* Vahl, Pineapple sage, Plate 31

One of the last sages to come into bloom before the end of autumn is the herbaceous perennial, *Salvia elegans*, also known as *Salvia rutilans* (Carrière). Seeing it bloom is a treat because most winters the plant is cut down by cold weather before it can flower. Its native habitat across central Mexico and into the Sierra Madre del Sur provides a long and mild season to mature, which can allow a bloom period of two to four months. Usually found at elevations of 6000–9000 ft (1800–2800 m), it colonizes on the edge of woodlands.

*Salvia elegans*

In the wild there are two distinct clones, as well as intergradations, of *Salvia elegans*. The clone with larger flowers, called pineapple sage, was known for over a hundred years as *Salvia rutilans* and was in cultivation before 1873. The British botanist James Compton (1994a) has proposed changing the name of pineapple sage to *Salvia elegans* in order to show its relationship within the species. He has also proposed that this cultivar be called 'Scarlet Pineapple'.

When able to reach maturity in the garden, *Salvia elegans*, the pineapple sage, is a somewhat shrubby plant about 4–5 ft (1.3–1.5 m) tall. Its roots extend on underground runners and in a moderate climate make a large clump. Deltoid, bright yellow-green leaves with a pale green, white-veined underside are covered with fine hairs and glands. They cover the branches fully and have a downy appearance. Deeply veined and graduated in size, the largest leaves measure 3 in (8 cm) in length and 2 in (5 cm) in width. Six to 12 scarlet-red flowers appear in widely spaced, loose whorls. Two stamens and a feathery red pistil protrude and are easily seen. The 8–10 in (20–25 cm) long inflorescence comes into bloom gradually, making the plant a valuable prolonged nectar source for hummingbirds.

Introduced to horticulture about 1870, few records and no lore exist to suggest where *Salvia elegans* came from or by what means, but its fragrance and form have given pleasure to scores of people. Prized for its pineapple scent, it is one of those beloved plants passed from gardener to gardener and wintered over indoors on many windowsills.

An area with mild winters, plus good drainage and garden soil enriched with humus are needed if *Salvia elegans* is to flower. Wind protection and weekly watering are also required. As to hardiness, pineapple sage prefers temperatures no lower than the low 30°s F (around −1° C). It will usually withstand winters in the San Francisco Bay area but on occasion will die down to the ground before returning from established rootstock in late spring. Cuttings and division of the rootstock are easy means of propagation. Seed sown in a warm greenhouse in early winter will produce a large plant by the following September or October. This sage grows rapidly and abundantly.

Easily placed in the garden with shrubs or tall perennials such as hollyhocks for shade, pineapple sage attracts hummingbirds and gives great enjoyment with its late flowering. In a mild climate, plant *Salvia elegans* in a protected nook in the garden. Its crisp foliage and showy blossoms will give the garden relief from the sparse look of winter. It makes a splendid greenhouse plant.

*Salvia elegans* 'Honey Melon' (plate 31) was introduced by the Huntington Botanical Gardens in the 1970s. This selection is from a seedling of *Salvia elegans* collected in 1968 in Jalisco, Mexico, by botanist Fred Boutin. A winsome plant, 'Honey Melon' resembles a miniature *S. elegans*. It is 1.5–2 ft (34–60 cm) tall, spreads on an underground rootstock, and in a short time will make a thick groundcover. Its leaves are smaller than the leaves of *Salvia elegans*, but when crushed, release the same fruity, pineapple fragrance.

'Honey Melon' begins flowering in early summer and erect stems carry many inflorescences of scarlet-red flowers that measure about 1 in (2.5 cm) in length. Many come into bloom at the same time and make a fine combination with the fresh looking, mid-green leaves. The leaves are deltoid in shape, about 1 in (2.5 cm) wide and as long. Hardy to 20° F (−7° C) or less, 'Honey Melon' renews itself from its rootstock. During the growing season, cut all inflorescences back as soon as they look spent. Very quickly the plant will come into bloom again. My growing season is a long one and I cut this salvia back three times for repeat bloom.

Flourishing in light shade, 'Honey Melon' will also take full sun. Give it good drainage, garden soil enriched with humus, and regular watering every 10 days to two weeks. It may be divided almost any time of the year and cuttings are also an easy form of propagation.

Try it as a groundcover at the base of shrubs such as *Osmanthus* or *Ilex* or at the base of tall salvias. The butter-yellow *Salvia madrensis* or the purple-blue *S. mexicana* would be enhanced with a liberal splash of the red of 'Honey Melon' at their feet.


## *Salvia farinacea* Bentham, Mealy sage

The herbaceous perennial *Salvia farinacea* occurs in a wide variety of habitats in central and eastern Texas into New Mexico and the neighboring Mexican province of Coahuila. Found at elevations varying from 165–6000 ft (50–1800 m), *S. farinacea* is usually found growing on rocky soil containing limestone. Described and named botanically in 1833, the specific epithet *farinacea* is derived from the Latin for "flour" and refers to the mealy looking dusting that covers the inflorescence. Mealy sage, as it is commonly called, was soon recognized as a fine plant and was being grown as a garden subject by 1850.

Growing 3–4 ft (1–1.3 m) in height and 2 ft (0.6 m) in width, mealy sage is heavily clothed with glossy mid-green, ovate, lance-like leaves. They are 3–4 in (7–10 cm) long and 1 in (2.5 cm) or more wide. The inflorescence is terminal, 6 in (15 cm) long, and tightly packed with whorls of flowers. The calyx that holds each flower is less than 0.5 in (1.3 cm) in length and appears farinose but is actually densely covered with mat-like woolly hairs that are tinged with white, blue, or purple. It is for this character that the plant is named. Flowers are less than 1 in (2.5 cm) in length and usually a dark violet color. It has a long blooming period beginning in April or May and flowering continues until cold weather and frost stop the display. Hardy to 25° F (−4° C), mealy sage will not come back from its rootstock after a cold winter.

A number of cultivars are offered by nurseries and seed catalogs. Some of the old-time favorites are 'Alba' and 'White Porcelain', which have white inflorescences; 'Blue Bedder', which has darker blue flowers than the typical species; and 'Victoria', which has violet-blue flowers and calyces. A smaller form of 'Victoria', called 'Mina', has been introduced. It grows about 1 ft (30 cm) in height, less in width, and is called by some gardeners "a weak perennial." All make good bedding plants with the exception of 'Mina'.

Undisturbed by pests or insects, mealy sage is a trouble-free plant either in the garden or in pots or tubs. Its attributes include plain and simple culture with little pruning or pinching and a long blooming period. Full sun and fast-draining soil enriched with humus are required, along with ample water. Because of heavy blooming, light applications of a balanced liquid fertilizer are helpful. If winters are mild, the root crown can be protected with lightweight straw or evergreen boughs. When all danger of frost has passed, prune for a shapely plant. Propagation is by cuttings or seed. Many *Salvia farinacea* cultivar selections will usually come true from seed, but plants are generally treated as annuals.

Mealy sage is often used as a filler in borders of all sizes because of its dependable flowering and very neat and trim appearance. Pamela J. Harper (1991) praises its ability to be grown as either an annual or perennial and its ability to mix well with either yellows or pinks.

Unexcelled as a pot plant or in a large container, a traditional plant combination includes *Salvia farinacea* 'Blue Bedder' and trailing ivy geraniums (*Pelargonium peltatum*) for an on-going floriferous display. An unconventional combination for a large tub includes the cultivar 'Victoria' with red lettuce, purple basil, and the large, gray leaved *Salvia argentea* at the edge and spilling over the side.

## *Salvia flava* Forrest ex Diels

Native to the province of Yunnan in China, *Salvia flava* is found there in large numbers on hillsides at altitudes of 7500–13,000 ft (2300–4000 m). It grows abundantly along streambanks in gravelly soil with maples, willows, viburnums, berberis, and clematis.

Sturdy and upright, *Salvia flava* is a perennial herb with a clump of basal-like leaves. It is sometimes under 1 ft (30 cm) tall but more usually over 2 ft tall (60 cm). The attractive leaves are a rich grassy-green color with a puckered surface, about 3 in (8 cm) in length with a pointed tip. In mid- to late summer, the salvia's flowering stalk elongates and blooms, reaching approximately 2 ft (60 cm) in height. The widely spaced flowers appear in whorls of four to eight. Individual flowers are covered with long, soft hairs and are tubular in shape, with the upper lip slightly curved at the apex. Flower color is yellow (*flava* means "yellow") or yellow-brown, with a conspicuous purple spot on the lower lip.

*The Flora of China* (1994) warns that *Salvia bulleyana*, also found in Yunnan, is very closely related to *S. flava*, and is repeatedly regarded as a synonym. In horticulture both in Great Britain and the United States, *S. flava* is frequently called *S. bulleyana*. The flowers of *S. bulleyana* are purple-blue, with no spotting on the middle lobe of the lower lip. There is no information about the two species hybridizing in the wild but it would be interesting to find out about that possibility. If they do not hybridize in the wild, then both species should be properly recognized.

The specific epithet *bulleyana* has its origins in a trip made by the famous plant collector Reginald John Farrer. The industrious and energetic Farrer needed subscriptions in order to finance his journeys to Japan, China, and other places in the East. Arthur K. Bulley, a wealthy cotton broker who in 1904 founded his own nursery, Bees, Ltd., was approached and was the principal contributor for two of Farrer's plant-hunting expeditions. The salvia that bears his name was collected on one of these trips.

Easy to situate and care for in the garden, *Salvia flava* needs friable soil that drains well, partial sunlight, and water on a weekly basis. Ascribed by some gardeners to be drought tolerant, I have not tested the plant in this regard but keep the soil around it from drying out. In my garden, *S. flava* is completely dormant in winter, returning from its root-stock in early spring after the soil has begun to warm. Plants are hardy to 0° F (−18° C) or lower. Stems hold well in flower arrangements if first conditioned by cutting them under water. Propagation is by division of an established clump or by seed.

*Salvia flava* is well suited for a subdued but important role in a partly sunny herbaceous border. When planning for mid-summer bloom, the yellow to cream flowered *Phlomis fruticosa*, reaching 4 ft (1.3 m), along with the 2 ft (60 cm) tall *Echinops ritro*, with its bristly, globular heads of light blue flowers, make fine companions for clumps of the subtly col-ored and long blooming *Salvia flava*. Space permitting, the off-white flowered *Verbascum chaixii* 'Album', which has a pronounced mauve eye and grows to 2–3 ft (60–90 cm), gives a strong vertical lift to the composition.

## *Salvia forskaohlei* Linnaeus, Plate 32

An endemic of the southeastern part of the Balkan Peninsula, *Salvia forskaohlei* is found from Bulgaria and Greece to the Black Sea coastline of Turkey. A hardy and handsome herbaceous perennial, in its native habitat it may be found at elevations of 6000 ft (1800 m) or less, growing in broad leaved and coniferous forests, in meadows, and on steep banks. Introduced to horticulture in 1800, it was named in honor of Peter Forsskal of Finland, who collected plants in southwest Arabia in the mid-1700s.

Being deciduous in cold climates, *Salvia forskaohlei* starts building its thick and plentiful basal leaves in early spring. Hairy on both surfaces,

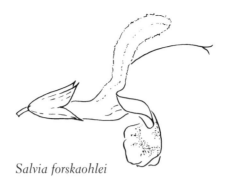

*Salvia forskaohlei*

the leaves are parsley-green in spring, turning dark green by summer. They gradually develop into a large basal clump 2 ft (60 cm) in height and as much across. In mid-summer, flowering stalks rise just above the ample foliage, with a blooming period of six weeks or so. The whorls of flowers are few in number and widely spaced, but make quite a show because the violet-blue, two-lipped flower has white streaks with yellow markings on the lower lip. This beeline tracks the most direct path to the nectar and pollen for insects. Fertile seed is plentifully produced and germinates readily. If you sow seed, try to find a strain that has flowers of deep violet-blue, which show up well in light shade. Inflorescences last well in bouquets.

Loamy soil and two-thirds to a half day of sun will promote a healthy plant and provide good flowering conditions. Weekly watering and sharp drainage are necessary, and a yearly dressing of humus will keep the soil in good tilth. A light application of fertilizer may be helpful in early summer. During a long, warm autumn, flowering will be repeated. *Salvia forskaohlei* plants can be protected with pine boughs in gardens that experience low temperatures. Plants are reported to be hardy to 0° F (−18° C).

For a border with some light shade, consider the evergreen western chain fern, *Woodwardia fimbriata*, which will grow in clumps 6 ft (2 m) tall, in the middle of the border along with *Salvia forskaohlei*. In front, *Geranium macrorrhizum* 'Album', with its creamy petals and pink stamens, will become a large mat. All have more or less evergreen foliage and will thrive with the same growing conditions in a mild climate. Gardens that have 0° F (−18° C) weather will find this salvia a valuable addition to a sunny herbaceous border. The 3 ft (1 m) or taller *Helianthus* × *laetiflorus* 'Morning Sun', with its clear yellow flowers, or the delightful, similar sized *Rudbeckia hirta* (black-eyed Susan), with its pale yellow rays and purple-brown discs, are worthy autumn companions.

## *Salvia* 'Frieda Dixon'

The herbaceous perennial *Salvia* 'Frieda Dixon' will reach 4–5 ft (1.3–1.5 m) in height in a growing season. Given a favorable situation in light shade, its rootstock increases rapidly and forms a large clump similar to *Salvia elegans*, the pineapple sage.

*Salvia* 'Frieda Dixon' is a chance seedling of *S. elegans* that was found by Jon Dixon in his greenhouse in Woodside, California, in the late 1970s or early 1980s. Only one parent is known since many different salvias were growing in the greenhouse and garden at that time. Dixon planted the seedling in a garden situation in order to evaluate its performance. When it proved to have an upright habit and an attractive appearance, he propagated it from cuttings and distributed it among gardeners. For well over 10 years it has been grown in gardens in the San Francisco Bay area and, as well as being beautiful, it has been found to attract hummingbirds and butterflies. During that period of time, it has demonstrated a pleasing vertical growth habit as well as hardiness during short periods to 20° F (−7° C). After one extended period of cold weather, when temperatures were about 11° F (−12° C) for several days, this salvia came back from its rootstock the following spring. By autumn, it was blooming as usual.

*Salvia* 'Frieda Dixon' can frequently be found in California nurseries and on mail order lists. It certainly merits its good reputation for reliable autumn flowering and unusual flower color.

Fast-draining soil enriched with humus and protection from the western sun are needed to bring the plant into flower by late summer or early autumn. Deep weekly watering is also necessary. *Salvia* 'Frieda Dixon' has the upright-growing habit of pineapple sage and the leaves have the same fruity fragrance. The leaves are lanceolate, the largest about 2 in (5 cm) long and 1 in (2.5 cm) wide and mid-green in color. The flowers are a peachy-red when fully open; when back lit, the peach color is prominent on the two lips of the flower. The color reminds me of tomato soup thinned with heavy cream. Pleasing as cut flowers, flowering stems have a long life in a bouquet. After all danger of a late frost, cut stems to the ground to ensure uniform spring and summer growth. Propagation is by cuttings or division of the rootstock.

A number of perennials and grasses require the same cultural conditions as *Salvia* 'Frieda Dixon'. A grouping that features beautiful foliage would include *Panicum virgatum*, the good-looking switch grass, which blooms in autumn and then turns a lovely shade of pale honey. The grass is 2 ft (60 cm) in height and its airy flowering stems rise an additional 2 ft (60 cm) and could be interspersed with clumps of the salvia. At the base of these plants, the 1 ft (30 cm) *Epimedium* × *rubrum* would tie the grouping together. Its handsome wine-red leaves with distinctive pea-green veining retain their color from the beginning to the end of the growing season. The shape and color of the three foliages, as well as the height of the plants, would be complimentary.

## *Salvia fruticosa* Miller, Greek sage, Plate 33

One of the earliest spring blooming salvias, *Salvia fruticosa* is evergreen and described as a shrub. Native to the eastern Mediterranean, including southern Italy, it is particularly abundant in Israel. It also occurs on the Canary Islands and in north Africa. Commonly found in several plant communities, populations comprised of *S. fruticosa* alone are not unusual. Valued for centuries for its bountiful beauty, Greek sage has medicinal and culinary properties as well as sweet nectar and pollen. On the Greek island of Crete at the site of reconstructed Knossos, Greek sage was depicted circa 1400 B.C. in the House of Frescoes.

In a garden setting the bushy *Salvia fruticosa* generally grows 2 ft (60 cm) in height and width and its flowering stalk rises 1 ft (30 cm) or more above the foliage. The entire plant is hairy and has a delightful frosty appearance. Its leaves are numerous, of different sizes, and in clusters—this accounts for the bushy look. A long, hairy petiole supports a three-part, artichoke-green leaf. The middle portion is obovate or lanceolate with two little segments at its base.

The blooming period usually begins in early March and continues for well over a month. Pinkish lavender flowers about 0.5 in (1.3 cm) in length are held in a small oxblood-red, five-pointed, hairy calyx, making a very pretty combination of colors. The flowers occur in whorls along the inflorescence.

When the plant was described by Linnaeus in 1781, he named it *triloba* to emphasize the unusual leaf. In actuality, the plant had already been described in 1768 by Philip Miller, who, among many other accomplishments, was Curator of the Chelsea Physic Garden for 22 years. According to the rules of botanical nomenclature, the earliest name stands. The specific epithet *fruticosa* means shrubby or bushy.

A full day of sun, well-draining soil, and good air circulation are all necessities for *Salvia fruticosa*. It is hardy to 20° F (−7° C) and is a drought tolerant plant that needs little additional water when established. After it blooms, it can be pruned to a desirable size. If flowers are needed for bouquets, this procedure can help with the shaping of the plant. Branches last well in arrangements. Propagation is by seed or cuttings. In June or July, cuttings strike roots rapidly.

Greek sage is highly variable in its form and structure. Its oils are variable too. Because of a high oil content, it has historical uses similar to *Salvia officinalis*, garden sage. The leaves contain chemicals similar to some lavenders, and druggists in some parts of the world sell them as *Folia salviae*. Dried leaves are used to make tea, and fresh leaves steeped with honey make a refreshing drink.

In its native habitat, *Salvia fruticosa* frequently develops woolly galls that range from the size of a cherry to the size of a walnut. The gall-producing insect is more than likely found only in the Middle East. Most galls are about 1 in (2.5 cm) in diameter and are called "apples." Often mistaken for fruit because of the resemblance to little apples, when young and still green they are very fragrant, juicy, and tasty. Considered delicious and healthful, Greeks and Arabs, among others, peel and eat them when they are soft.

On a dry hillside with other evergreen Mediterranean plants such as *Artemisia arborescens*, *Euphorbia rigida* or *E. myrsinites*, and *Rosmarinus officinalis* 'Collingwood Ingram', a group of *Salvia fruticosa* will add variety of leaf form to a combination of plants with interesting foliage. All require the same culture, including good drainage and only occasional summer water.

## *Salvia fulgens* Cavanilles, Cardinal sage, Plate 53

Botanically classified as a perennial herb, *Salvia fulgens* resembles, in stature, a shrub. Native to Mexico, its range is limited to the central mountains in the province of Puebla. It is found there on the edge of oak and coniferous woodlands, particularly in clearings of *Picea religiosa*, at elevations of 8700–11,000 ft (2700–3400 m). These mountains receive moisture in the form of fog practically year round and in the form of rain during the late spring and the end of summer and beginning of autumn. Its common name, cardinal sage, is appropriate, for the flowers stand out as brightly in its native green woodland as the eastern cardinal stands out in its home territory. This salvia is also known by the synonym *Salvia cardinalis* (Kunth).

Growing 4–5 ft (1.3–1.5 m) in height and 3–4 ft (1–1.3 m) in width in a season, cardinal sage needs a long, warm autumn in order to produce heavy flowering. The rather pale, yellow-green, heart-shaped leaves are about 1.5 in (4 cm) long and 1 in (2.5 cm) wide and cover the plant amply. Inflorescences are short, usually 4 in (10 cm) in length, and are terminal. Very rarely, an inflorescence 12 in (30 cm) long may be found. The flowers are fire-engine red, 2 in (5 cm) in length, and in loose whorls. The upper lip of each flower is covered with red hairs. These hairs catch moisture from dew and glisten in the morning light. The specific epithet, *fulgens*, means glitter, glisten, or shine. After the flowers have bloomed, they drop, leaving a reddish-brown, 0.5 in (1.3 cm) calyx. Frequently, the calyx drops too, precluding seed production.

Site cardinal sage in full sun, being careful that the slanted October and November sun still reaches the plant. Well-draining soil enriched with humus and regular summer watering are needed. Fertilizer in early summer may help the salvia get off to a fast start. Some staking is necessary. I usually tie twine around the middle of all the stems of the plant to hold them up in order to see the flowers. Other plants will camouflage the twine. Hardy to 20° F (−7° C), cut cardinal sage within 1 ft (30 cm) of its crown after all danger of frost has passed. Propagation is by seed, cuttings, and division of the rootstock.

During the autumn and winter of 1993–94 temperatures were mild and the soil remained warm in my garden, with no killing frost. These unusual weather conditions allowed me to have a bouquet of cardinal sage for my desk on the 23rd of January. This was a particular pleasure during the short days of winter.

Introduced to horticulture in the 1800s, cardinal sage has been grown in Britain for many years. Harold and Joan Bawden (1970) call its flowers startling and write that it is at its very best in their Sussex garden in September. They regard it as well worth the extra trouble of keeping it in a greenhouse over winter and finding a warm wall for it in the garden in spring.

A composition of autumn blooming salvias is outstanding and a joy to behold. For height, the yellow flowered *Salvia madrensis* and vermilion flowered *S. confertiflora* will make a 5–7 ft (1.5–2.3 m) tall background. In the midground, clumps of cardinal sage can be interplanted with white and scarlet *S. coccinea*. For the front of the border, a wide ribbon of *S. elegans* 'Honey Melon' will hold the mass of foliage and colorful flowers together. All plants require the same culture and care. In my own garden, *S. fulgens* is allowed very little space and must compete for sun with the rich violet flowered *S. mexicana* and violet-blue flowered *Aster × versicolor*. These plants are in the range of 4–5 ft (1.3–1.5 m) and when crowded together help hold each other up. For well over a month their various colored flowers are a treat.

## *Salvia gesneraeflora* Lindley & Paxton, Plate 34

A robust, winter into spring flowering perennial or sub-shrub, *Salvia gesneraeflora* is found in many mountainous provinces of the Sierra Madre Occidental in Mexico. Growing at elevations ranging from 7500–10,000 ft (2300–3100 m), it is apparently tolerant of cold temperatures into the low 20°s F (around −6° C). Named to honor Conrad von

Gesner of Zurich, a celebrated 15th-century naturalist and botanist, the long tubular flowers of this salvia resemble the flowers in the genus *Gesneria*. The family *Gesneriaceae* is named for Conrad von Gesner, as well as this genus.

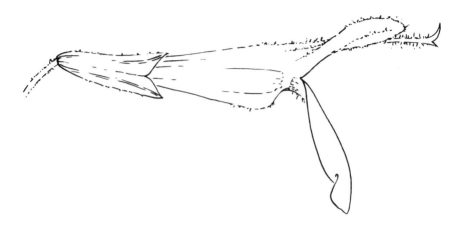

*Salvia gesneraeflora*

    Reputed to grow to 25 ft (7.6 m) in height in its native habitat, *Salvia gesneraeflora* usually attains approximately 5–6 ft (1.5–2 m) in height and 4 ft (1.3 m) in width as a garden plant. Pruning is a contributing factor to the smaller plant size, whether brought about by the gardener or by windy weather. Because it builds multiple woody stems that are heavy with foliage, this salvia is a ready candidate for rain and wind damage. Leaves are graduated in size, heart-shaped and mid-green, and strongly aromatic. Large, vivid orange-red flowers, 1–1.5 in (2.5–4 cm) long, are held in an 1 in (2.5 cm) yellow-green calyx, tinged with purple glands. Whorls of showy flowers are closely spaced on inflorescences that are 8–12 in (20–30 cm) long. This plant tends to stay in bloom for an extended period during the late winter and early spring. In late May when the weather is very warm, it is advisable to cut the whole plant back to leaf nodes near its base even though it may still be in bloom. Hard annual pruning will ensure new growth, which will build approximately 6 ft (2m) in height, and will encourage flowering in the coming year.

A collecting trip to Mexico was made in 1970 by botanists at the Huntington Botanical Gardens. At this time, Fred Boutin collected seed of *Salvia gesneraeflora* from two distinctly different populations—a form with green calyx and a form with purple calyx and stem. The collection site was at 8500 ft (2600 m) on the Volcan de Tequila in the province of Jalisco. The green calyx form is the one commonly found. The dark purple calyx and stem form was given the name 'Tequila' (plate 34). Sometime around 1979, John MacGregor, who was on the staff at the Huntington, selected a seedling from 'Tequila' and called it 'Mole Poblano'. It is reputed to be more floriferous than 'Tequila', with a longer bloom season, but I have been unable to verify this. It is entirely possible that these two selections have become confused, since they are similar.

A sunny spot with good drainage and protection from wind is ideal for *Salvia gesneraeflora* and its two cultivars. Some regular water is needed throughout the summer and autumn. Propagation is by seed or cuttings. It is not unusual to find seedlings near the mother plant from time to time. Remember, late May is the time to cut the plant back even though it may still be blooming. If branching occurs at awkward angles, and it probably will, remove shoots at the main stem in order to keep a shapely plant. Proven to be cold tolerant into the low 20°s F (around −6° C), I would not advise planting this salvia unless your winter climate is both sunny and mild, conditions which are necessary to generate good flowering. These salvias are striking companions in gardens with mild climates and, in addition, are a generous nectar source for over-wintering hummingbirds.

Because of its large stature, *Salvia gesneraeflora* and *S. gesneraeflora* 'Tequila' combine beautifully with large clumping grasses such as *Miscanthus sinensis* (Japanese silver grass), which reaches 6–8 ft (2–2.5 m) at maturity. Flowering in August, the dried inflorescence of the grass holds right through the winter months, complementing the winter blooming salvia. Late in the season the foliage of Japanese silver grass turns purple-red and then dries to a warm beige, giving form and motion to the garden during the shortest days of the year.

## *Salvia glechomaefolia* Kunth

Native to at least three provinces in central Mexico, *Salvia glechomae-folia* is found at altitudes ranging from 7500–10,500 ft (2300–3200 m). Not a well-known plant in horticultural circles, it became available to gardeners through California nurseries in 1992. The specific name, *glechomaefolia*, is derived from the Greek and means with foliage like *Glechoma*. Linnaeus gave this name to a small genus in the mint family comprised of creeping and stoloniferous plants.

A creeping perennial herb, *Salvia glechomaefolia*, when established, will make an airy colony of yellow-green foliage that is upright and almost sparse. The leaves reflect light and appear to be in widely spaced whorls. Stems are short and reach about 1–1.5 ft (30–40 cm) in height. Flowering lightly throughout the summer, the long, blue-violet flowers have two prominent white lines leading to the nectary and seem to bloom without interruption. The small flowers are less than 1 in (2.5 cm) long and occur in unevenly spaced whorls, usually with fewer than 12 flowers in each whorl. The overall effect is of daintiness.

A half day of sun along with loamy soil enriched with humus are needed for *Salvia glechomaefolia*. Friable soil enriched with a large handful of bloodmeal will encourage the plant to colonize. In fact, a small amount of bloodmeal every spring will give plants strength and good foliage color. Soil that drains well and deep watering at least once a week are also recommended. Colonies of the salvia profit from the humidity created by the leaves of nearby plants. The removal of spent inflorescences will help keep the plants flowering over a three month period during summer. Known to be hardy to 32° F (0° C), *Salvia glechomaefolia* has survived without damage when temperatures fell to the high 20°s F (around −2° C) for short periods of time. Propagation is by division of the rootstock, seed, or cuttings. Cuttings for overwintering in the greenhouse can be taken in late summer or early autumn.

Another native of Mexico, *Echeveria elegans* (sometimes called white Mexican rose) would make an admirable partner for *Salvia glecho-maefolia*. The leaves of *Echeveria elegans* are a year-round garden feature and grow in bold rosettes. Flat and silver-gray, they are covered with a fine white powdery meal. Short flowering stalks appear in spring with pinkish, bell-like flowers that are orange and yellow inside. Another possible companion for *Salvia glechomaefolia* is *Anthemis cretica* if you want a gray foliaged plant that will bloom at the same time as the salvia. It is an uncommon, cushion-forming perennial that is well worth looking for. About 1 ft (30 cm) in height and width with deeply divided grayish foliage, its small daisy-like flowers make a floriferous display. It is easy to grow from seed. If you are looking for a long blooming companion, the California native *Erigeron glaucus*, with basal leaves in clumps, is a good companion with lots of color. Adaptable to most growing conditions, it has lavender, daisy-like flowers and is under 1 ft (30 cm) when in bloom. Suitable for a large container, *Salvia glechomaefolia* combines well with the old-fashioned favorite *Glechoma hederacea* 'Variegata'. These plants will thrive with similar culture.

## *Salvia glutinosa* Linnaeus, Jupiter's distaff

Found across Europe and western Asia, the native habitat of *Salvia glutinosa* includes central France through central Russia, reaching south to Spain, Italy, and Greece. Usually occurring in mountainous areas, it is found in woodlands and protective, shaded environments. Described by Linnaeus in 1753, *S. glutinosa* was known long ago in central Europe for its pleasant smelling flowers and leaves that were used to give flavor to homemade wines.

A deciduous perennial, *Salvia glutinosa* is a rangy plant that frequently reaches 3 ft (1 m) in height. Hairy, hastate leaves, about 5 in (13 cm) in length, are widely spaced on the plant's ascending stems. Parsley-green in color, the leaves have petioles that are practically as long as the leaf itself. The flowers, in whorls of two to six, are pale yellow in color with the upper lip heavily flecked with maroon dots. Both the flowers and the small, lime-green calyces are sticky, hence the specific name *glutinosa*. Flowering begins in early summer and continues for about a two-month period. Be sure to look for the flowers. Even though the inflorescences can be 1 ft (30 cm) in length, flower color is subtle and flowering can easily be overlooked. *S. glutinosa* bears a remarkable resemblance to *S. nubicola*, a species from China. In a mild climate, flowers can be found in late autumn. Propagation is by seed or cuttings.

Friable garden soil containing humus and a shady area are specific cultural requirements for *Salvia glutinosa*, along with water on a weekly basis. This deciduous plant is cold tolerant and withstands temperatures below 0° F (−18° C). Remove the season's top growth when tidying the garden in late autumn or early winter. The practice of removing withered stalks prevents decomposers getting into the crown of the plant.

Gardeners in England have made use of the salvia's tendency to reproduce itself freely by seedlings. The Bawdens (1970) credit it as a tall groundcover plant with an outward sprawl. Their plants flowered over a period of three months. Graham Stuart Thomas (1990a) calls it coarse but recommends it for rough places. The experience of these writers will help other gardeners in placing *Salvia glutinosa* to cover shady areas that require only occasional water and care.

### *Salvia greggii* Gray, Autumn sage, Plate 35

Occurring in rocky soil at elevations of 5000–9000 ft (1500–2800 m), *Salvia greggii* has a lengthy and narrow distribution from southwest Texas throughout the Chihuahuan deserts into the province of San Luis Potosi, Mexico. An evergreen shrub that is common throughout this region, autumn sage is usually found in sunny and dry locations. Described and named by Asa Gray in 1870, the name commemorates J. Gregg, a Mexican trader, who found and collected the salvia in Texas.

*Salvia greggii*

Closely related to *Salvia microphylla*, *S. greggii*, according to Epling (1939), can be identified by the lack of a pair of papillae inside the corolla near its base. Both of these species hybridize freely and James Compton (1994a) has named a hybrid swarm of S. *microphylla* and S. *greggii*, found in the wild, as *Salvia* × *jamensis* (see entry for *Salvia* × *jamensis*). In my experience, S. *greggii* and its hybrids are fecund, and every summer both the species and their hybrids produce numerous seedlings.

Defying its common name, autumn sage flowers throughout the summer and autumn until short days and cool weather slow then stop their production. A highly variable plant reaching 1–4 ft (0.3–1.3 m) in height and less in width, this salvia's growth habit ranges from upright to mounding. Leaves vary in shape and tend to be less than 1 in (2.5 cm) in length. Mid-green in color and glabrous, they can lightly or profusely cover the plant. Flower size, 0.25–1 in (0.6–2.5 cm), is highly variable. Color is variable too. Tints and shades of scarlet and red are the most common colors in the wild, but rose, white, and occasionally pink, lavender, and violet may also occur. From time to time, plants are found that exhibit unusual attributes. For example, *Salvia greggii* 'Big Pink' was introduced by garden writer Scott Ogden, in Austin, Texas, because of the plant's larger than usual lower lip, which clearly flaunts the flower's deep pink color with a lavender tint. The cultivar 'Furman's Red' is a selection made in Texas, probably in the 1970s, and named for W. A. Furman, a distinguished plantsman from Kerrville, Texas. It is known for its profuse production of dark red flowers in autumn. Nurseryman Pat McNeal of Austin, Texas, has introduced the small and charming 'Purple Pastel', which repeats bloom heavily in autumn. Another of his introductions is 'Purple Haze', with small but intensely colored violet-purple flowers. 'Cherry Red' (plate 35) was introduced by nurseryman Richard Dufresne, of Greensboro, North Carolina, because it blooms reliably in the humid south. These plants have proved to be hardy and suitable for shady spots such as an eastern or northeastern exposure, making them valuable additions to horticulture. Their glossy green foliage intensifies the bright colors of the flowers.

Easy to grow in areas with low humidity, *Salvia greggii* needs excellent drainage, a half to full day of sun, and loamy soil. Reported to be drought tolerant, I find plants will tolerate regular water on a weekly basis. Some pinching and pruning will be necessary throughout the long growing season to induce continued flowering. Cut back spent inflorescences periodically. Before active growth begins in spring, prune all dead wood and shape the plant for the season ahead. In my mild climate, S. *greggii* blooms from May until November and is tolerant of temperatures into the teens (around −11° C). Because wood builds in the center of the plant, be sure to start afresh with cuttings every four to five years. Propagation is usually by cuttings because of the great variability of seedlings.

*Salvia greggii* was introduced to cultivation in 1885 and became popular in the United States on the west coast a hundred years later. Nurseries propagate reams of attractive cultivars—the white flowered 'Alba', red flowered 'Cherry Queen', orange-red flowered 'Keter's Red', pale red flowered 'Rosea', reddish pink flowered 'La Encantada', and pink flowered 'Big Pink' and 'Dwarf Pink'. Several undesignated forms have peach or salmon flowers. Sizes and growing habits differ. Two hybrids that are fine ornamental plants with graceful growing habits are 'Plum Wine' and 'Raspberry Royale'. These measure 3 ft (1 m) in both height and width.

Known and valued for its long flowering period, *Salvia greggii* can be smoothly slipped into many different kinds of sunny borders. In an area designed to be attractive from late summer through autumn, the purple leaved *Cercis canadensis* 'Forest Pansy' will anchor a number of pink flowering S. *greggii* cultivars along with drifts of *Aster* × *frikartii* 'Monch', with its deep, clear, violet-blue flowers, and *Aster lateriflorus*, with its purple foliage and pink ray flowers. The self-seeding *Viola tricolor* 'Johnny Jump Up', which is purple and gold with a white eye, can fill the bare spots between the other plants. All require the same culture.

## *Salvia guaranitica* Saint-Hilaire ex Bentham, Anise-scented sage, Plates 36, 37, & 70

From a wide geographical region in South America, including Brazil, Paraguay, Uruguay, and Argentina, comes the exceedingly long blooming herbaceous perennial *Salvia guaranitica*. Described and named in 1833, it has long been favored by gardeners both in the United

States and elsewhere because of its adaptability and brilliant, almost true-blue flowers.

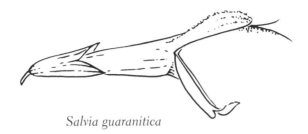

*Salvia guaranitica*

Sometimes called anise-scented sage, referring to the scent released from bruised leaves, this salvia begins blooming in early summer and continues until frost—flowering being heaviest throughout the hot summer months. *Salvia guaranitica* will reach 4–5 ft (1.3–1.5 m) in height in a season and become a large patch in a few years due to its running rootstock. Its roots sport little nodules that look like miniature cigars. The rootstock is quite easy to divide, or propagation can be by seed and cuttings.

Inflorescences are 8–10 in (20–25 cm) long and fairly sparkle with rich blue-violet flowers. Leaves are ovate in shape, 1.5 in (4 cm) long, and almost the same in width. They are a fresh mint-green in color and remain so throughout the prolonged flowering period. The calyx is small, usually a dark purple-green on the side facing the sun and green on the underside. Good for cut flowers, this salvia lasts well in arrangements if stems are conditioned by first cutting them under water.

The culture of *Salvia guaranitica* is similar to that of many of the salvias that come from Mexico. Situate plants in full sunlight or at least in three-quarters of a day of sun. Fast drainage and soil enriched with humus are required. Also, watering on a weekly to 10 day basis is advised in hot weather. Plants may be pruned to the ground in late winter and clumps divided every three years or so. Anise-scented sage has proved hardy to 10° F (−12° C) when given the protection of pine boughs, but it will be completely dormant in a cold climate. Penelope Hobhouse (1985) admires it but warns that cuttings should be taken in autumn and a protective mulch used since it is not reliably hardy in Great Britain.

A number of cultivars are being grown in Britain, France, and the United States. 'Argentina Skies' (plate 37) has pale blue flowers, 'Blue Enigma' has a green calyx, 'Blue Ensign' has large, Cambridge blue flowers, 'Black and Blue' is a subshrub with a very dark violet-blue calyx, and 'Purple Splendour' has rich purple flowers. In my experience, none of the cultivars develop in the same substantial clumps as the species, neither do they flower as profusely. A cultivar that reaches 6 ft (2 m) in height is 'Costa Rica Blue'. It blooms for a long period in autumn. I have found it to be more tender than the other cultivars. In 1993 in my garden, a dark violet flowered sport occurred that has thick stems and a sturdy and upright habit—proving the plant's propensity to variability.

Easy to situate in the garden because of its dependable upright habit, *Salvia guaranitica* can be the mainstay at the back of a herbaceous border. For a pleasing color scheme a clump can be planted with the polyantha rose 'Nathalie Nypels', a repeat blooming, rosy-pink, 3–4 ft (1–1.3 m) shrub. A start of *Geranium dalmaticum*, with its rich green, lush foliage and pink flowers will, in time, make an admirable carpet. Another color scheme combines *Salvia guaranitica* with the yellow-gold, 1.5 ft (45 cm) tall perennial *Coreopsis* 'Early Sunrise'. Known for flowering early from seed, 'Early Sunrise' can be treated as an annual. At their base, the reliable, trailing *Lobelia* 'Crystal Palace' would complement both. The green foliage of the plants is restful and brings the cold blues and warm yellow-gold colors together harmoniously.

## *Salvia hians* Royle ex Bentham, Plate 38

A herbaceous perennial, *Salvia hians* is found in many locations in mountainous regions from Pakistan to Bhutan. Commonly occurring in the Kashmir alpine region at elevations of 7800–13,000 ft (2400–4000 m), its habitats are open slopes and forests. It was first described in 1830 by the naturalist John Forbes Royle, who was superintendent of the East India Company's two hospitals at Saharunpur and curator of the botanical garden there. The gardens were redesigned by Royle and contained both medicinal and economically useful plants that had been collected in the high mountain areas of Kashmir.

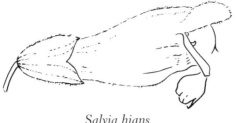

*Salvia hians*

Withstanding temperatures below 0° F (−18° C), in a normal growing season *Salvia hians* makes a mound that measures 2–3 ft (0.6–1 m) in height by 2 ft (0.6 m) in width. The slightly hairy leaves vary in size and shape, the largest being about 10 in (25 cm) long. Usually lanceolate in shape, with a petiole as long as the blade itself, the leaves appear linear because they are slightly folded in half along the mid-rib. Deep pea-green in color, the leaves are deciduous in winter, even in a mild climate. Flowering stems are branched and rise well above the foliage. Whorls of only a few dusky violet flowers are airily spaced towards the top of the stem. The calyx is frequently less than 0.5 in (1.3 cm) in length but though it is small, it is an important adjunct to the flower. It is covered with sticky, glandular hairs and is an unusually dark brown-red color. This rather strange color somehow intensifies the inflated violet flower. The specific epithet *hians* means gaping, referring to the gap between the two lips of the flower.

*Salvia hians* adapts well to many garden situations. A friable, loamy soil with good drainage is recommended along with a half to full day of sun, and deep watering once each week. Flowering occurs during the summer with repeat bloom where the autumn is long and mild. Propagation is by seed and division. Frequently, plantlets (leaves with roots) appear in late summer that can be teased away from the base of the plant.

*Salvia hians* is known to gardeners on the U.S. west coast and may be seen at Quarry Hill Botanic Garden near Glen Ellen, California, as well as the University of California Botanical Garden, Berkeley. It appears with regularity on seed lists. Gardeners in Britain have appreciated this salvia for many years. William Robinson (1933) wrote that it was free in growth and flower. Graham Stuart Thomas (1990a) found its plentiful spikes of purplish blue flowers and purplish brown, hairy calyces an unusual and attractive color scheme.

Well-suited for a sunny border, *Salvia hians* combines nicely with many other sun loving perennials. Planted with groups of the 2 ft (60 cm) tall, pale yellow flowered *Achillea* 'Taygetae', it will flower during the same period and the achillea's ferny foliage contrasts with the somewhat long and slender leaf blade of the salvia. Included for its eye catching pale gray, heart-shaped foliage, *Helichrysum petiolare* will complement the other two plants. Another combination includes the 9 in (22 cm) annual marigold *Tagetes patula* 'Legion of Honour' massed in front of the salvia. The marigold has single, golden yellow flowers with dark brown markings. In the background, the gray leaved, shrub-like *Senecio* 'Sunshine' supplies substance and light. Space permitting, the vertical *Salvia farinacea* 'Victoria' adds another shade of purple and another shape to the picture.

## *Salvia hirtella* Vahl, Plate 39

A long blooming perennial herb, *Salvia hirtella* is found in Ecuador, both north and south of the equator, in the province of Cotopaxi. The distribution of *S. hirtella* is limited to high elevations in the Andes Mountains and collections have been made in the range of 12,000 ft (3600 m). My plants come from seed collected in Valle del Rio Mestizo by Jim and Jenny Archibald of Wales in July 1993, made available the same year through their enticing seed list.

In my garden *Salvia hirtella* is an evergreen, branching herb that grows just under 2 ft (60 cm) in height. When the weight of its stems and inflorescences bend it to the ground it will root at the node if the soil is loose and friable. It is not unusual for a single plant to cover 3 ft (1 m) in two years. The appearance of the salvia is very erect in spite of its mat-forming growth habit. The glossy, grass-green leaves are graduated in size and triangular. The average size is about 2 in (5 cm) in width at the base of the leaf and 2 in (5 cm) in length. Inflorescences are usually about 1 ft (30 cm) in length and held upright. Richly colored orange-red flowers are 1.5 in (4 cm) in length and in verticils of six. Even though a whorl has 12 flowers, only a few bloom at the same time. The calyx and stem of the inflorescence are covered with conspicuous dark purple hairs with glands that enhance the beauty of the plant. The calyces remain after the flowers have bloomed and dropped, giving the plant an additional attractive feature. The specific epithet *hirtella* literally means "rather hairy." Blooming begins in early summer and continues until the days shorten noticeably.

Place *Salvia hirtella* in the garden where it receives direct sun for a half day but has the protection of surrounding plants. Well-draining, friable soil amended with compost for a good root run is recommended as well as deep watering on a weekly basis. Seed is usually produced in small amounts by garden plants and is easy to germinate. Cuttings taken during the active growing season are virtually sure to strike roots. Layering is another means of propagation. *S. hirtella* has remained evergreen and unharmed when temperatures have dropped into the high 20s° F (around −2° C) in my garden. Its high elevation habitat implies hardiness to an even lower temperature and tolerance of light frosts.

Along the edge of a woodland border that receives filtered light, the evergreen *Viburnum japonicum* or *V. cinnamonifolium*, both about 9 ft (3 m) in height, will in time make an impressive background. While the viburnums mature, the blue flowered *Salvia cacaliaefolia* and bright red flowered *S. hirtella* provide excellent patches of summer color. If there is space, consider adding the evergreen *Viburnum davidii*, 3 ft (1 m) in height, and the creeping, orange-red flowered *Salvia blepharophylla*, 1 ft (30 cm). These three salvias are colonizers and make fine fillers in the border. All plants require high or light shade and regular deep watering.

## *Salvia holwayi* Blake, Plate 40

Throughout Guatemala, *Salvia holwayi* is found at elevations of 3000–9000 ft (900–2800 m). Prevalent at similar elevations in the Mexican province of Chiapas, it frequently makes an understory in thickets and mixed forests of pine and oak. Flowering in abundance in November, at the end of the rainy season, Guatemalans call it one of the most attractive plants of their western highlands. It was named to honor the plant and fungi collector, Edward Willet Dorland Holway of Michigan, who made four collecting trips to Mexico at the turn of the nineteenth century.

A herbaceous perennial 3–5 ft (1–1.5 m) in height, *Salvia holwayi* grows profusely and will easily cover 8–10 ft (2.5–3 m) in a year. Its long stems are lax and look beautiful in its native habitat when it grows over and is supported by other shrubs. Many inflorescences are produced along each stem. After they expand they measure about 8 in (20 cm) in length, creating a sea of subtle color. Whorls of cardinal-red flowers almost 1 in (2.5 cm) long and inflated in the center are spaced closely together and make a splendid show because large numbers of flowers expand and open at the same time. Blooming begins in late autumn or early winter and will usually continue through February and March. Established plants in mild climates bloom earlier and for a longer period. Leaves are yellow-green, deltoid in shape, and have pronounced veining. They vary in size, the average being about 2 in (5 cm) long by 1 in (2.5 cm) wide. The overall effect of the plant is one of luxuriousness.

Some shade, good drainage, and soil enriched with humus are needed for *Salvia holwayi*. Deep watering once every two to three weeks is advisable. If temperatures dip below 20° F (−5° C) much of the top growth may be damaged, but the plant will come back from its strong roots, possibly because the heavy top growth protects the base of the plant. After the blooming season is over and the danger of frost is past, prune the plant hard in order to keep it in bounds during the coming growing season. It is vigorous and 8–10 ft (2.5–3 m) of growth each summer is usual for a mature plant.

After *Salvia holwayi* becomes well established, you may find small plants under or near it that are the result of adventitious roots. These plants may be removed and shared with other gardeners. Layering also frequently occurs when a lax stem becomes covered with soil. This promotes rooting at the nodes. Both forms of propagation produce desirable offspring. Because of the rampant growth during each season, the removal of additional plants usually becomes a necessity. Cuttings taken in summer root quite readily.

Here is a wonderful winter blooming plant with many uses. It will camouflage fences that are 5–6 ft (1.5–2 m) in height or hide unsightly rough and weedy places. It makes a fine background for other plants when placed at the back of the border with something it can climb. Flowering stems hold well in flower arrangements and are handsome in winter bouquets. Hummingbirds find its nectar a fine food source at the time of year when little food is available.

## *Salvia* 'Indigo Spires', Plates 41 & 73

Rapidly growing into a large shrub 4 ft (1.3 m) tall and as wide, *Salvia* 'Indigo Spires' is a spontaneous garden hybrid. It was found growing near S. *longispicata* and S. *farinacea* at the Huntington Botanical Gardens by John MacGregor, horticulturist, and was introduced to gardeners in 1979. A chance seedling, MacGregor refers to the plant as a "sterile hybrid, courtesy of the bees."

Blooming begins in early summer and continues until frost. The long, 10–12 in (25–30 cm) inflorescence is spike-like and crowded with rich violet flowers. Individual flowers are small, 0.5 in (1.3 cm) in length, closely spaced together in whorls, and a fine violet-blue color that does not fade in the hot summer sunlight. The upper lip has two very narrow white bee lines leading insects to nectar, and the lower lip is covered with small violet-blue hairs. The 0.5 in (1.3 cm) long calyx is dark purple and remains intact on its violet stem after the flowers have dropped. The leaves are primarily ovate in shape and widely spaced along the branches. Mid-green in color, they appear slick and their margins are serrated and dark.

Full sun and fast-draining soil enriched with humus are essential for this salvia, which develops and blooms for such a long period of time. Deep weekly water is advisable too. Pinching and pruning throughout the growing season is vital in order to keep the plant shapely. Be sure to remove inflorescences when most of the flowers have dropped. This kind of grooming will take excess weight off the shrub and encourage repeated flowering. Propagation is by cuttings.

Probably hardy to the mid 20's F (around −4° C), *Salvia* 'Indigo Spires' slowly came back from its rootstock when temperatures in my garden dipped to 11° F (−12° C) one December. It is wise to have cuttings in the greenhouse in case of a sudden drop in temperature. After all danger of frost has passed, prune the shrub heavily. When the earth has been warmed by the sun in late spring, a thick, 2–4 in (5–10 cm) mulch of humus at the base of the plant will provide food and help prevent water evaporation.

To take advantage of a salvia that blooms continually, plant *Salvia* 'Indigo Spires' in a herbaceous border designed for leaf texture and summer bloom. The back of the border might include several plants of 'Indigo Spires' interplanted with a few *Gaura lindheimeri*, the graceful white and pink, 3–4 ft (1–1.3 m) tall Louisiana and Texas native. In front, drifts of *Artemisia absinthium* 'Lambrook Silver', which has silver-gray foliage, and the pink flowered soapwort, *Saponaria ocymoides* 'Splendens', would round out the composition. All require the same culture, including similar amounts of water. For a cottage garden border, plant over-wintered cuttings of 'Indigo Spires' in the background with masses of annuals in the foreground. In situ, sow seed of cosmos, cleome, zinnia, and *Salvia viridis*. All of these annuals are more or less the same size and will develop concurrently. At any stage of growth, unwanted seedlings may be easily thinned.

## *Salvia interrupta* Schousboe, Plates 42 & 90

A perennial with some wood at the base, *Salvia interrupta* occurs throughout the range of the Atlas Mountains in Morocco. When in bloom, it is a dignified and beautiful plant. It grows at elevations of 1300–5000 ft (400–1500 m) on rock covered limestone slopes and in lightly shaded forests. Described botanically in 1801, it was introduced to horticulture before 1870 and has become a favorite of gardeners both here and abroad since the 1970s.

*Salvia interrupta* appears to grow in a basal rosette. It has apple-green leaves of varying sizes that are covered with short white hairs on the underside. The leaf is three lobed and the lobes can be situated at different angles at the base of the leaf. Flowering is usually in late spring or early summer and frequently repeats quite heavily in October. At that time, the flowering stalk elongates approximately 2 ft (60 cm). Verticels

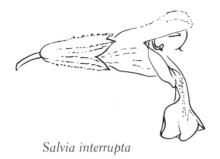

*Salvia interrupta*

of five to 10 flowers are held on small stems called peduncles and are widely spaced along the stalk. This spacing is the reason for the plant's specific name, *interrupta*, and contributes to the plant's elegance. Large, fat, violet flowers, just less than 1.5 in (3.5 mm) long, come into bloom a few at a time. The lower lip of the flower is wide and in the center are two distinct white lines that lead insects to pollen and nectar glands. Flowering stalks last well as cut flowers. Be sure to condition them by cutting the stems under water. Interestingly, the stalks of this salvia are square when they are young, but with age become round. At maturity they have two distinct, dark purple-brown lines that run the length of the stalk. This salvia is sometimes confused with *S. candelabrum* from Spain because the inflorescences are similar. However, the leaves of *S. candelabrum* are not divided.

*Salvia interrupta* thrives best in full sun but will survive with less direct light. Loamy, friable soil that has good drainage is necessary, and a small handful of ground oyster shells worked thoroughly into the soil when preparing a place for each plant is desirable. Fertilizer is not required but deep weekly watering is recommended. This salvia is a tender plant, and will probably not survive temperatures that fall under 25° F (−4° C) for long periods. It is a short-lived perennial that should be replaced every third year. Propagation is usually by seed, although cuttings can be taken.

Though described by William Robinson (1933) as one of the most beautiful border plants, *Salvia interrupta* is difficult to place in a herbaceous border because its tall and dramatic flowering stalks tend to get lost in a sea of flowers and leaves. Since its tidy foliage stays in a loose and low mound, it can be planted at the front of a border. Matting groundcover such as the silver leaved *Achillea ageratifolia* with its white flowers allows a good view of the salvia. For background, the rich, green leaved sweet nancy, *Achillea ageratum* 'W. G. Childs', with its large, flat heads of white flowers, is a substantial but not fussy possibility. This grouping can be planted alone or alongside other combinations. All plants flower at more or less the same time and require the same simple cultural conditions. As a single specimen in a large pot, *Salvia interrupta* makes a dramatic presence when in bloom. A sun-filled terrace or sunny garden steps provide an appropriate and striking setting for pots or containers during the full month the salvia blooms.

### *Salvia involucrata* Cavanilles, Roseleaf sage, Plates 43 & 44

A perennial herb that builds some wood at its base, *Salvia involucrata* is not usually deciduous in a mild climate. Sometimes called roseleaf sage, the common name refers to the specific epithet, *involucrata*, which literally means having an involucre. This is a botanical term for bracts — those leafy parts that are situated under the flowers. In this case, the involucres that surround the flowers are large and colorful and contribute greatly to the plant's charm and attractiveness. Roseleaf sage has been collected in its native habitat in at least three Mexican provinces, Puebla, Tamaulipas, and Vera Cruz. It is usually found established in shady places, such as the edges of forests.

Growing consistently throughout the late spring and early summer, *Salvia involucrata* will reach 5 ft (1.5 m) or more before it starts blooming in late summer. Both its flowers and bracts are a beetroot color. The colorful bracts occur in pairs and usually envelop three flowers. As the flowers expand, the bracts fall away. The leaves are a flat looking mid-green, with petiole and veins reflecting the beetroot color of the flowers and bracts. Stems of flowers hold well in arrangements.

Individual plants of *Salvia involucrata* that merit attention have been collected in the wild, and after evaluation have been given cultivar names. For example, 'Bethellii', introduced in 1881, was praised for its compact habit, and large, ovate, cordate leaves. 'Deschampsiana' was selected in 1869 for the bright rose color of its inflated flowers. In France

and Britain these cultivars are still found today, but they are seldom listed by nurseries in the United States. Other selections of roseleaf sage
have been made in the wild for hardiness and flower color and these are
being distributed in the United States. These particular plants usually
carry the name of the place in Mexico where the cultivar was collected,
'Hidalgo', 'El Butano', and 'El Cielo' (plate 43) are three examples.

*Salvia involucrata* is known for its propensity to cross freely with
other salvia species, and hybrids have occurred at the University of
California Botanical Garden, Berkeley. These plants show hybrid vigor,
attaining approximately 6 ft (2 m) in height, and have a long blooming
period. They are being evaluated as garden subjects. In the summer of
1991, a 4 ft (1.3 m) tall spontaneous hybrid of *S. involucrata* bloomed in
my garden. Smaller in stature than the species, this hybrid is well suited
for a small garden. The plant holds itself upright because its
stems are thin and woody. A well-behaved and handsome addition to the
summer/autumn border, it was introduced in the fall of 1995 as
'Mulberry Jam' (plate 44).

Roseleaf sage performs best when given good drainage, soil enriched
with humus, half to three-quarters of a day of sun, and deep watering at
least once a week. Half-strength liquid fertilizer given every two weeks
when the plant starts making active growth is often helpful. Flowering
begins in mid- to late summer and continues until frost. If old inflorescences are removed throughout the blooming season the tall flowering
stems will stay erect. Propagation is by division of the rootstock or by cuttings. Cuttings taken in late summer or early autumn will strike roots
rapidly. In my garden roseleaf sage has come back from its rootstock after
light freezes of 25° F (−4° C). In early spring, cut the plant back to active
nodes a few inches above the crown.

*Salvia involucrata* or one of its cultivars planted with a tall clumping
grass such as *Miscanthus sinensis* 'Condensatus', a purple blooming
Japanese silver grass that has a dark green color through the growing
season and then turns reddish purple in autumn, makes a very dramatic
combination. Roseleaf sage benefits from the protection of other plants
and, due to its stature, combines well with roses. The threesome of
*S. involucrata* planted between the old-fashioned, pink flowered tea rose
'Duchesse de Brabant' and the white sport of that rose, 'Mrs. Joseph

Schwartz', gives pleasure in summer and autumn. Consider the new hybrid musk 'Ballerina' for a companion. It is of medium size and repeats bloom almost without pause.

## *Salvia iodantha* Fernald

Generally found in the mountainous region of central Mexico, *Salvia iodantha* usually grows at altitudes of 2600–10,500 ft (800–3200 m). Even at high altitudes these mountains rarely experience low temperatures. This salvia has a wide distribution and occurs in seven or more provinces.

Described by the botanist Merritt Lyndon Fernald in 1900, it has only come to the attention of gardeners since the 1980s. Mature plants may be seen at Strybing Arboretum, the University of California Botanical Garden in Berkeley, and the Arboretum at the University of California at Santa Cruz. Also, Conejo Valley Botanic Garden in Thousand Oaks, California, has a large salvia collection where *Salvia iodantha* flourishes.

A herbaceous perennial, *Salvia iodantha* grows robustly to 10 ft (3 m) or more in height and 6 ft (2 m) or so in width. It tends to be scandent and I have seen it supported by a deciduous tree with its flowering branches hanging from the tree's limbs in the late winter and early spring. Many branches rise from the base and are covered with mistletoe-green leaves that are ovate or lanceolate in shape. Leaves can vary greatly in size as well as shape; the average is 2–3 in (5–8 cm) in length by 1–1.5 in (2–4 cm) in width. The cyclamen-purple flowers have a velvety appearance due to the many small hairs that closely cover them. Less than 1 in (2.5 cm) in length, it is the quantity of the flowers that makes the colorful, 6 in (15 cm) long inflorescence so showy. The flowers, sometimes numbering as many as twelve, are tightly packed in whorls. The whorls too are tightly packed on short inflorescences. Flowering begins in autumn with peak bloom coming during a mild, sunny spell in December or January.

In my own garden this salvia tends to be shrub-like and around 5–6 ft (1.5–2 m) tall. Even in a mild winter it seldom flowers. Though it can survive temperatures in the 20°s F (−6° to −1° C), low temperatures most certainly prohibit flowering. In a warmer area, where frost seldom occurs, it becomes scandent and many racemes of vivid flowers are produced over a long period of time.

A position sheltered from cool air and wind is essential in siting this salvia. Sun for at least half the day throughout the year along with deep weekly watering is vital. It should be planted in good garden soil with fast drainage, and humus can be added each summer to keep the root-run of this salvia friable and cool. Propagation is by cuttings.

In a benign climate, *Salvia iodantha* can be the focal point of a subtle winter garden. Place it to grow on a wall or into a tree and on each side plant an early winter blooming *Arctostaphylos stanfordiana* subsp. *bakeri* 'Louis Edmunds'. Clusters of urn-shaped, pink flowers remain on this purple-brown trunked manzanita for over a month. Another combination features *S. iodantha* grown as a shrub with the 3 ft (1 m) tall, evergreen *Ceanothus maritimus* 'Roger's Dark'. This wild lilac has textured leaves and clusters of violet-blue flowers that persist for about a month. The blooming periods of all three plants overlap. Both the manzanita and the wild lilac, even though California native plants, will tolerate occasional summer water.

## *Salvia* × *jamensis* J. Compton, Plate 45

A newly discovered hybrid swarm of colorful salvias from Mexico, *Salvia* × *jamensis*, was described by the English botanist James Compton (1994a). Collected in 1991 near the village of Jame in the province of Coahuila, *S.* × *jamensis* is found in the Sierra Madre Oriental at elevations of 6500–9800 ft (2000–3000 m). Plants are also found in the adjoining provinces of Nuevo Leon and San Luis Potosi.

The parents of these hybrid salvias are *Salvia greggii* and *S. microphylla*, and the hybrids are found where the habitats of the two parent species coincide. Usually *S. greggii* tends to grow in more open and sunnier spots than *S. microphylla*. At the collection site a bank alongside a road furnishes the shade and exposure required for *S. microphylla*, while more open habitat needed for *S. greggii* is close by.

*Salvia × jamensis* is a shrub, usually under 3 ft (1 m) in height and width. Some plants are more rounded in shape than others. Small, glossy green, ovate leaves, usually less than 1 in (2.5 cm) in length, lightly cover the shrub. The corollas vary in size and color, as do the calyces. Flowers may be found in many shades of red, rose, rose-pink, orange, salmon, or pale yellow, and some are bicolored.

Easy to grow in a climate with low humidity, *Salvia × jamensis* requires full sun, good drainage, friable garden soil, and deep weekly water. Plants will tolerate overhead irrigation. Temperatures in my garden have not fallen below 20° F (−7° C) in the years that I have been growing these plants; because of their high altitude habitat, an established plant would probably survive a lower temperature. Flowering begins in early summer and continues until frost. Some pruning is needed throughout the growing season in order to promote repeat bloom. In early spring, remove old wood and shape the plant to a compact form. Propagation is by seed or cuttings. Seedlings germinate around these hybrids throughout the growing season—a few resemble the parent plant, others introduce flowers of different colors.

In 1988, Yucca Do Nursery found plants of what is now known as *Salvia × jamensis* in the wild. Selections were made and introduced in their 1991 catalog as 'Cienega de Oro' (plates 45 and 84) (pale yellow); 'Sierra San Antonio' (plate 45) (peach-rose with yellow lower lip); and 'San Isidro Moon' (pale creamy pink with a dark purple calyx). These cultivars are popular on the west coast. Many seedling cultivars are available in England, such as 'El Duranzo' (peach) and 'La Luna' (creamy yellow with upper lip covered in buff colored hairs).

A sunny slope facing south or west can be filled with these long blooming and nicely shaped small shrubs. Their delicate colors combine beautifully. Dot one or two dasylirions or yuccas among the salvias for a sharp contrast in habit and foliage. Another plant that complements these colorful salvias is *Carex buchananii*, brown sedge. About 2 ft (60 cm) or a little more in height, its very narrow, glossy, light brown leaves grow in delicate arches. All respond well to the same culture.

## *Salvia jurisicii* Kosanin, Plates 46 & 86

A petite herbaceous perennial, *Salvia jurisicii*'s native habitat is the former southern Yugoslavia, spilling over into Bulgaria and Albania. Its high mountainous home is reflected in its hardiness to 0° F (−18° C).

Small and compact, with pinnate leaves that have linear segments, *Salvia jurisicii* grows about 1 ft (30 cm) in height and width. Reported to develop into a 2 ft (60 cm) tall plant, it has never attained this in my garden. The pinnate leaves are much branched with hairs on the back of each rib and vein, giving a frothy effect. Olive-green in color, the leaves are eye catching whether the plant is in bloom or not. Flowers appear in whorls that are closely spaced and turned upside down. They are small, usually 0.5 in (1.3 cm) in length, and covered with hairs. Flower color is variable but in the violet range. A white flowered form, 'Alba', comes true from seed.

*Salvia jurisicii*

Easy to grow, *Salvia jurisicii* needs sun for half a day at the very least, good drainage, soil enriched with humus, and weekly water. Propagation is usually by seed but cuttings will strike roots. Seedlings appear sporadically in the garden near the mother plant.

*Salvia jurisicii* is one of very few salvias that are appropriate for rock gardens, since it is small, compact, and hardy. Plants with these characteristics are often sought for rock gardens or other small or contained areas. Well-known to European gardeners, this salvia also remains evergreen in a mild climate and has a delightful appearance. Because of its size, *S. jurisicii* can be observed more easily in a bed that is raised. A group of plants chosen for complimentary foliage texture includes the silky, tufted, low-growing *Achillea clavenae*, with gray leaves and white flowers. *Artemisia schmidtiana* 'Nana' adds gray-white foliage with linear leaves, and *Geranium sanguineum* 'Minutum' has small dark green leaves and tiny, unexpected, magenta flowers. All plants are either smaller than *Salvia jurisicii* or in proportion to it. This salvia also makes a very nice container plant.

## *Salvia karwinskii* Bentham, Karwinski's sage, Plate 47

From moist mountain forests in southern Mexico, Guatemala, El Salvador, Honduras, and Nicaragua comes *Salvia karwinskii*. Grown as a garden plant throughout its native habitat, it is a stout, winter blooming shrub that is found in abundance in the wild—usually in or near oak or pine forests at 4000–8000 ft (1200–2500 m). There, it is known as a honey producing plant. Rarely seen in private gardens, fine specimens may be seen at Strybing Arboretum, the University of California Botanical Garden, Berkeley, and Huntington Botanical Gardens.

In mild California gardens during a long growing period, *Salvia karwinskii* usually attains 8 ft (2.5 m) in height and 4 ft (1.3 m) in width. In the wild it reaches anywhere from 3–12 ft (1–4 m). Sometimes Karwinski's sage comes into bloom before Christmas, developing a few short inflorescences. In January these elongate, and by February the shrub carries many 15 in (37 cm) racemes of brick-red, rose-red, or scarlet flowers. The two-lipped flower is inflated and about 1 in (2.5 cm) long. It is held in a long, showy, dark red, 0.5 in (1.3 cm) calyx. The stems and petioles of the leaves are covered with short woolly hairs, giving them a grayish appearance. The evergreen leaves are large, often 6 in (15 cm) long, and look rough on the surface. On the underside, the veining is prominent and covered with light, cream colored hairs.

Because of the luxuriant growth of Karwinski's sage, it is a good idea to remove some of the flowering branches or to shorten them periodically. Branches of flowers hold well in flower arrangements if they are conditioned by cutting the stems under water. Prune the shrub almost to the ground as it nears the end of its flowering period once the danger of frost has passed. This encourages a more upright and compact habit. April or May is the usual pruning time in the San Francisco Bay area. Propagation is usually by cuttings taken at this time and rooting is rapid. *Salvia karwinskii* will produce viable seed, though pruning of course precludes it. It is known to hybridize with other Mexican autumn flowering salvias in the Berkeley, California area.

A warm, protected spot in the garden is a necessity for Karwinski's sage. Be sure it receives full sun in winter. Over the years I have noticed that it flowers more profusely in mild winters but on quite a few occasions it has withstood temperatures in the low 20°s F (around −6° C) and still produced a few flowers. A rooted cutting in the greenhouse is wise insurance against low temperatures.

A south-facing wall or hedge is an ideal location for *Salvia karwin-skii*. Because of its uncommon blooming period, background becomes very important for its protection and appearance. A green hedge would certainly highlight its unusual reddish flowers. At the base of the salvia, a carpet of the dark green foliage of *Iberis sempervirens* 'Purity' would complete the composition. This perennial candytuft, with its sea of white flowers, blooms in very early spring, often at the same time as the salvia. A large and sunny shrub border of winter blooming plants could feature *Salvia karwinskii* and *Chimonanthus praecox*, the fragrant and beloved wintersweet. Supposedly deciduous, on occasion wintersweet's tattered leaves refuse to drop, obscuring its pale yellow flowers. They can easily be removed. Undisturbed shrub areas are excellent places to establish drifts of bulbs. *Narcissus jonquilla*, known and prized as a winter cut flower, could be established between the large shrubs.

## *Salvia koyamae* Makino, Shinano-akigiri

Rarely found in the wild, *Salvia koyamae* comes from a limited habitat on the largest island of Japan, Honshu. It has affinities with two other salvias that occur on Honshu, *S. glabrescens* and *S. nipponica*.

*Salvia koyamae*

A lax perennial with decumbent stems sometimes reaching 2 ft (60 cm) or more, *Salvia koyamae* appears to creep through beds or borders, forming a loose groundcover. Roughly 1 ft (30 cm) in height, this salvia has large, cordate leaves, heartshaped in outline. They measure 6 in (15 cm) in length and 5 in (12 cm) in width and have a 5 in (12 cm) long petiole. Yellow-green in color, the leaves are lightly covered with fine hairs. Whorls of pale yellow flowers are spaced along an inflorescence that sometimes reaches almost 1 ft (30 cm) in length but is usually half that. Blooming occurs in late summer and autumn. There are so few flowers in bloom at a given time the plant seldom commands attention; however, the heartshaped leaves are luscious looking and a perfect foil for the subtle, pale yellow flowers. Leaves and flowers are attractive in bouquets.

Easy to grow and preferring shade, *Salvia koyamae* needs deep, rich soil, good drainage, and a generous supply of water. When well-established this sage will climb through shrubs and between low-growing plants, easily filling a woodland border with handsome leaves. Propagation is by seed or cuttings taken after active spring growth or in late summer.

Sometime around 1990 *Salvia koyamae* was grown at the University of California Botanical Garden, Berkeley, and subsequently introduced to gardeners. At about that time its name appeared in nursery catalogs. It has not been in horticulture long enough to test its ultimate hardiness, but it certainly withstands short periods of light freezes.

Here is a plant that can easily be tucked into an existing shaded border. In time it will weave itself through and around established plants, making a handsome cover throughout the growing season. In a mild climate, leaves tend to be evergreen. In a new border with filtered light, the 5 ft (1.5 m) tall, semi-evergreen *Viburnum* 'Anne Russell', combined with clumps of the 4 ft (1.3 m) tall *Miscanthus sinensis* 'Morning Light', which has a narrow band of white on the leaf margins, make a splendid pair. *Salvia koyamae* weaving around them unifies the composition.

## *Salvia lavandulifolia* Vahl, Spanish sage

A small, woody based herbaceous plant with gray-white foliage, *Salvia lavandulifolia* is native to central, southern, and eastern Spain, extending into southern France. It is frequently found growing with rosemary, *Lavandula lanata*, and *Genista cinerea* in a habitat that is dry in summer and wet in winter.

Usually 1.5 ft (45 cm) in height and width, Spanish sage is somewhat lanky in habit. The narrow, whitish-gray, lanceolate leaves, less than 2 in (5 cm) in length, are evergreen and rather meager in number, giving the salvia a rangy appearance. When rubbed, the oils in the leaves release a scent similar to rosemary. These oils are of economic value and are used to scent soaps. Flowering for about one month in early summer, *Salvia lavandulifolia* has short inflorescences of pale, rather washed-out lavender-blue flowers that are less than 1 in (2.5 cm) long. These leafless flowering stems have but a very few flowers in widely spaced whorls. Clones with a dark calyx are frequently found. Propagation is by cuttings taken either before or after flowering, or by seed.

A subspecies of *Salvia lavandulifolia* that is found in southern Spain and Algeria is S. *lavandulifolia* subsp. *blancoana*. The two plants have similar leaves and flowers but the growing habit of subspecies *blancoana* is almost prostrate. It is well-suited to a hot, rocky hillside or a container. Both S. *lavandulifolia* and its subspecies *blancoana* are grown as ornamental plants in southern France.

Full sun, friable clay soil with fast drainage, and good air circulation are the cultural needs of Spanish sage. Occasional deep watering throughout the summer is advisable. In areas of high humidity and heat, this sage seldom succeeds. However, it is tolerant of temperatures as low as 20° (−7° C), possibly to 10° F (−12° C).

The preceding description of *Salvia lavandulifolia* and the subspecies *blancoana* might lead one to think the sage uninteresting, almost dull. However, the leaves of Spanish sage give texture and reflect light in the garden throughout the year. In a dry border filled with plants with rich green foliage, such as rosemary and myrtle, the whitish-gray leaves of Spanish sage planted in groups will lighten the foreground. In a rock-filled sunny border, its ability to fit into nooks and crannies because of its rangy habit is a great advantage in filling a difficult site.

## *Salvia leucantha* Cavanilles, Mexican bush sage, Plate 48

Reported to occur in tropical and subtropical conifer forests in central and eastern Mexico, *Salvia leucantha* is a small shrub or herbaceous perennial. It grows about 4 ft (1.3 m) in height in a season and develops a great many flowering stems from its rootstock. In several years the plant may quickly spread from 3 ft to 6 ft (1 m to 2 m) in width.

The leaves of *Salvia leucantha* are linear-lanceolate, a soft mid-green color with a grayish cast. The underside is white and hairy, making the leaves very attractive. The inflorescence is 6–12 in (15–30 cm) in length and extends well beyond the foliage. Individual flowers are white and project from a purple calyx. They are arranged in whorls and many come into bloom at the same time. Fine hairs covering both flower and calyx give the look and feel of velvet. The specific epithet *leucantha* means white flowered. Flowering begins in summer and continues until frost.

To promote flowering, remove inflorescences as they show signs of fading. This procedure takes excess weight off the tops of stems and allows the extension of more inflorescences. Deadheading of this kind, practiced throughout the long flowering period, will enable the plant to stay more upright. Both flowers and leaves are useful in flower arrangements. When dried, the flowers and calyces retain their color.

Mexican bush sage prefers full sun, ordinary garden soil, good drainage, and infrequent water during the summer. It has proved to be cold tolerant to about 25° F (−4° C). Prune it to the ground in late February or early March. This is also a good time to remove excess rooted stems for gardening friends. In cultivation since 1846, *Salvia leucantha* has probably been shared more frequently than it has been purchased because of its ease of propagation and prolific flower display. It is commonly grown in the United States, Britain, and mainland Europe.

One form of *Salvia leucantha* has deep violet flowers and calyces. It differs from the typical form described above only in the different violet color of the flowers. It is quite common in cultivation and can be seen in gardens and nurseries in California and Arizona. For a number of years it has been listed in catalogs as *Salvia leucantha* 'Midnight' (plate 48).

Known to be easy to establish, Mexican bush sage is also able to survive where choicer but choosier plants would fail. This advice is helpful in placing *Salvia leucantha* in the garden. It combines well with the thin, dark green foliage of rosemary and the gray foliage of lavender. A good border of drought tolerant plants giving successive bloom consists of rosemary (flowering in winter), lavender (flowering in early summer), and Mexican bush sage (continuing until frost). In a large border of summer flowering plants, *Gaura lindheimeri*, with its wonderful wands of almost pink flowers, can be interplanted with either form of Mexican bush sage. The upright, summer blooming *Verbascum olympicum* has a 6 ft (2 m) high candelabra of bright, golden yellow flowers that appear imbedded in white wool, and this, along with the beautiful, bright blue *Linum narbonense*, would add an intriguing touch to the composition. All plants will adjust to similar cultural conditions.

### *Salvia leucophylla* Greene, Purple sage or gray sage, Plate 49

An extraordinarily beautiful California native shrub, *Salvia leucophylla* is found in the wild in the southern coast ranges from Santa Barbara to Orange County. Hot, dry hillsides and gravelly soil seem to determine its habitat. It has two appropriate common names: purple sage reflects the pale purple flowers seen in swatches on slopes in the wild, and gray sage reflects the color of the evergreen leaves. The specific epithet, *leucophylla*, refers to the plant's whitish leaves. David Douglas, the ardent Scottish plant explorer, collected the herbarium specimen from the vicinity of Santa Barbara and the species was named from this plant by the botanist Edward Lee Greene in 1892.

Reaching 3–5 ft (1–1.5 m) in both height and width, gray sage begins its blooming period in early March and continues for a solid month or more. Tight whorls of many flowers open gradually on an inflorescence that elongates to 6–8 in (15–20 cm). The short flowering stem is usually pinkish purple and adds intensity to the color of the flowers. Pinkish purple flowers, about 1 in (2.5 cm) in length, are held in a 0.5 in (1.3 cm) gray calyx tinged with purple. Leaves are an apple-green in spring, becoming grayer and whiter as the days get hotter. The habit of growth of gray sage is graceful, with the uppermost branches swooping downward. When limbs touch the ground they frequently root, expanding the volume of the plant. Propagation is usually by cuttings, since branches strike roots so readily, though the salvia does set viable seed. Reputed to be frost sensitive, in my garden it took blasts of 11° F (−12° C) on one occasion and has withstood 20° F (−7° C) frequently.

Carl Epling (1939) writes of gray sage growing so densely that it gives a velvety texture to the rounded coastal hills of southern California, noting that it frequently occurs with *Salvia mellifera* and *S. apiana*. It is indeed a choice plant whether in the wild or in the garden.

Some years ago, James Roof, former director of the Regional Parks Botanic Garden in Berkeley, California, visited many of the native habitats of *Salvia leucophylla* and on his return to Berkeley cultivated the species in the garden. In a 1981 article, he warned of the tendency of the plant to decline and die after five or six years in cultivation. However, the *S. leucophylla* he collected at Point Sal in Santa Barbara County, California, remained healthy for several years. My own experience is that *S. leucophylla* and its hybrids and cultivars live much longer, perhaps because of the influence of the ocean storms, winds, and heat on my garden. All the *S. leucophyllas* that I planted between eight and 15 years ago remain vigorous and handsome.

Gray sage is easy to care for if given full sun, fast drainage, and water as it is becoming established. A sloping hillside with two or three 15 ft (4.5 m) tall western redbuds (*Cercis occidentalis*) interplanted with three or more *Salvia leucophyllas* will make a flowering display for almost a two-month period. The silvery bark of the redbuds in winter will be complemented by the gray-green foliage of the salvias. All of the varieties of *S. leucophyllas* described below are substantial plants that are handsome and easy to place in a dry garden. Their care is minimal. Gray sage is not only beautiful, but it is an important nectar source for hummingbirds. Its canopy of attractive, aromatic foliage can also provide a refuge for small animals.

Over the course of the years, many selections of *Salvia leucophylla* have been made, each chosen for a unique characteristic. Because of the tendency to use the collection site as a cultivar name, it is sometimes confusing and difficult for nursery people and gardeners to keep cultivars clearly defined. In addition, hybridization in the wild and in the garden has given rise to a number of plants with *Salvia leucophylla* as one parent—making matters more complicated. Incidentally, the seed-bearing parent of these promiscuous hybrids cannot usually be determined even with expensive laboratory work. Consequently, when the two parents are cited they are given alphabetically. The list that follows will demonstrate how confusing the situation has become:

*Salvia leucophylla*: A low coastal form from Point Sal. Introduced by East Bay Regional Parks Botanic Garden in the early 1950s, it is without a cultivar designation.

*Salvia leucophylla*: A large, pink flowered shrub form. Introduced by Saratoga Horticultural Foundation in the 1970s. Probably the most hardy and most beautiful of all the selections. It may reach 7–8 ft (2.3–2.5 m) in width and height.

*Salvia leucophylla* 'Point Sal': Selected by Dale Smith of the University of California in Santa Barbara for Santa Barbara Botanic Garden and introduced by Randy Baldwin through San Marcos Growers in 1986. Commonly referred to as "Point Sal Spreader" because of its draping habit, it is notable for its broader and grayer foliage.

*Salvia leucophylla* 'Point Sal': The name signifies the collection site. This selection was made by David Fross of Native Sons Nursery in Arroyo Grande in the 1990s. It is remarkable for its 6 ft (2 m) by 12 ft (4 m) size and spread.

*Salvia leucophylla* 'Figueroa': A selection from Figueroa Mountain made by Nevin Smith for hardiness and introduced through his Wintergreen Nursery in the 1980s.

*Salvia* 'Bee's Bliss' (*S. leucophylla* × *S. clevelandii* or *S. sonomensis*) (plate 49): A selection made in 1989 by Roger Raiche of the University of California Botanical Garden, Berkeley, for its low growth and beautiful spreading habit. Its rich gray foliage and prolific spring flowering make it an unusually handsome garden subject. Long spikes, 1 ft (30 cm) or more in length, of large lavender-pink flowers adorn the plant for a full month.

## *Salvia littae* Visiani, Plate 50

A late blooming herbaceous perennial, *Salvia littae* is native to the Mexican province of Oaxaca and is found at altitudes of 8000–10,000 ft (2500–3100 m). Plants are usually established in groups growing at the edge of wet oak forests in some shade, these areas are referred to as cloud forest habitats.

Reaching 4–5 ft (1.3–1.5 m) in height and frequently 6 ft (2 m) across, *Salvia littae* becomes thicket-like when left untended. Many leafy

*Salvia littae*

stems rise from the base and when they touch the ground they often root. The plant is generously clothed with 1–3 in (2.5–8 cm) long, medium green leaves that are glabrous and rounded. Flowers in tight verticils elongate and some inflorescences are 1 ft (30 cm) or more in length. Brilliant magenta flowers covered with hairs are just less than 1 in (2.5 cm) in length. When open, the upper lip is upright and the lower lip is opened wide and gaping. The two-parted lower lip appears to be curled and turned under. (I know of no other salvia flower with this form.) The calyx is small and a bright lime green that heightens the colorful inflorescence.

Plant *Salvia littae* where it will receive a half day of sun in well-draining garden soil amended with humus. Use humus regularly as a mulch, not only to retain moisture but to improve the soil. Simple cultural requirements involve watering on a regular basis throughout the growing season. This autumn blooming salvia is hardy to about 25° F (−4° C) and propagation is by cuttings. In case of frosty weather, cuttings taken in late August can be wintered over in the greenhouse. In early spring prune stems to more or less 3 ft (1 m) in order to achieve a shapely and controlled plant during the coming season. Blooming branches last well as cut flowers if stems are conditioned by cutting under water and displayed in a cool place.

To help control the plant's lax growth, in late spring place a piece of wire fencing 3 ft² (1 m²) over the plant, parallel to the ground at a height of about 2 ft (60 cm). Drive four stakes in the ground and secure the fencing with staples in each stake. As the plant develops, it can then be trained up and through the wire.

*Salvia littae* produces abundant foliage and flowers, and combines beautifully with the 6 ft (2 m) evergreen, *Viburnum tinus* 'Spring Bouquet'. The handsome, mulberry colored buds of the spring blooming viburnum appear as the salvia reaches the end of its blooming period. Another fine companion is the 3–4 ft (1–1.3 m) shrub rose 'Lyda Rose', which produces continuous large, white, single flowers edged in lavender-pink. Penstemon cultivars that repeat bloom such as 'Garnet', 'Midnight', and 'Sour Grapes' would also make colorful partners.

## *Salvia longispicata* Martius & Galeotti

*Salvia longispicata* is found in southwestern Mexico, usually at elevations of 1000–6500 ft (300–2000 m). Even though classified as a perennial, it has the size and stature of a small shrub. In one season it grows 4–5 ft (1.3–1.5 m) in height and a good 3–4 ft (1–1.3 m) across. Regardless of its size, this salvia cannot be described as a showy plant for the garden, but it has interesting, dark purple flowers and a splendid upright habit—two characteristics that hybridizers seek and value.

The specific epithet *longispicata* would suggest that the plant has long spikes. As a matter of fact, this is not the case, and the meaning refers to the plant's projecting or extending many clusters of short flowering spikes resembling ears of corn.

Leaves are many different sizes, mid-green, ovate, and connected to the petiole at the broader end, giving the plant a bumpy look. Small dark purple flowers less than 0.5 in (1.3 cm) in length start appearing in summer and continue to bloom until late autumn. The calyces are a light, pale green and about the same length as the flower. Tight whorls of flowers elongate on inflorescences to 6–8 in (15–20 cm) but do not stand erect above the foliage. Hardy to 20° F (−7° C), *Salvia longispicata*, if struck by a freeze, will eventually come back from its rootstock.

Cultural requirements are a half to full day of sun, regular garden soil amended with humus, quick drainage, and water once every week or two. Propagation is by seed or cuttings. In early spring, prune all stems to two active nodes just above ground level to encourage healthy and uniform growth during the coming growing season.

*Salvia longispicata* is thought to be a parent (along with *Salvia farinacea*) of a spontaneous sterile hybrid that was found at the Huntington Botanical Gardens in 1979. This hybrid was introduced as *Salvia* 'Indigo Spires' and has proved to be quite ornamental in the garden.

*Salvia longispicata* is rarely seen in gardens or in nurseries in the United States, but it may be found in the national collections of salvias in both Britain and France.

This is clearly a plant for the collector or hybridizer. In a garden setting it attracts little attention and could easily be overlooked. However, placed as a filler between large shrub roses such as the rugosa 'Roseraie de l'Hay', which has violet-red flowers, or the hybrid rugosa 'Blanc Double de Coubert', which has almost pure white flowers, its most noteworthy attributes are emphasized—namely, its sturdy upright habit and deep purple flowers.

## *Salvia lycioides* Gray, Canyon sage, Plate 51

A small, shrub-like plant that builds wood at its base, *Salvia lycioides* was described botanically by Carl Epling (1939) as a perennial herb. Found in a wide territory, from west Texas into New Mexico then south through Mexico to the province of San Luis Potosi, canyon sage is reported to be established on dry limestone hills and canyons at high elevations, usually 5000 ft (1500 m) or more.

Canyon sage fairly twinkles with bright cornflower-blue flowers in the spring and again in the fall. From time to time during the summer a few flowers appear, but it tends to bloom best when nights are cool. Usually reaching 1–1.5 ft (30–45 cm) in height and width, the plant has a graceful sprawl. From its base many small branches grow up and then out. Little mistletoe-green leaves, less than 1 in (2.5 cm) long and 0.5 in (1.3 cm) wide, cover the plant well and tend to be evergreen in a mild climate. Its hardiness is reported to be in the low 10°s F (around −12° C).

A selection of *Salvia lycioides* was made by nurseryman Pat McNeal of Austin, Texas, and introduced as 'Guadalupe Mountain Form'. It is similar to the plant described above except its flowers and leaves are smaller. The flowers are a deep and vibrant delphinium-blue.

Situated in ordinary garden soil with good drainage and in full sun, this drought tolerant salvia needs little, if any, additional summer water. I have found regular dressings of humus to be helpful in conserving water and furnishing food for the plant. Also, light dressings of lime on a yearly basis will keep the soil sweet. It is usually propagated by seed and cuttings.

Named by Asa Gray in 1886, canyon sage is relatively unknown and rarely seen in gardens and nurseries. However, it has been cultivated at the Texas Agricultural Experiment Station since 1976. It is not known when it was introduced to horticulture. The specific epithet, *lycioides*, from the Greek, refers to the plant's resemblance to *Lycium*, a genus called boxthorn in the nightshade family.

Here is a plant made to order for the rock garden, where it can climb or nestle among rocks and other plants. Because of *Salvia lycioides'* neat growing habit, it has many possibilities for placement in the garden. One planting might include groups of *S. lycioides* along with 'Dark Dancer', a hybrid of *S. greggii* that has dark raspberry flowers. The two salvias are more or less equal in size and produce quantities of flowers during late summer and autumn. A composition eminently suited for siting on a mound includes the prostrate and spreading evergreen shore juniper, *Juniperus conferta*, and canyon sage. To add a little dark green foliage to anchor the planting, *Teucrium lucidum*, the clumping, evergreen, 4–6 in (10–15 cm) germander, suits very well. The texture of the foliage is eye catching year round. Canyon sage does very well as a container plant or on the perimeter of a dry border.

## *Salvia macellaria* Epling, Plates 52 & 91

A small, sweet-smelling herbaceous perennial, *Salvia macellaria* can be found in limited mountainous areas in central Mexico. In its native habitat it is found growing on open hillsides with many other species of salvia.

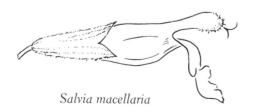
*Salvia macellaria*

The specimens described and named by Carl Epling (1939) came from the province of San Luis Potosi. Collections made by Strybing Arboretum in 1991 were from the province of Coahuila. It is from this latter collection that cuttings and plants were distributed, introducing *Salvia macellaria* to horticulture in this country. In France this salvia is grown at the Nice Botanical Garden and in the National Collection at Pépinière de la Foux.

A slight and slender plant, less than 2 ft (60 cm) in height and width, *Salvia macellaria* has a woody base as well as woody branches. Mid-green, ovate leaves are scarcely 1 in (2.5 cm) long and 0.25 in (0.6 cm) wide. Evergreen, they appear in little clusters along each stem and are fragrant. The flowers are about 1 in (2.5 cm) long with a wide and showy lower lip. The color of the flowers varies according to the clone. I grow two clones, one a pale brick-red, and the other a ripe peach color. Both are delicate shades and hard to describe because a subtle pale yellow streak on the lower lip subdues the intensity of the color.

Three-quarters to a full day of sun and quick-draining soil enriched with humus are advised for this salvia. Regular watering throughout the summer is needed, frequent if the weather is hot and dry. If temperatures are moderate, watering twice each week is sufficient. Shy to bloom, I have found applications of a balanced liquid fertilizer at half strength on a monthly basis encourage modest growth and flowering. Occasional pinching or light pruning will keep *Salvia macellaria* in fine shape. Never in heavy bloom, a smattering of flowers may be seen throughout summer and autumn, particularly during cool spells. Propagation is by seed or cuttings. Because of its mountainous habitats and close kinship with *S. greggii*, *S. lycioides*, and *S. muelleri*, *S. macellaria* is probably hardy to 20° F (−7° C) but it has not been in cultivation in the United States long enough to be tested for ultimate hardiness.

With its unusual flower color, *Salvia macellaria* can be shown to advantage against a background of green. Place it in front of 3 ft (1 m) tall boxwoods or euonymous and interplant with the 3 in (8 cm) *Alyssum* 'Apricot Shades' for a visual treat. Evergreen foliage keeps this salvia looking good year round while making a fine background for its unusual flower colors. Yellow roses for the back of the border might include David Austin's 4 ft (1.3 m) introduction 'Windrush', or *Rosa* 'Golden

Wings', one of its parents. For structure and color of foliage, add three plants of the dwarf *Nandina domestica* 'Gulf Stream', which grows to 3 ft (1 m). For the front of the border, combine *Salvia macellaria* with the annual *Calendula* 'Apricot Beauty' in a mass for a blending of complimentary hues. The soft and warm colors of foliage and flowers will make a rich but subdued picture.

## *Salvia madrensis* Seemann, Forsythia sage, Plate 53

A slow developing and late blooming perennial from the Sierra Madre Oriental in Mexico, *Salvia madrensis* has been given the common name forsythia sage, referring to the rich yellow color of its flowers. The specific epithet *madrensis* describes the plant's origin, which indicates cultural conditions. Occurring at 4000–5000 ft (1200–1500 m) in warm and often wet areas, it is reported to be hardy to 25° F (−4° C). In my garden it has come back from its rootstock after withstanding 11° F (−12° C) for short periods.

*Salvia madrensis*

To watch *Salvia madrensis* push up its square stems and heart-shaped leaves from underground rhizomes is to see a marvel in slow motion. All summer the plant builds, and by early September, stems measure 4–7 ft (1.3–2.3 m) in height and are 2 in (5 cm) wide on each of their square sides. A ridge at each corner of the stem emphasizes the squareness. Rough-textured, heart-shaped, spinach-green leaves are graduated in size from large at the bottom to small at the top. In spite of being widely spaced along the stem, the leaves give a lush covering to the plant. Many 12 in (30 cm) inflorescences develop and are covered with softly colored, butter-yellow flowers, and calyces that are aromatic and sticky with glands. Blooming begins in late August and continues until frost. The flowers are arranged in whorls and hold well as cut flowers.

*Salvia madrensis* prefers a warm growing season and placement in light to medium shade, in soil mixed with humus. Even though it will tolerate high humidity, good drainage is essential for this salvia as well as regular water. It will take full sun but will need more water and the protection of other plants. I have never found fertilizer necessary, but by mulching regularly the food supply for the plant is increased and water is preserved. In a few years plants will multiply by spreading rootstock into a colony and may easily be divided. In the wild, fertile seed is set but this occurs only occasionally in cultivation. Divisions and cuttings are the usual methods of propagation. Cut the plants back to 6–8 in (15–20 cm) above the ground after flowering for good air circulation and a tidy border.

The upright, autumn blooming, orange-red *Salvia regla* makes a striking companion for *S. madrensis*. Also, the old-fashioned snowball, *Viburnum opulus* 'Roseum', which colors wonderfully in the autumn, brings a range of reds to complement the soft yellow flowers of *Salvia madrensis*. The repeat blooming *S. elegans* 'Honey Melon', with its lush green foliage and bright scarlet-red flowers, makes a fine groundcover at the base of all these plants.

## *Salvia melissodora* Lagasca, Grape-scented sage, Plate 55

At elevations ranging from 4000–8000 ft (1200–2500 m) in the Sierra Madre Occidental, *Salvia melissodora* is found in the Mexican provinces of Chihuahua in the north all the way to Oaxaca in the south. Both leaves and seed of grape-scented sage have been used by the Tarahumara Indians for medicinal purposes for several hundred years.

A woody shrub 6 ft (2 m) in height and 4 ft (1.3 m) in width, *Salvia melissodora* has an upright and graceful habit. Ovate leaves 1–1.5 in (2.5–4 cm) in length cover the shrub lightly and tend to be evergreen in a mild winter. Mid-green in color, the veins on the back stand out because of the chamois colored pubescence that covers them. When partially dry the leaves emit a pleasant fragrance. The flowers are frequently described as being grape-scented. Blooming continually from late spring until frost, *S. melissodora* attracts bees, insects, butterflies, and hummingbirds because of its dependable nectar supply. Short inflorescences hold several whorls of flowers with upper lips of violet-lavender. The lower lip is pale lavender, as is the back of the upper lip. This light lavender color probably lures and directs insects to the nectary. The specific epithet *melissodora* comes from two Greek words, *melissa* (honeybee) and *odora* (fragrant). Melissa is also the name of a Cretan nymph who discovered how to collect honey. It is a fitting name for an appealing and useful plant.

Undemanding in culture, *Salvia melissodora* likes full sun, quick drainage, good air circulation, and regular watering on a 10-day basis. Once established it will produce viable seed and, occasionally, seedlings. Propagation is also by cuttings. Pruning and pinching of new growth will help in shaping the plant. If entire branches need to be removed the active growing season is the best time for heavy pruning. I have found grape-scented sage to be hardy to 20° F (−7° C). On one occasion when the temperature fell to 11° F (−12° C) in December, the mother plant was killed but the following spring we found seedlings had germinated at the base of the original plant.

A delight to have in a border, *Salvia melissodora* along with *Aloysia triphylla* (lemon verbena) will make the backbone of a border designed for fragrance. The plants are similar in size and stature. The small and compact shrub rose 'Wise Portia' is strongly scented and a lovely magenta color. This rose reaches 3 ft (1 m) in height and width and makes a floriferous filler. Several groups of the white *Dianthus* 'Jealousy' and *Dianthus* 'Danielle Pink', both about 1 ft (0.3 m) in height and very fragrant, would help in unifying the scented border.

## *Salvia mellifera* Green, Black sage, Plate 54

Commonly found on dry slopes under 2000 ft (0–600 m), *Salvia mellifera* has a lengthy coastal distribution in California that stretches from Contra Costa County south into Baja. It is one of the chief components of the coastal sage scrub plant community. Both in the wild and in gardens, it hybridizes freely with *S. apiana*, *S. columbariae*, and *S. leucophylla*, and sometimes with *S. carduacea* and *S. clevelandii*. The specific epithet *mellifera* means honey-producing. Beekeepers have long been aware of this nectar and pollen source and often place their hives in chaparral where large stands of black sage thrive.

Relatively unknown to gardeners until the early 1950s, even today black sage is rarely seen outside nurseries that specialize in California native plants. However, fine specimens can be seen at the University of California Botanical Garden, Berkeley, and the Arboretum of the University of California, Santa Cruz, as well as Strybing Arboretum, East Bay Regional Parks Botanic Garden, Santa Barbara Botanic Garden, and Rancho Santa Ana Botanic Garden.

With water shortages occurring frequently on the west coast of the United States and elsewhere, designers are searching for tough, drought tolerant plants to bring into dry garden settings. California native salvias and their hybrids provide many examples of such plants, with *Salvia mellifera* prominent among them. A 3–6 ft (1–2 m) evergreen shrub that sometimes mounds 3–5 ft (1–1.5 m) across, black sage has an overall look in keeping with a Mediterranean or dry garden setting. Its small leaves clothe the shrub but do not give it a predominantly leafy look. Blooming takes place in late spring, with tight whorls of flowers that hardly attract attention. They are small and whitish or pale lavender. However, the flowers do attract bees. The leaves are a strong mid-green color, 1–2 in (2.5–5 cm) in length, with indented veins giving the surface a textured appearance. If stroked, the leaves release a pleasant scent.

Usually placed in full sun in the garden, black sage will also succeed with some shade. A gritty soil with a light texture is needed for quick drainage, and fertilizer is not recommended. Additional water is not necessary once the plant becomes established. It is reliably reported that deer never browse *Salvia mellifera*, its hybrids, or its cultivars.

Many California native plants make inestimable companions for black sage. *Rhus ovata* (sugar bush), with its slick and shiny dark evergreen leaves, is about the same size as *Salvia mellifera*. The sugar bush's fat, eye catching buds and flowers emerge before the sage comes into bloom. Various species of evergreen *Ceanothus* are other good partners. In areas with relatively cool summers, the 2–3 ft (0.6–3 m) tall *Ceanothus gloriosus* var. *porrectus*, with its narrow holly-like leaves and lavender-blue flowers, does well. C. 'Dark Star', which has masses of cobalt-blue flowers, tolerates more heat and is usually under 6 ft (2 m) in height. Both are drought tolerant.

Several selections of the prostrate form of *Salvia mellifera* have been made. *S. mellifera* 'Little Sur' is a selection made in the 1990s from the mouth of the Little Sur River by David Amme, a nurseryman specializing in California native plants. It is prostrate in growth and notable for draping over walls or among rocks. *S. mellifera* 'Terra Seca' was introduced in the 1970s by the Saratoga Horticultural Foundation from a plant from the University of California Botanical Garden, Berkeley. This selection was made in the 1950s by the California nurseryman Louis Edmunds. Sold by some nurseries as 'Prostrata', it is hoped that name will be abandoned in favor of its correct name, 'Terra Seca'. Reaching 2 ft (0.6 m) in height and over 6 ft (2 m) in width, *S. mellifera* 'Terra Seca' will endure the toughest conditions. An early spring blooming plant with tiny white flowers, its mid-green leaves appear rough and are both aromatic and shiny. Drought tolerant when established, be sure to prune or pinch all upright growth regularly as the plant develops in order to keep it both prostrate and leafy. A good groundcover, it is particularly nice at the base of the upright, 8–12 ft (2–4 m) *Fremontodendron californicum* subsp. *crassifolium*, a small evergreen tree with primrose-yellow flowers.

*Salvia* 'Mrs. Beard', a hybrid of *S. mellifera* and *S. sonomensis*, is described under *S. sonomensis* because of its strong resemblance to that parent.

## *Salvia mexicana* Linnaeus, Mexican sage, Plates 56 & 92

A highly variable plant in the wild, *Salvia mexicana* is distributed over a wide area throughout central Mexico. Its habitat includes arid subtropical regions in the north and tropical areas in the south. Growing at elevations ranging from 2600–8500 ft (800–2600 m), Mexican sage is frequently found growing at the edge of forests where it receives some protection from the elements.

Described as a shrubby perennial, in cultivation Mexican sage grows 3–9 ft (1–3 m) in height and 3–4 ft (1–1.3 m) in width. Leaves are variable in size and color—some plants have mid-green, glabrous leaves

*Salvia mexicana*

and others have gray-green leaves with short hairs covering the surface. Leaves are sufficient in number to give the plant a clothed look. Inflorescences are variable, both in length and size of flowers. The size and color of the calyces and flowers vary as well, ranging from purple-blue to midnight-purple. Beginning in late summer, midnight-purplish flowers in whorls are abundantly produced for several months. Flowering branches are beautiful and are long lasting in bouquets. Stems can be conditioned by cutting them under water.

*Salvia mexicana* is best grown in a climate where temperatures do not fall below 20° F (−7° C). In my garden this sage has come back from its rootstock after 11° F (−12° C), but it took two summers for it to regain its former vigor and stature. Situate plants so they receive half to a full day of sun and have fast drainage. Occasional deep watering is necessary but excessive watering stimulates the plant to produce lots of branches that break quite easily. In spring, after the danger of frost has passed, prune *S. mexicana* to a pleasing shape approximately 2 ft (0.6 m) in height and width to prepare for the coming season's growth. Prune plants throughout the flowering season by removing spent inflorescences. This procedure will reduce the plant's bulk and weight. Remove crossed or weighted branches in order to encourage upright growth. Propagation is by seed and cuttings.

I am unable to find a record of when *Salvia mexicana* came into cultivation, but collection records from several botanic gardens show that it was grown in these gardens in the early 1970s. Distinctive plants without cultivar names are being propagated by nurseries and gardeners. One plant collected in Mexico by the Huntington Botanical Gardens has gray leaves and attracts several species of butterfly. Another undesignated plant, collected in Guanajuato province by the University of California Botanical Garden, Berkeley, has short, showy, chartreuse-green calyces. Still another plant was collected in 1978 by botanist Robert Ornduff for the University of California Botanical Garden, Berkeley. Found on the Quertaro Province line at the edge of a fir and oak woodland in abundant litter, it has large chartreuse-green calyces and vibrant violet-blue flowers. It was designated a cultivar and given the name 'Limelight' (plate 92). Two additional cultivars appear frequently on nursery lists: 'Lollie Jackson' (plate 56) is a compact, 4 ft (1.3 m) plant, and 'Ocampo' is upright in growth to 7 ft (2.3 m) and survives low temperatures for short periods. All of these cultivars grow well under high tree canopies, making them fine understory plants.

For continued autumn bloom, *Salvia mexicana* is one of the most reliable plants for the border. It is a nectar source for many insects, butterflies, and hummingbirds. Because of its brittle branches, it needs wind protection and some pruning throughout the summer. Try growing it next to upright trees or shrubs. By chance I planted it between *Magnolia dawsoniana* and a 4 ft (1.3 m) tall fence and found it had no choice but to grow upward in this wind protected position. A border of evergreen shrubs interplanted with *Salvia mexicana* gives the gardener subtle color until the end of the season.

## *Salvia microphylla* Kunth, Cherry sage, Plate 59

Covering an immense geographical area, *Salvia microphylla* may be found in the wild in southeastern Arizona and in the mountains of eastern, western, and southern Mexico. Carl Epling (1939) considers *Salvia microphylla* to consist of three geographical races that are difficult to define because they are currently in the process of emerging. Known to show great variation, it is conceivable that this species has even more than three variants. James Compton (1994a) devised a key to varieties of *S. microphylla* using leaves and bracts as characters. To my knowledge, gardeners are growing four different forms of *S. microphylla*. See the following entries for *S. microphylla* (grahami), *S. microphylla* var. *neurepia*, and *S. microphylla* var. *wislizeni* (lemmoni). To complicate matters further, *S. greggii* is frequently confused with *S. microphylla*. Epling (1939) distinguishes between the two by a pair of papillae inside the corolla near the base of *S. microphylla*.

*Salvia microphylla* comes into full bloom in late spring and again in autumn and throws a few sporadic flowers practically year round in mild areas. Flowering ends only with the onset of cold weather and short days. Measuring 3–4 ft (1–1.3 m) in height and width, cherry sage has small, 0.5–1 in (1.3–2.5 cm) leaves, deltoid in shape and a bright green color with a yellow undertone. They have a grayish cast. A pronounced, pleasing fragrance is released when the leaves are rubbed. The specific epithet *microphylla* is from the Greek and means small leaved. Flowers appear in whorls, with great variation in color—pink, rose, red, magenta, and others. Flowering stems hold well in arrangements.

The plant described here is the form commonly found in nurseries under the name *Salvia microphylla*. Called *mirto de montes*, myrtle of the mountains, this is a tough, wiry looking plant that will take full sun or a little shade. It is drought tolerant and usually ignored by deer. Hummingbirds adore it. It has escaped from gardens in the San Francisco Bay region and become naturalized in a number of small areas in that benign climate. Given good drainage and only occasional water it requires no other ongoing care. In late winter, remove all woody stems as close to the ground as possible to encourage new and more succulent growth. It may be propagated by seed or cuttings. Because of its wide distribution in the wild, some strains are probably more frost tolerant than others. In my garden it has withstood temperatures into the teens (around −10° C) with no apparent damage.

The Huntington Botanical Gardens collected a form of *Salvia microphylla* in Belize that differs from the plant described above. It has vibrant red flowers and a more leafy and succulent look. I have found it tender to light frosts in my garden, though it will come back from established rootstock. In the Monterey Bay area of California, it flourishes and looks good year round.

Even in cultivation, *Salvia microphylla* varies in flower color. For example, Merritt College in Oakland, California, has a large planting of the red flowered *S. microphylla* that is perhaps 8–10 ft (2.5–3 m) in length and width. At the edge of the planting I found stems with pink flowers. Along with variations, cherry sage is notorious for hybridizing with other salvias in the garden. Since 1960, many collections have been made in Mexico by botanists and plantspeople and subsequently introduced to the gardening public.

Two cultivars of *Salvia microphylla* that are exceptional garden plants were introduced in the early 1990s. 'Rosita', a bright candy-pink flowered plant with a graceful mounding habit, was selected by Don Mahoney and introduced by Strybing Arboretum. 'San Carlos Festival', with rich magenta-pink flowers, a leafy look, and a pleasing habit, was introduced by Yucca Do Nursery of Texas. Both plants are about 2 ft (0.6 m) tall and bloom profusely from early summer until late autumn. Cultivars that are grown in England include 'Cerro Potosi', with large and vibrant magenta flowers, and 'Oxford', with deep magenta-crimson flowers and small deltoid leaves. In France 'Pink Blush' is a border favorite.

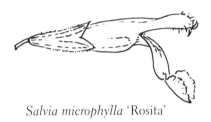

*Salvia microphylla* 'Rosita'

For a dry landscape, combine *Salvia microphylla* with drought tolerant plants such as *Romneya coulteri* (Matilija poppy) and the dark, shiny leaved, evergreen shrub *Prunus ilicifolia*. Together, they give cover and texture to an exposed, south-facing bank. Cherry sage tolerates some additional water and can be combined in a border with the stately *Euphorbia characias* subsp. *wulfenii* and *Artemisia* 'Powis Castle', which has gray, filigree-like foliage. Add the 3 ft (1 m) blue oat grass, *Helictotrichon sempervirens*, to give motion to the entire planting.

## *Salvia microphylla* Kunth, Graham's sage, Plates 16 & 57

Central Mexico, in the Sierra Madre west of Durango at 7500–8000 ft (2300–2500 m), is the native habitat of Graham's sage, known as both *Salvia microphylla* and *S. grahami*. Its distribution is apparently limited, but it has been grown in Britain since the 1880s as a prized ornamental plant. It is obscure to gardeners in the United States, where, to my knowledge, it remained unknown until the late 1980s.

The salvia Bentham described as *Salvia grahami* raises botanical questions. According to Carl Epling, the botanist who did major work on the salvias of the new world in the 1920s and 1930s, *S. grahami* is not distinguishable from *S. microphylla*. James Compton (1994a) and Gabriel Alziar (1988) both concur with Epling and state the epithet *grahami* is synonymous. The description that follows is from plants grown in horticulture from seed collected in Mexico west of the city of Durango, at about 7800 ft (2400 m) in the Sierra Madre. The seed was collected by Southwestern Native Seeds of Tucson, Arizona. The plant is horticulturally distinctive in habit, leaf shape, and flower size, and by calling it Graham's sage, I am optimistic that it can be separated from other forms of *S. microphylla*. See also the entries for *S. microphylla*, *S. microphylla* var. *neurepia*, and *S. microphylla* var. *wislizeni* (lemmoni).

Graham's sage is a handsome perennial that forms a little wood at its base and will reach 3 ft (1 m) or more in height and width. Delightful rose-red flowers appear in whorls and rise only inches above the small, mid-green, crisp looking foliage. The leaves are ovate in outline, 1 in (2.5 cm) long, and 0.5 in (1.3 cm) wide. With a hand lens, these slick looking leaves are seen to be covered with fine hairs on both surfaces. When they are brushed, they release an odor that I associate with a chaparral habitat. It is both fresh and pungent. The plant has a well-clothed look and may be easily propagated by seed or cuttings. Remember that seedling plants will show variation.

Three English writers praise the value of Graham's sage in the garden. William Robinson, Eleanour Sinclair Rohde, and E. A. Bowles all write of the plant's beauty and charm and their delight with its long bloom season.

In 1991 a purple flowering form of Graham's sage was introduced by Southwestern Native Seeds. It is found in two Mexican provinces at approximately 7000 ft (2100 m): the southwestern part of San Luis Potosi and western Zacatecas. The flowers are small, close to 0.5 in (1.3 cm) in length, and a vibrant beetroot-purple color. The leaves are obovate, scarcely 0.5 in (1.3 cm) long and wide, and lettuce-green in color. Arranged in clusters along the stems, when bruised they release a pleasant odor similar to that of *Salvia greggii*. Flowering begins in early summer and continues until frost. Not even short days stop its blooming.

Cultural requirements for both color forms of Graham's sage are full sun, good drainage, ordinary garden soil with some humus, and weekly water. The blooming period is from early summer until frost. Plants are cold tolerant to 20° F (−7° C).

Either color form of Graham's sage combines nicely with the well-branched mugwort, *Artemisia stelleriana*, which has beautiful, dissected, gray-white foliage, and with the upright, handsome, late blooming anise hyssop, *Agastache foeniculum*. This old-fashioned plant has violet flowers and blooms repeatedly. *A. foeniculum* 'Alba' is a stately, white flowered form that is a good alternative. A suitable groundcover for this combination is the low, creeping *Veronica* 'Waterperry Blue'. Flowering continually throughout the warm months, both color forms are fine plants for borders or containers.

## *Salvia microphylla* var. *neurepia* Epling, Delta leaf sage, Plate 58

*Salvia microphylla* var. *neurepia* comes from a wide area in central Mexico and can be found at altitudes ranging from 3000–7000 ft (900–2100 m) from Coahuila Province in the north to Guanajuato Province in the south. This striking deltoid and truncate leaved form is particularly prevalent in San Luis Potosi Province.

The varietal name *neurepia* is of Greek origin. It combines two words; *neure* for nerve or vein, and *pia*, a perennial herb producing arrowroot. This salvia is usually referred to by its complete botanical name.

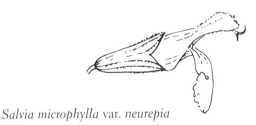

*Salvia microphylla* var. *neurepia*

The plant I grow and will describe below came from a cutting from a plant that has been nurtured in a greenhouse by a family in England for over one hundred years. It has proved to be hardy in my garden, probably reflecting its high mountainous origin. Seed from *Salvia microphylla* var. *neurepia* appears on the seed list of the Royal Horticultural Society's garden at Wisley from time to time. My plant produces seed and abundant cutting material; both methods have proved easy and reliable means of propagation. See also the entries for *Salvia microphylla*, *S. microphylla* (grahami), and *S. microphylla* var. *wislizeni* (lemmoni).

At maturity, *Salvia microphylla* var. *neurepia* is a full and rounded plant about 3 ft (1 m) tall and 4 ft (1.3 m) wide. It is shapely and sends out its flowers above the foliage so they are easily seen. Bright, signal-red flowers in verticils of two appear throughout the summer. Heavy blooming periods occur in early summer and in autumn. Deltoid leaves with a yellow-green cast range in size from 3 in (8 cm) in length and 1.5 in (4 cm) across to one quarter that size. If rubbed, they release a light, rather pleasant medicinal odor. When conditioned by cutting stems under water, the flowers hold well in arrangements.

Full sun, good drainage, soil enriched with humus, and weekly watering are needed for *Salvia microphylla* var. *neurepia* to produce flowers over a long period of time. Before new spring growth begins, prune all woody parts and reshape the plant. Humus may be added as mulch and for food during the growing season. Hardy to 20° F (−7° C), this salvia eventually comes back from its rootstock if cut down by frost.

The English botanist James Compton (1994a) writes of *Salvia microphylla* var. *neurepia*, "In cultivation this species is one of the most desirable of all salvias, liberally covered in strikingly colored flowers, often of intense and vibrant hues, for 6 months or more." Beth Chatto (1978) commends its good looks and hardiness in her Essex garden. Grown in England since the late 1800s and on the French Riviera, it is rarely seen in gardens and is rarely available through nurserymen's lists in America.

Here is a plant that has endless possibilities in the garden. It is beautiful combined with pink and white roses in a herbaceous border. The David Austin shrub roses 'Mary Rose' and 'Winchester Cathedral' are admirable companions. White cleome and cosmos along with lavender-blue asters and erigerons planted with this cheery sage make an striking summer into autumn display.

## *Salvia microphylla* **var.** *wislizeni* Gray, Little leaf sage

*Salvia microphylla* var. *wislizeni* is described by botanists as a perennial, but it quickly builds up wood at its base and appears shrub-like. Found at high elevations of 6000–8000 ft (1800–2500 m) in the mountains of southern Arizona and northern Mexico, it probably came into cultivation in Arizona and California in the early 1980s. Asa Gray described it and named it for John Gill Lemmon, the pioneer California botanist, who had collected it in Arizona in 1885.

For many years this plant was always referred to as *Salvia lemmoni*, probably because Asa Gray named it after Lemmon when he first looked at the dried specimens that had come from Arizona. Later, in looking at material from Mexico, Gray called the plant *Salvia microphylla* var. *wislizeni* because of its differences from the type. Its rangy habit and leaves arranged in clusters are marked differences from the type. Carl Epling studied the plant from many collections and contends that *Salvia microphylla* embraces a great variety of forms, distinguishable chiefly by the habit of foliage. Apparently it is a species in which three geographical races are emerging. See also the entries under *Salvia microphylla*, *S. microphylla* (grahami), and *S. microphylla* var. *neurepia*.

In a mild climate, little leaf sage tends to keep its small, mistletoe-green leaves throughout the winter. They seldom measure more than 0.5 in (1.3 cm) in length and less in width and are arranged on the stem in tight clusters. A light minty odor is released when they are crushed. Flowering begins in summer and continues until frost. The problem for gardeners is to keep this sage cut back to promote more flowering and to encourage a shapely plant. Neat flowers that are a bright shade of fuchsia-pink are produced a few at a time all summer. Though they are small, they are persistent, and furnish food for insects and hummingbirds. The calyx is small and the color of rich red wine.

Good drainage, full sun, ordinary garden soil, and infrequent water are the plant's requirements. Definitely drought tolerant, little leaf sage performs best in a dry and sunny location. However, in areas with very low humidity, it will tolerate normal garden watering, in which case, foliage will be produced abundantly. In arid and desert areas of Arizona, large colonies are reported to die in extremely dry summers. One of the hardiest sages native to the United States, little leaf sage will endure temperatures of 10° F (−12° C) or less for short periods of time. It has a good reputation for hybridizing—being one of the parents (along with *Salvia greggii*) of the beautiful hybrid 'Plum Wine'. Little leaf sage is easily propagated by seed or cuttings.

A dry hillside planted with drifts of little leaf sage among Mediterranean plants such as rosemary, lavender, and ballota makes an attractive composition of varied leaf textures and flower colors. All require little care and very little summer water. In climates that experience temperatures as low as 10° F (−12° C), *Salvia microphylla* var. *wislizeni* should prove cold tolerant. In a cold zone it is an attractive feature in either a herbaceous or shrub border.

## *Salvia miniata* Fernald

From Belize and the Mexican province of Chiapas comes the handsome and luxuriant *Salvia miniata*. In the wild it grows on shaded hillsides at elevations of around 2000 ft (600 m). These are warm, moist mountains with precipitation in the form of rain or fog occurring throughout the year—the winter months being the driest.

The specific epithet *miniata* means red, vermilion, or scarlet, in particular the red used in illuminating or decorating letters in a manuscript. The salvia's flowers reflect this name, being clear red with an orange undertone. The glossy green foliage helps intensify the rich vermilion flower color.

A herbaceous perennial, *Salvia miniata* is quite tender and will not survive a light freeze. In the ground it grows robustly, reaching 3 ft (1 m) in height and width during the summer. Well-branched from the base, the myrtle-green leaves are glistening and hairless, and amply clothe the plant. The glossy leaves reflect light, which in turn brightens the shaded plant. The largest leaves measure about 5 in (12 cm) in length and 2 in (5 cm) in width and are the perfect foil for the 1 in (2.5 cm) long, signal-red flowers. Flowers are loosely spaced in whorls on an inflorescence that will reach a good 12 in (30 cm) in length. Many flowers elongate simultaneously, making a visual treat. Flowering begins in mid-summer and tapers off as the days grow shorter. However, if autumn weather is warm the plant will persist in producing flowers. Flowering branches last well in bouquets if stems are conditioned by first cutting them under water. A frost-free and mild climate will permit S. *miniata* to persist in the garden throughout the winter. For a nicely shaped plant, wait until just before active growth begins and then cut stems to two active nodes about 6 in (15 cm) above the ground.

*Salvia miniata* is a well-proportioned salvia that requires high shade and moisture. The soil must have good drainage and be prepared with humus. A half day of sun is needed along with weekly deep watering. S. *miniata* will not succeed in a hot and dry climate. Like many salvias that produce a lot of growth, it needs protection from winds. Easily propagated by cuttings, it may be over-wintered by this method.

It is not known when *Salvia miniata* was introduced to horticulture, but the botanist Merritt Lyndon Fernald described it in 1900. Few people have seen it in gardens although it is an excellent garden plant — in spite of having to lift it for the greenhouse or take cuttings each autumn. It has been grown outdoors at Strybing Arboretum in San Francisco for many years and is propagated regularly for their plant sales. Since the early 1990s, quite a few nurseries have offered it on their lists. Gardeners in the southern part of the United States and England find it worth the effort of wintering cuttings in a greenhouse in order to enjoy it in the garden.

A group of *Salvia miniata* plants, growing with clumps of *Chasmanthium latifolium* (sea oats), the handsome grass from the eastern United States, will reach the same height, and the two plants make remarkable partners. Their profuse and contrasting foliages have a rich and plentiful look. Both require high shade and similar cultural conditions.

## *Salvia moorcroftiana* Wallich ex Bentham

Found throughout the Himalayan mountains from Pakistan to western Nepal, *Salvia moorcroftiana* is particularly common in the Kashmir valley area of India. Not fussy as to habitat, it grows on open slopes and disturbed areas between 5000–9000 ft (1500–2800 m). The leaves of *S. moorcroftiana* are reported to be used medicinally in Kashmir.

A robust herbaceous perennial, *Salvia moorcroftiana* builds mostly basal leaves to 2.5 ft (0.8 m) in height and a little less in width. They are long-stalked, covered with white wool, and have a toothed margin. The inflorescence rises just above the foliage, making a mass of pale lilac or nearly white flowers. Individual flowers are about 1 in (2.5 cm) in length and are held in a hairy calyx. Showy, green-veined bracts add to the plant's charm. Flowering takes place during early summer and usually lasts for a solid four-week period.

Easy to situate in a border, *Salvia moorcroftiana* prefers full sun, friable garden soil, good drainage, and regular water. Large leaves make a damp and attractive haunt for snails and should be inspected occasionally. Little attention is required to keep this salvia in good condition because its needs are simple—only the removal of spent inflorescences and tattered leaves is needed. Reflecting its high mountain habitat, *S. moorcroftiana* is hardy to 0° F (−18° C). Propagation is by seed.

Because of this salvia's late spring into early summer blooming period, it combines beautifully with the fragrant, one-time blooming, pale pink rose 'Baltimore Belle'. This rose is a vigorous climber and when it is covered with flowers on a high trellis, the flowering salvia gives an echo of a similar effect at a lower height. Another rose, 'Kathleen', a hybrid musk that repeat blooms, is also a desirable companion. Fragrant, almost single flowers of soft pink to pale yellow bloom repeatedly and are followed in autumn by outstanding hips that are the color of the flesh of a perfectly ripe cantaloupe. In a mild climate there is an additional reward—the large woolly-gray leaves of *Salvia moorcroftiana* are evergreen and remain to enhance the winter garden.

### *Salvia muelleri* Epling, Royal purple sage, Plate 60

*Salvia muelleri* has a very limited natural range and distribution in the Mexican province of Nuevo Leon in the mountains near Monterrey. At the time of publication, there have been no other sitings or habitats reported. Almost never seen in nurseries or gardens before 1987, royal purple sage remains scarcely known to horticulture. It is closely related to *S. greggii*.

When Carl Epling described and named *Salvia muelleri*, he called it a perennial herb. In my garden it builds up light wood very rapidly and looks shrubby by the end of the growing season. However, in late winter when pruning takes place, one can see many underground runners with wiry stems. About 2.5 ft (0.8 m) tall and 4 ft (1.3 m) wide, royal purple sage may be found in bloom from spring through autumn. It blooms more freely when the days are short. The royal purple flowers are less than 1 in (2.5 cm) in length, two-lipped, with the lower lip 0.5 in (1.3 cm) wide and showy. The small calyx is dark purple and intensifies the color of the royal purple flower. Small, shiny, grassy green leaves lightly cover the plant, allowing its woody structure to be seen. They measure less than 1 in (2.5 cm) in length and 0.5 in (1.3 cm) in width and are ovate. In small flower arrangements, its leaves and inflorescences are a rich addition.

The culture of royal purple sage entails full sun, fast drainage, and soil enriched with humus. It is drought tolerant and needs little water to survive. However, for constant bloom it is advisable during hot weather to water deeply every week. A top dressing of humus once a year helps with moisture retention and nourishment. Some pruning throughout the growing season will keep the plant's growth in check. Propagation is by seed, cuttings, or division of the rootstock. Once established, the roots of the plant will send out fresh stems. These new plants can be divided from the mother plant and shared with other gardeners or simply removed in order to maintain a well-shaped plant. Royal purple sage is hardy to 10° F (−12° C).

*Salvia muelleri* is eminently well suited for a drought tolerant garden. Placed among rocks, it looks natural and fills niches freely. A sunny rock garden might include clumps of *Helictotrichon sempervirens*, a grass with evergreen, blue-gray foliage from southwestern Europe, along with patches of the native California *Eriogonum grande* var. *rubescens* (red buckwheat), with its rosy balls of flowers, and the Eastern European *Limonium latifolium* (sea lavender) with its basal rosettes of dark green leaves and sprays of lavender flowers. Several or more royal purple sages would complete a picture of harmonious flower color and varying leaf textures.

## *Salvia nubicola* Wallich ex Sweet, Plates 61 & 93

A full leaved, summer blooming herbaceous perennial, *Salvia nubicola* has a wide distribution, including Afghanistan, Bhutan, India, Pakistan, southwest Asia, and Europe. Found at elevations of 7000 ft (2100 m) or higher, it has been collected many times and grown frequently as a garden subject. In 1993, botanists from Quarry Hill Botanic Garden, Glen Ellen, California, and the Royal Botanic Gardens, Kew, collected seed at 9200 ft (2850 m) on a heavily grazed hillside in northern India where it grew in full sun on light loam along with *Agrimonia*, a *Polygonum* groundcover, and a giant thistle.

*Salvia nubicola*

Holding its stems erect, *Salvia nubicola* reaches 3 ft (1 m) in height and close to the same in width. The leaves have a fresh green color and are triangular. The largest grow at the base of the plant and measure about 5 in (13 cm) in length. The petiole is more or less the same length as the leaf blade. Inflorescences are numerous and about 10 in (25 cm) long. Pale yellow flowers with finely spotted maroon markings on the upper lip appear in whorls of 2 to 6. They are held in a bright green, hairy calyx that is glandular and sticky. A light medicinal odor is released when the calyx is rubbed. Flowering is in summer and seed frequently matures in autumn. Propagation is by seed or cuttings. Superficially, this salvia resembles the early summer blooming Jupiter's Distaff, *S. glutinosa*.

The specific epithet *nubicola* means dweller among clouds and underlines the plants high mountainous home. Hardy to 0° F (−18° C), *Salvia nubicola* also performs well at low elevations in warm climates. Regular, fast-draining garden soil along with protection and some shade from other plants are the main requirements of this salvia. Regular water will insure flowering and seed production. In a cold climate, the plant is dormant. In a mild climate, the plant will frequently retain a few leaves.

*Salvia nubicola* makes a fine filler in a border of summer blooming perennials. The lax, 4–5 ft (1.3–1.5 m), spreading *Buddleja davidii* 'Nanho Purple', which has dark red-purple flowers with an orange eye, would make a focal point at the back of the border. Several of the 4 ft (1.3 m) tall *Salvia* 'Purple Majesty' along with the butter-yellow *S. madrensis* would fill in the back and middle of the border. In groups of three, mix plants of *S. nubicola* along with the 2 ft (60 cm) tall, red-purple flowered *Agastache barberi*. These will fill the front and probably overflow. If any space can be found in the front of the border, the matting, pale yellow yarrow *Achillea* 'King Edward' grows quickly and would soon cover the bare spots.

## *Salvia officinalis* Linnaeus, Garden sage, common sage, Plates 31 & 62–64

Described in 1753 by Carl Linnaeus, a great and creative naturalist, *Salvia officinalis* has long been known and grown. Old herbal books tell of the miraculous properties attributed to it:

> He who would live for aye
> Must eat sage in May.

Called sage or garden sage in early times, the specific epithet *officinalis* refers to the plant being sold in shops for its medicinal virtues. Found in the wild on the northern shores of the Mediterranean, including Asia Minor, it is renowned for its culinary and medicinal properties. Cultivated for centuries in England, France, Germany, Spain, and Italy for these attributes, it is also valued throughout the temperate world as a handsome and well tested garden subject. Through widespread cultivation it has become naturalized in a few benign climates.

Described by botanists as a shrub because of the woody stems at the base, to the gardener its appearance is more like a well-branched, evergreen, herbaceous perennial. With a height and width of 2 ft (60 cm), the handsome gray-green leaves have a rugose surface and are almost white underneath because of short, soft hairs. Oblong in shape, the leaves vary in size, the largest being about 2.5 in (6 cm) in length and 1 in (2.5 cm) in width. The leaves give the sage a well-covered look both summer and winter. Flowering occurs in late spring or summer. *Salvia officinalis* is exceedingly variable in flower and leaf color. You may find white, pink, purple, or lavender flowers—the latter being most common. Highly variable in size, the foliage is variable too. Leaves can be variegated with yellow, cream, purple, or rose in different patterns.

These varied characteristics have given rise to many different cultivars. The weak 'Aurea' has golden leaves. 'Berggarten', meaning mountain garden, was introduced by Herrenhausen Grosser Garten in Hannover, Germany, and has wide, rounded leaves and few flowers. 'Compacta' is a narrow leaved and compact form. 'Icterina' (plates 31 and 63) has green leaves with a wide golden margin. 'Purpurascens', the favored sage of medieval times, has purple-red leaves and was commonly called red sage (plate 64). 'Tricolor' has gray-green leaves that are zoned creamy yellow and rose. 'Holt's Mammoth' has long, wide, gray-green leaves and is a compact form. All of these cultivars hold their foliage and flowers well in bouquets. Other cultivars are more familiar in Britain and Europe than in the United States. 'Albiflora' has long leaves and white flowers. 'Crispa' has variegated leaves with wavy margins. 'Grete Stolze' has pointed, pale gray leaves. 'Milleri' has spotted red leaves. 'Salicifolia' has long narrow leaves, and 'Sturnina' has white-green leaves.

*Salvia officinalis* is hardy and reputed to withstand temperatures of 0° F (−18° C) or less. All cultivars are much less hardy and need protection from freezing and thawing.

Quick-draining garden soil and full sun are necessities for these sages. Some kind of grit or coarse sand can be incorporated in the soil and the plant elevated on a small mound in order to ensure fast drainage. Somewhat drought tolerant, garden sage needs moderate additional summer watering and will withstand overhead irrigation if given fast drainage. Though perennial, these sages are short-lived plants—usually looking good for three to four years. Propagation is by cuttings or divisions in late spring or early autumn. Seeds germinate readily, but because of the plant's variability, vegetative propagation is advised. Just before the plant comes into bloom is when its leaves have the highest concentration of volatile oils. This is the most advantageous time to gather leaves for drying. A saying from the Middle Ages is "Why should a man die whilst sage grows in his garden?"

Garden sage and its many cultivars need little if any attention when well-placed in the garden. I frequently squeeze *Salvia officinalis* 'Purpurascens' into the front of my border or into spots where its purple-gray leaves bring out the color of other plants. I find this plant indispensable. Trevor Nottle (1984), an Australian garden writer, advocates its placement in the front of the border combined with a plant or two of *Geranium sanguineum* (bloody cranesbill), which has finely divided, dark green leaves and magenta flowers. The cultivar 'Berggarten' is choice for the border too. Its large, rounded, gray-green leaves make a quiet pool of color, and it is longer lived than the species or any cultivars that I have grown. 'Icterina' is also especially useful; Penelope Hobhouse (1985) laments the fact that it is usually described as having variegated green and golden-yellow foliage. She insists that the green is yellowish and the golden-yellow almost honey colored. This gives the plant a subtlety of hue which is softer than gold. A good choice for small, tight spaces is the cultivar 'Compacta'. Its small, gray-green leaves look good throughout the year. All of these plants add color and texture to designs and provide short-term reliability.

## *Salvia patens* Cavanilles, Gentian sage

Since *Salvia patens* was introduced to horticulture in 1838, it has been extensively grown and deservedly praised. William Robinson (1933) says that without question, *Salvia patens* is one of the best plants in cultivation. Many gardeners today wholeheartedly agree with him.

Found in the wild over a large section of central Mexico, *Salvia patens* is a herbaceous perennial that will overwinter with protection in areas where the temperature dips down into the 20s° F (around −6° C). Beth Chatto (1988) confirms the plant's hardiness in her Essex garden but cautions that cuttings should be kept under cover as insurance. It is

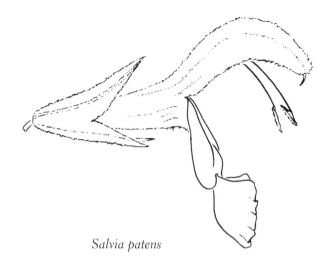

*Salvia patens*

frequently treated as an annual, and new plants can be bedded out in mid-spring. A few color selections are offered on seed lists and at nurseries from time to time, such as 'Oxford Blue' (dark blue), 'Cambridge Blue' (light blue), 'Chilcombe' (lilac), and 'Alba' (white). Seeds have been available from Holland of special selections with large and richly colored flowers.

*Salvia patens* is tuberous and easy to lift for greenhouse protection if winters are cold and unpredictable. Mature plants reach 1–2 ft (30–60 cm) in height and width and are generously covered with mistletoe-green leaves that are hastate in shape. The inflorescence rises well above the foliage, extending 6–12 in (15–30 cm), sometimes more. Rich, cornflower-blue flowers over 1 in (2.5 cm) in length are spaced along the inflorescence. On close examination, the hood of the flower is a lighter color (probably because of the hairs that cover it) than the wide, two-parted lip. Both parts are violet-blue. The specific epithet *patens* refers to the two spreading parts of the flower, which make it easily accessible to pollinators. The calyx is green, about 0.5 in (1.3 cm) long, with an upper and lower lip. It is a graceful appendage and adds to the beauty of each flower. Propagation is by seed and cuttings. Established plants can be carefully divided from the rootstock.

*Salvia patens* needs some shade and good garden soil that drains well and is enriched with humus. Deep weekly watering and fertilizer once a month will stimulate reblooming if spent inflorescences are removed. Peak bloom is in early summer and lasts close to a month. A 2–4 in (5–10 cm) mulch will conserve water and improve the soil around the plants.

A versatile plant because of its neat growing habit, groups of gentian sage are a good choice with the wonderful dark red Gallica roses 'Tuscany' or 'Tuscany Superb'. Another rose that might be considered is *Rosa rugosa* 'Rubra', which frequently produces violet-red hips. An effective planting is *Salvia patens* massed in formal beds or areas that are edged with clipped boxwood. Another fine edging plant is the handsome, low-growing *Tanacetum haradjanii*. Its gray-white, feathery foliage along with the blue flowers of the sage make a striking combination.

## *Salvia penstemonoides* Kunth & Bouche, Big red sage

*Salvia penstemonoides* is a rare plant in nature, occurring in only three locations in Texas, including the Edwards Plateau in central Texas. It was first sighted and documented in 1849 growing along the Salado Creek near San Antonio. In 1946 it was thought to be extinct, but it was rediscovered in 1987. Marshall Enquist, a botanist who was taking photographs for his book *Wildflowers of the Texas Hill Country*, rediscovered it. A large colony was found at that time but the plant remains endangered and on the verge of extinction because of destruction of its habitat and browsing by deer. It is speculated that a severe drought in the early 1950s in Texas contributed to its decline.

A herbaceous perennial, big red sage grows to 5 ft (1.5 m) in height in its native habitat of limestone rock along seeps or creeks. This information gives a good clue as to its requirements in the garden. In a mild climate, the flowering stalks will reach a mere 3 ft (1 m) and have a tendency to be lax. It has a slick and healthy looking basal rosette of leaves that are lance-like in outline and mistletoe-green in color. From the rosette, numerous stalks arise bearing flowers 1 in (2.5 cm) in length and beetroot-purple in color. The calyx is 0.5 in (1.3 cm) long and the color of red wine. Whorls of loosely packed flowers are spaced along an inflorescence that sometimes measures 8–12 in (20–30 cm). As its name suggests, *Salvia penstemonoides* resembles a penstemon. Flowering can begin in early summer but more frequently starts in August. Quite hardy to the low 20°s F (around −5° C), big red sage is most easily propagated by seed. Cuttings are possible and large clumps, with care, can be divided. Plants and seed are available from a limited number of sources.

Before planting *Salvia penstemonoides*, it is a good idea to incorporate humus and ground oyster shells or lime into the soil. The plant requires fast drainage and enough space for the roots to develop deeply. A half day of morning sun with the protection of high shade is desirable. Deep weekly watering will encourage good growth. It is reported to grow in full sun in areas where the humidity is high.

If you are fortunate enough to have limestone rocks, this is the perfect plant to grow among them. Other rocks are suitable if the soil is adjusted. A possible companion plant for *Salvia penstemonoides* is one of the cotoneasters, which are notable for their preference for sweet soil. There are many species to choose from, offering an array of habits and sizes. *Cotoneaster horizontalis* is known for its low-growing and spreading habit. It prefers north or east light and deep weekly watering. Ferns are an interesting group of plants to grow in a border with big red sage. One possible combination is *Cyrtomium falcatum* (Japanese holly fern) and *Pteris cretica*—both enjoy the same cultural conditions as *Salvia penstemonoides*. With or without rocks, the contrast in foliage makes a pleasing and graceful combination.

## *Salvia polystachya* Ortega, Plate 65

A tall perennial herb, *Salvia polystachya* has a wide distribution from central Mexico reaching south through Guatemala into Panama. It is found at altitudes of 3000–10,000 ft (900–3100 m) that have a mild climate and some summer rain. Rarely seen in gardens or on nursery lists, it deserves to become better known.

Shrub-like, *Salvia polystachya* grows 3–9 ft (1–3 m) in a season. Like so many of the late blooming Mexican salvias, it is brittle and needs the protection of other plants. By late September, *S. polystachya* begins to show a few violet-blue flowers less than 0.5 in (1.3 cm) long, but it does not come into full bloom until the middle of October. Then, many short and slender spikes composed of verticils of tightly held flowers provide a burst of color. The specific epithet, *polystachya*, refers to the many flowered branches or spikes. Leaves are small, barely 1 in (2.5 cm) in length and width, yellow-green in color, and held in little clusters. They clothe the stems of the plant without obstructing the spikes of sparkling flowers, which are violet blue at the edge, gradually fading to white in the center.

The flowering of this salvia came as a delightful surprise to me for it had been in my garden two years before it began its autumnal display. Before it will flower, the plant must build a strong root system. Then, leafy stems about 5 ft (1.5 m) in height and 4 ft (1.3 m) in width develop during the summer. A few flowers are seen in September but as October gradually rolls into November, the plant continues flowering through rainy autumn days and nights of light frost. Hardy to 20° F (−7° C), it is advisable to take cuttings for the greenhouse in early autumn. Propagation is by cuttings.

In the border, place *Salvia polystachya* so that it receives half to three-quarters of a day's sun. Well-draining soil amended with humus is advised, as well as a mulch of humus during the summer months. The additional humus helps keep the soil friable and moist. Deep watering is required once or twice a week throughout the growing and flowering periods. More water may be needed if temperatures are high. Prune the plant back to two active nodes about 1 ft (30 cm) from the ground in early spring to encourage shapeliness during the coming season of growth. Cut flowers are a disappointment because once they are brought inside they loose their brilliant sparkle and merely look gray.

This salvia complements many herbaceous perennials and shrubs. For example, its height and sparkling flowers add an additional touch to an autumn blooming border of asters and penstemons. A fine companion for shrub roses, *Salvia polystachya* will hardly be noticed until it comes into bloom late in the season, complementing reblooming roses such as the single, buff-yellow 'Mrs. Oakley Fisher', the warm pink 'Mary Rose', or the clear, light pink 'Duchesse de Brabant'. In my garden it grows behind the handsome, shrub-like *Salvia microphylla* var. *neurepia*. The combination of red and blue flowers on two dissimilar salvia plants is impressive.

## *Salvia pratensis* Linnaeus, Meadow sage, Plate 66

A widely scattered species, *Salvia pratensis* is found throughout Europe, including Great Britain. It is also reported in North Africa. An erect perennial, it grows in sunny meadows along with other wild flowers and grasses. *Pratensis* means growing in meadows.

Making a basal clump of rich green leaves, meadow sage has a leafy, herbaceous look. The margins of the leaves are slightly ruffled and toothed and the wrinkled surface is rugose. The upper leaves clasp the stem and twist in an attractive way. Flowering spikes are usually branched, with four to six flowers held in each verticil. Rich violet flowers, less than 1 in (2.5 cm) long, open from the base of the inflorescence as it elongates to about 12 in (30 cm). Each flower is held in a tiny, dark brown calyx that sits on a platter of small green bracts. The seedlings of *Salvia pratensis* vary in flower color from violet-blue to bluish white, and from pure white to pink. The plant is usually in bloom for three or four weeks if early spring weather stays moderate. The selection 'Tenorii' has especially fine rich blue flowers.

*Salvia pratensis* subsp. *haematodes* is widely grown and admired for its erect sprays of large, summer blooming, lilac-blue flowers. Flower arrangers in particular prize its endurance as a cut flower. It is not apparent why it is called *haematodes*, which means blood-red.

Indigenous to areas with hard winters as well as frost-free areas, the deciduous meadow sage can be tried in all kinds of climates. Full sun and good garden loam that drains readily are needed, as well as occasional water throughout the year. In a very mild climate, meadow sage comes into bloom in March and makes a wonderful display of rich purple spikes. Areas in the north or with hard winters may not get bloom until June, even July. If the plant is cut back before it makes seed it will probably re-bloom if summer temperatures are warm and the autumn long. Meadow sage makes a long-lasting and handsome cut flower.

As long ago as 1968, the seed of *Salvia pratensis* was not permitted to be shipped to California because it was thought to have naturalized in the wild in three locations. In 1983 this naturalized salvia was correctly identified as *S. virgata*, another widely distributed European native. Botanists at the State of California Department of Food and Agriculture have decided that *S. virgata* is no longer a threat. Seed catalogs for 1995 from other countries still warn that seed of *Salvia pratensis* may not be sent into California. It probably will take quite some time to unravel this tangle.

A meadow-like border in full sun might include *Leucanthemum vulgare*, the single, white ox-eye daisy, along with clumps of meadow sage and quantities of *Stipa pulchra*. *Stipa pulchra* (purple needlegrass) is the grass that gives California the name the Golden State. By mid-spring its green foliage begins to recede and its beautiful and delicate flower panicles rise 2 ft (0.6 m) or more. The entire plant dries to a rich tawny color. Even though it is considered drought tolerant, some additional summer water may be necessary, even in its dormant state. Another grass that can be interplanted with meadow sage and ox-eye daisy is *Koeleria cristata*. It is a clumping evergreen perennial under 2 ft (0.6 m) in height with rich green foliage and flowering stems that rise 12 in (30 cm) above the foliage. Sweet vernal grass, *Anthoxanthum odoratum,* is another choice. About 6–8 in (15–20 cm) in height, its flowers rise 12 in (30 cm) above the clump. In June it turns a warm golden color. These grasses are particularly effective because they respond so gracefully to the movement of the wind.

## *Salvia przewalskii* Maximowicz, Plate 94

In the wild *Salvia przewalskii* is found in China in the provinces of Gansu, Hubei, Sichuan, Xizang, and Yunnan. A freely seeding herbaceous perennial, this salvia establishes itself along streamsides and forest margins, among shrubs, and on granitic hillsides. Described and named by the indefatigable Russian botanist Carl Johann Maximowicz in 1881, it has been collected in China by many famous plantspeople on a number of occasions. In naming the salvia, Maximowicz honored the Russian zoological and botanical explorer Nicolai M. Przwalski, who himself made four collecting trips to China between 1872 and 1884. Botanists have specified four varieties—their identification being determined primarily by leaf covering and shape. One variety, *Salvia przewalskii* var. *przewalskii*, has a wide distribution and is known throughout its native habitat for its medicinal properties. Its leaves have very long petioles. *Salvia przewalskii* is usually seen growing only in botanic gardens but since the 1980s it has appeared on seed lists that are available to gardeners.

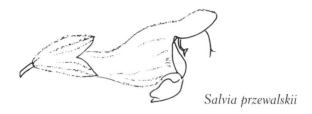

*Salvia przewalskii*

From a clump of basal leaves between 1–2 ft (30–60 cm) in width and height, flowering stalks of 3 ft (1 m) rise above yellow-green foliage in mid-summer. Leaves are 6–12 in (15–30 cm) long with veins clearly delineated on the underside. On the tall, branched inflorescence, widely spaced whorls of flowers open a few at a time. The flowers are about 1 in (2.5 cm) in length, fat, and an unusual purple-red or red-brown color. The hairy and glandular calyx is red-brown and two-lipped. These handsome flowering stems are subtle in color and make fine cut flowers. Be sure to condition each stem by cutting it under water. The blooming period usually lasts for well over three weeks. Propagation is by seed. Self-seeding becomes evident when plants are established.

Well-draining, friable garden soil is needed for *Salvia przewalskii*. Plants will bloom liberally if situated in full sun, and they will bloom fairly well with a half day of sun. Mulching with compost provides food and helps with water retention. Deep weekly watering is also necessary. Established plants are hardy to 10° F (−12° C).

This plant is a handsome addition to a high-summer flowering bed of purple-red and pink cut flowers, including both annuals and perennials. The purple-red leaved *Perilla frutescens* interplanted in threes or fives with *Datura wrightii* (formerly known as *Datura meteloides*), with its handsome gray leaves and a trumpet flower of soft white tinged with purple, make harmonious companions for *Salvia przewalskii*. This composition of subtle colors would be brightened with a few pastel pink zinnias. To enliven the color combination further, add one or two plants of wispy, white flowering cosmos. If there is space, the continually blooming

*Salvia microphylla* 'Rosita', which has candy-pink flowers, would add substance as well as uninterrupted color. All require the same culture and some cutting-back in order to encourage repeat bloom.

## *Salvia puberula* Fernald, Plate 67

Rarely seen in the wild, *Salvia puberula* has been reported to be found in the Mexican provinces of San Luis Potosi, Tamaulipas, Hidalgo, and Nuevo Leon. It is usually found in small colonies near oaks, yews, liquidambers, lindens, and dogwoods. It may be found at elevations varying from 4500–8000 ft (1400–2500 m). *S. puberula* is also known by the synonym *S. involucrata* (Cavanilles).

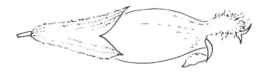

*Salvia puberula*

Growing 3–5 ft (1–1.5 m) in height, this shrub-like herbaceous perennial comes into glorious bloom in autumn. From October until frost, terminal clusters of bright magenta flowers are displayed at the top of long stems. The inflated flowers are about 1 in (2.5 cm) in length and are two-lipped. The upper lip is heavily covered with magenta hairs that fairly sparkle in sunlight. The 0.5 in (1.3 cm) calyx is also magenta and adds to the colorful display. Leaf-like bracts surround the expanding flowers and soon drop. The leaves are hastate in shape and the largest are 4 in (10 cm) long and 2.5 in (7 cm) wide. Pea-green in color, they are widely spaced along the stems. Short, soft hairs cover the stems and leaves, and the upper lip of each flower has magenta hairs. This characteristic probably led to the specific epithet *puberula*, meaning soft and downy. *Salvia puberula* was described and named in 1900 by the American botanist M. L. Fernald.

Fine specimens of *Salvia puberula* may be seen at the University of California Botanical Garden, Berkeley. Gardeners have quickly discovered its long autumn flowering season. Yucca Do Nursery in Waller,

Texas, has introduced plants collected in two different locations in the province of Nuevo Leon in Mexico. One selection comes from an elevation of 4500 ft (1400 m). The other selection comes from El Butano at an even higher elevation, 7000 ft (2100 m). Both clones were found to be growing in well-draining but moist soil in association with dogwoods, yews, and oaks.

Cultural requirements are simple. Well-draining soil enriched with humus and at least a half day of sun are needed. Deep watering on a one to two week basis is desirable. Depending on its collection site, *Salvia puberula* is probably hardy to 20° F (−7° C). Do take cuttings for the greenhouse in autumn. In early spring prune the plant almost to the ground; it grows prolifically once the weather warms. Propagation is by seed or cuttings.

*Salvia puberula* likes close association with other plants. Small trees, such as cherries, redbuds, and arbutus are fine companions and give added protection from both wind and strong sunlight. A border of shrubs interplanted with *Salvia puberula* is handsome as well as practical. Good companion shrubs with an upright-growing habit and dark green foliage are *Osmanthus heterophyllus*, *Rhamnus alaternus*, and *R. californicus*. Because the weight of foliage and flowers gives the salvia a tendency to lean, the thick green foliage of the shrubs acts as support as well as a foil for the yellow-green leaves and distinctive magenta flowers.

## *Salvia* 'Purple Majesty', Plate 68

A large herbaceous shrub, the hybrid *Salvia* 'Purple Majesty' comes from an artificial cross made at the Huntington Botanical Gardens by Fred Boutin in 1977. The parents are S. *guaranitica* and S. *gesneraeflora* 'Tequila'. From that cross pollination, three seeds were produced and from those seedlings, one plant was chosen for introduction because of its garden merit. *Salvia* 'Purple Majesty' was introduced to horticulture around 1980 and has proved to be a tireless bloomer with rich and color-ful flowers.

*Salvia* 'Purple Majesty' reaches 3–4 ft (1–1.3) in a growing season and comes into bloom in mid-summer, flowering until frost. Ovate, serrated, yellow-green leaves amply cover the plant. They measure about 3 in (8 cm) in length and 2 in (5 cm) in width. Spike-like inflorescences, 8–10 in (20–25 cm) long, form at the top of stems. Individual flowers are about 1 in (2.5 cm) in length and a rich violet color. The calyx is 0.75 in (2 cm) long and an even darker purple than the flowers, adding to the beauty of the inflorescence. The inflorescences are handsome and make fine cut flowers if conditioned by cutting each stem under water. They last for many days in an arrangement. Their color remains when they are dried for winter bouquets.

Full sun, fast-draining soil, and regular dressings of humus are needed to keep this salvia flowering for a long period. Also, three applications of liquid fertilizer spread out over the growing season are helpful. Deep watering once every week or two is desirable. The frequent removal of spent flowering parts is a necessity for two reasons: the weight of the spent inflorescences will break stems and branches if not removed, and new flowering is stimulated by this kind of pruning. Propagation is by cuttings in order to secure identical plants. When taken in late summer, cuttings strike roots readily. *Salvia* 'Purple Majesty' is reported to be hardy to 10° F (−12° C) when the crown is protected with straw or some other light mulch. In a moderate climate no protection is needed. When all danger of frost has passed, prune all stems back to the lowest active nodes. This procedure will assure a well-shaped plant for the coming season.

This is a fine plant for the summer into autumn border. *Salvia* 'Purple Majesty' combined with the 6 ft (2 m), yellow flowering *Salvia madrensis* makes an admirable background for drifts of the 4 ft (1.3 m) *Boltonia asteroides* 'Snowbank' and 3–4 ft (1–1.3 m) Michaelmas daisies. (Both *Aster novae-angliae* from New England and *A. novi-belgii* from New York have been used in hybridizing work and the name Michaelmas daisy applies to their hybrids.) A selection of lavender-blue, violet, white, and purple Michaelmas daisies looks handsome in the border or in bouquets with this salvia.

## *Salvia purpurea* Cavanilles, Plate 69

An autumn into winter blooming herbaceous perennial from Mesoamerica, *Salvia purpurea* is distributed from the province of Jalisco in Mexico south into Guatemala, El Salvador, and Honduras. It is widely spread through six Mexican provinces. Epling (1939) states that great variation in the length of the corolla is typical throughout the range of the species. The plant was described in 1793, though I can find no mention of it in horticultural literature. Huntington Botanical Gardens, Strybing Arboretum, and the University of California Botanical Garden in Berkeley have examples of the plant collected in Mexico. It is likely that its introduction to horticulture came from those institutions. This desirable salvia is rarely seen in nurseries or on seed lists.

A striking plant because of the color of its flowers, *Salvia purpurea* is shrub-like in stature, about 3–7 ft (1–2.5 m) in height, and a little less in width. Ovate, yellow-green leaves with serrated margins cover the plant well. Branched inflorescences begin to appear in mid-autumn and the flowering period is usually two, even three months long. When the plant breaks into bloom it is a surprise to see pinkish purple-violet flowers, rather than the more common warm autumnal reds and yellows. Flowers are in tight verticils that appear to be swept to one side of the spike. Small, individual flowers about 0.75 in (2 cm) in length are crowded together at the ends of numerous branches. These inflorescences of pinkish purple flowers make a rich display. Flowering stems hold well as cut flowers if kept in a cool place.

Provided with a few basic conditions, *Salvia purpurea* is easy to establish in a garden. Place it to receive a half day of sun in both summer and winter, in well-draining soil that has been amended with humus. A mulch of humus and regular weekly water are needed to imitate conditions in its native habitat. In order to ensure a shapely plant, prune stems back to active leaf nodes near the base in early spring. This salvia is tender but withstands temperatures of 25° F (−4° C) for very short periods. Propagation is generally by seed or cuttings.

An unusual plant because of its flowering period and flower color, *Salvia purpurea* is not easy to place in an autumn garden design. However, companion plants can be found for its pinkish purple flowers. *Osmanthus heterophyllus*, an evergreen shrub with dark green, shiny leaves, makes a splendid backdrop for the salvia. It too, blooms in late autumn with tiny, fragrant, creamy-white blossoms. The compact Australian shrub *Westringia* 'Wynyabbie Gem', growing to 3–4 ft (1–1.3 m) with silky gray-green leaves and lavender flowers that appear from time to time throughout the year, would complete the picture.

### *Salvia recognita* Fischer & Meyer, Plates 70, 73, & 95

*Salvia recognita*, an endemic, comes from central Turkey and is found in light shade at the base of cliffs at an elevation usually of 4000 ft (1200 m) or less. Described as a woody-based perennial, its mass of divided leaves forms a small to medium basal clump. Leaves vary in size from 3–4 in (7–10 cm) to almost 1 ft (30 cm) in length with three or more leaflets. Light green leaves with a grayish cast appear thick in texture due to a covering of long, soft hairs. Each leaf blade has a wine colored petiole, or leaf stalk. The cyclamen-pink flowers appear in whorls and the calyces that hold them are covered with glands and hairs. These shaggy hairs and dew-like viscid glands add further interest to this handsome plant. Round flowering stalks elongate to 2–3 ft (0.6–1 m) and hold many whorls of widely spaced flowers at the top. The long blooming period begins in spring, continuing into warm weather with an occasional inflorescence seen throughout the growing season.

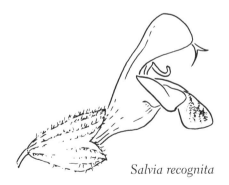

*Salvia recognita*

Reported to be hardy to 0° F (−18° C), *Salvia recognita*'s springtime display is something to look forward to. This salvia may be short-lived but once established it seeds itself freely and usually there are many seedlings of varying sizes around it. Cuttings are possible but propagation is usually by seed. Planted in full or partial sun, it needs fast drainage, good garden loam, and weekly water. A light dressing of lime in late winter may be added at its base.

Described by botanists in the 1800s, *Salvia recognita* has only come to the attention of gardeners in the past few years. It was in the 1980s that Jim and Jenny Archibald of Wales made seed they had collected in Turkey available through their seed list. My records show my seed germination was poor but one small plant survived and was planted in the garden in May of 1986. It soon died. The following spring, one plant again germinated and was planted in the garden in the early autumn of 1989. This plant did well from the start and by the winter/spring of 1990–91, many seedlings were germinating all around the mother plant.

A bed or border of small shrubby roses that are of similar size, such as the 2 ft (0.6 m) tall and 3 ft (1 m) wide 'Little White Pet' along with the soft pink *Rosa* 'The Fairy', is enhanced by patches of *Salvia recognita*. To give depth of color to the composition, add drifts of *Nepeta × faassenii* with its gray foliage and rich lavender flowers. If there is space, a small 4–5 ft (1.3–1.5 m) shrub with wine colored foliage such as *Berberis thunbergii* 'Red Chief' would add substance to the composition. Requiring the same culture, all of these plants except the berberis are remontant.

### *Salvia regla* Cavanilles, Mountain sage, Plates 71 & 96

*Salvia regla* comes from a small area in the Chisos Mountains in western Texas and a large area in Mexico from Coahuila and Durango to Oaxaca. It is probably named after the town of Regla in the province of Hidalgo, though the specific epithet *regla* also means a standard or model. Mountain sage certainly is a model specimen—whether in the wild or in the garden. Called the queen of the Chisos Mountains, *S. regla* has been planted on the Texas flyway for migrating birds and has become an important food source for hummingbirds making their return migration to the tropics in September and October.

A deciduous shrub, *Salvia regla* will reach 6 ft (2 m) or more in height and about 4–5 ft (1.3–1.5 m) in width over several years in the

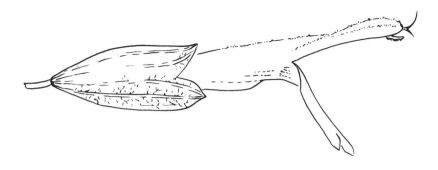

*Salvia regla*

garden. It builds on upright woody stems that give it a regal appearance. Flowering begins in late summer or early autumn and continues until frost. Mistletoe-green, deeply veined leaves are deltoid and 1 in (2.5 cm) wide and long. The tube of the flower is usually 1 in (2.5 cm) long. Frequently, the calyx is 1 in (2.5 cm) long, signal-red on the side that is turned to the light and chartreuse on the underside. It is a striking plant when in bloom.

Introduced into cultivation in 1839, it was rarely seen in gardens until the 1980s. At present several cultivars of mountain sage are grown and distributed by nurseries. The selection *Salvia regla* 'Royal' was first introduced by a nursery in Texas and later, in California, by the Saratoga Horticultural Foundation. It resembles the species described above. 'Mount Emory' is a selection from the Chisos Mountains in Texas and was introduced in 1983 by the Texas A & M University Research and Extension Center. 'Mount Emory' has large glossy leaves, 2 in (5 cm) long and as wide. Its calyx is large and 1 in (2.5 cm) long—mostly signal-red in color. The tubular flowers are 2 in (5 cm) long and repeat the vivid orange-red color of the calyx. The overall plant is lush looking and literally bends to the ground with the weight of its flowers and foliage. To prevent collapse, judicious pinching and pruning is necessary through-out the growing season. Another selection has been made by Yucca Do Nursery in Texas. Called 'Warnocks Choice', it grows 4–6 ft (1.3–2 m) in height, is woody and cold tolerant to 20° F (−7° C), and is very florifer-ous. Another selection collected in Coahuila by Yucca Do Nursery is being tested in Texas and California for introduction. In the wild it is tree-like and reaches 12 ft (4 m) in height.

Planted on an east-facing wall or in dappled shade, mountain sage needs good drainage and ordinary garden soil. After it becomes established it is a drought tolerant plant, requiring only occasional deep watering in long periods of drought. Because it is a woody and deciduous shrub, it should be pruned lightly by removing flowering branches or, occasionally, an entire stem from the base during its active growing period. Beware of heavy pruning during the dormant season. In my experience it does not bloom well with winter pruning. Mountain sage does not show any signs of life until late spring, when it seems the entire shrub breaks into leaf at once. It is hardy to 15° F (−9° C) and propagation is by cuttings.

Botanists and others who have seen its spectacular bloom on mountainsides in the wild agree that mountain sage is eminently worthy of cultivation. In garden settings it is an exciting, autumn blooming plant and can be grouped with the compact form of the evergreen *Arbutus unedo*, which has red fruits and deep brown, shredding bark. Both require the same culture, including slightly sweet soil. For a smaller grouping, the graceful 3 ft (1 m) tall and wide *Bracteantha bracteata* 'Dargan Hill Monarch', frequently called *Helichrysum bracteatum*, with its felt-like, gray-green leaves, makes a handsome companion, and the golden brown centers and glossy yellow bracts of its flowers add more harmonizing colors to the grouping.

## *Salvia reptans* Jacquin

A salvia with an unusual habit of growth, *Salvia reptans* produces numbers of lax or decumbent stems. It has a large distribution and is found in the mountains of the Trans-Pecos in Texas and also in Mexico and Guatemala. Dry washes and gravelly soils in stream beds are its usual habitat in the wild. Introduced to cultivation in the early 1800s, *Salvia reptans* was previously known as *Salvia angustifolia* (narrow leaved) or *Salvia leptophylla* (slender leaved). The specific epithet *reptans* refers to the plant's creeping habit and nicely describes a graceful salvia that has been grown in cultivation for many years.

*Salvia reptans*

In nature there are two distinct clones of *Salvia reptans*. The clone grown in gardens is lax in habit. The other clone is approximately 3 ft (1 m) tall and upright. It is found in western Texas and has not been introduced as a garden subject. In addition, S. *reptans* var. *glabra* occurs naturally in Texas but is not grown horticulturally.

A perennial herb, *Salvia reptans* sprawls about 3 ft (1 m) or more in width and has handsome, thin, dark, almost black stems. Very narrow mistletoe-green leaves, most measuring less than 0.25 in (0.6 cm) in width are sparsely set along the stem. The stems are abundant and virtually cover the ground. The flowers are a lovely wisteria-blue and about 0.5 in (1.3 cm) in length. They are held in a tiny, dark calyx that enhances the flowers' beauty. Blooming begins in summer, becoming sparse by October until frost. Hardy in the San Francisco Bay area, S. *reptans* dies to the ground when temperatures fall below 30° F (−1° C). In spring, new growth will emerge from the tuberous rootstock. Cut S. *reptans* back to its crown in early spring to encourage the growth of multiple stems. If it is not cut back a woody base will develop and prohibit plentiful new growth. A half day of sun, quick drainage, ordinary garden soil, and weekly water are its cultural needs. Propagation is easily achieved by seed, cuttings, or division.

Even though *Salvia reptans* has been grown as a garden subject for a long time, it is seldom seen outside botanic gardens. It makes an ideal plant for a warm, sloping rock garden in moderate shade, or as a groundcover among shrubs. Because of its lax growth, which will spill over the side of a large container, it can be successfully combined in planters with reliable space fillers such as fancy leaved lettuces, parsley, and basil. I have seen it in window boxes with stiff pink pelargoniums, where it added a note of grace to the planting. Another combination capitalizes on a red, white, and blue theme—*Salvia* 'Red Velvet' for the background, S. *reptans* to trail over the side, and a white flowering filler such as petunias or *Chrysanthemum paludosum*. Elevating the plant in a container or planting it on top of a low wall is another way of taking advantage of its sprawl.

## *Salvia roborowskii* Maximowicz

Regarded as an annual or occasionally a biennial herb, *Salvia roborowskii* has a wide distribution that includes Tibet, Sikkim, and five provinces in China. Found at elevations of 8000–12,000 ft (2500–3600 m), its habitat includes grasslands and hillsides as well as wet streamsides.

This salvia is scarcely known in horticulture but merits the gardener's awareness and attention. My plants came from seed collected in China in 1991 by botanists from Quarry Hill Botanic Garden and the Royal Botanic Gardens, Kew. Plants were growing at 10,000 ft (3100 m) on an east-facing meadow. This open hillside had pines and dogwood nearby as well as roses, clematis, and nepeta.

Small and upright, *Salvia roborowskii* usually reaches 1.5 ft (45 cm) in height in cultivation, but in the wild it has been recorded as reaching 3 ft (1 m). Rosemary-green leaves are mainly triangular in shape and neatly cover the plant. The margins of the leaves are scalloped and the surface is hairy with indented veins. Flowering takes place in summer. Small lemon-yellow flowers about 0.25 in (0.6 cm) in length emerge from a rosemary-green calyx. Each whorl has eight to 12 flowers but only a few come into bloom at the same time. Far from being showy, S. *roborowskii*'s beauty lies in its precise erectness and fine green color. The miniature flowers hold well in arrangements.

A spot in the garden with at least a half day of sunlight and the protection of other plants is the ideal setting for a group of these salvias. Be sure well-draining soil has been enriched liberally with compost, and water deeply every few days.

This annual is easy to grow and has the tendency to self sow once it is established. Sow seed of *Salvia roborowskii* in pots and then transplant young seedlings into the garden where a colony is desired. After summer flowering, allow plants to set and drop seed *in situ*. A few seeds can be gathered and saved in case the first attempt at establishing a colony fails.

Another tactic is to prune inflorescences after seed production in order to encourage plants to live another year. With either approach, it may take several attempts to have a colony sustain itself but this tidy salvia is worth the effort.

*Salvia roborowskii* is a perky filler for the front of the summer border. In my garden it grows next to the 1.5 ft (40 cm) high *Salvia elegans* 'Honey Melon'. Behind the salvias are long sweeping branches of *Cotoneaster horizontalis* 'Variegatus', which has cream colored, variegated leaves that are suffused with red in the autumn. A dahlia with flat, dark red flowers the size of a small grapefruit completes the picture. The name of the dahlia has been long forgotten—it is one of those favored plants that gardeners pass from friend to friend.

### *Salvia roemeriana* Scheele, Cedar sage, Plate 72

*Salvia roemeriana* is found in the Edwards Plateau area of Texas, as well as in Arizona and several provinces in Mexico. Its specific epithet honors a professor of botany from Zurich, Johann Jacob Roemer (1763– 1819), while its common name refers to the cedar brakes where it is found growing in patches. It grows prolifically in oak woodlands and on rocky outcroppings as well.

Cedar sage has rounded leaflets of a good grassy green color that wither and die to the ground in winter. Its flowering stalk is 8–10 in (20–25 cm) in length, with bright scarlet flowers in loose whorls rising at angles above the foliage. Each plant has a great many flowering stalks, and when a patch of sage comes into bloom it is a very pretty sight. Plants are hardy to 10° F (−12° C). Plants with larger leaves and flowers have been found in limestone areas of Sierra Chiquita, Tamaulipas, Mexico, by John Fairey and Carl Schoenfeld.

A small perennial, less than 1 ft (30 cm) in height and width, *Salvia roemeriana* will quickly become established and make a nice colony of plants by freely seeding itself. New plants appear throughout the spring and summer. A half day of shade, good garden soil with humus, and weekly watering will encourage the multiplication of plants and prolong the blooming season from late spring to late autumn. Removal of spent flowering stalks during the summer is necessary for a long flowering period.

Both foliage and flowers hold well in arrangements. Propagation is by seed or cuttings. Seedlings appear throughout the summer months once the parent plant is established and may be replanted or shared with other gardeners.

Introduced into cultivation in 1852, *Salvia roemeriana* was grown and admired by William Robinson (1933), who commended its neatness to other gardeners for edgings or the front of the border. Cedar sage can brighten plantings in many parts of the garden. For example, the evergreen needles of mugo pine or other conifers will look darker and greener in combination with the salvia's scarlet flowers. Since it needs some shade, *Salvia roemeriana* makes a fine groundcover for rhododendrons — covering the ground with green foliage when the rhododendrons are in bloom. Later, after the rhododendrons have flowered, the scarlet flowers will sparkle alone in a pool of green during the summer and autumn. A group of *Hydrangea quercifolia*, native to the southeastern section of the United States, with its large and strongly lobed leaves that color so well in the autumn, would be enhanced throughout the growing season by a large patch of cedar sage at its feet. All of these plants require the same culture.

## *Salvia sclarea* Linnaeus, Clary sage, Plates 70, 73, & 74

A striking herbaceous plant that is classified both as biennial and perennial, *Salvia sclarea* has been recognized for its essential oils and used extensively since well before the birth of Christ. Theophrastus, Dioscorides, and Pliny all wrote at length about its useful properties. In the wild, it is found throughout the northern Mediterranean region, and in limited parts of north Africa and central Asia. It is commonly known as toute-bonne or sauge sclarée in France, sclarea in Italy, hierba de los ojos in Spain, and clary in Britain. Requiring little water or attention and being adaptable to temperatures below 0° F (−18° C), it has become naturalized in central Europe.

An early summer blooming plant, *Salvia sclarea* can develop in a year's time from a seedling to a plant 3–4 ft (1–1.3 m) tall when in flower.

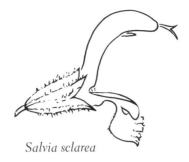

*Salvia sclarea*

Stems are square and covered with hairs and oil globules. Leaves vary in size from 1 ft (30 cm) in length at the bottom of the plant, to less than half that size at the top. They may be sessile or have a short petiole when growing at the top of the plant. The length of the petiole varies too. The leaf surface is rugose and covered with short hairs and oil globules. Grassy green in color on the surface, the underside has pronounced creamy white veins. The entire edge is saw-toothed. Flowers number between two and six in each verticil and are held in large, colorful floral bracts that are pale mauve to lilac floral or white to pink with a pink marking at the edge. The corolla is lilac or pale blue, about 1 in (2.5 cm) in length, and the lips are held wide open in the shape of a scythe. The colors referred to here are only an indication of the range that may be observed.

Eleanour Sinclair Rohde (1936) refers to an unusually tall and handsome form of clary sage as the "Vatican strain." Jim and Jenny Archibald of Wales saw such plants in Turkey in 1984 and collected seed. They subsequently gave reports of large and grand plants from that seed.

Occasionally, a form may be found in the wild with white flowers and white floral bracts tinged with pink. This is the cultivar 'Turkestanica' (plate 74) and will come true from seed. In my garden, this cultivar has pinkish stems and petioles and leaves that are more yellow-green than the clary sage described above. It requires weekly water in order to attain 3–4 ft (1–1.3 m).

Full sun, a soil low in nutrients, and fast drainage are needed for clary sage. Watering on a weekly basis will make plants in a border flourish. Once flowers start to look shabby and tan at the edges, cut flowering stems back to encourage perennial vigor. This procedure precludes seed production and avoids large numbers of seedlings germinating at the base of plants. Even with this prudent practice, plants may be short-lived, so it is judicious to have a few young plants developing. Propagation is quite easily accomplished from seed.

Clary sage is not suitable as a cut flower because of the powerful odor of penetrating oils. These essential oils are widely used in making perfume and in imparting a muscatel flavor to wines, vermouths, and liqueurs. The oils are one source of the plant's healing qualities; seed is another. A long-standing usage of the seeds of clary sage is to place them in the eye, thus producing a thick mucilage. This practice is said to clean the eye of impurities. The name *sclarea* carries the connotation of clear and bright. It is also said that clary is an English corruption of clear-eye.

Stately in stature, *Salvia sclarea* is one of our most arresting border plants. In a bed filled with old fashioned, early summer blooming plants such as roses, foxgloves, Canterbury bells, hollyhocks, delphiniums, pinks, dill, fennel, larkspur, and love-in-a-mist, clary sage gives height and color for almost a full month. It will bloom even longer if inflorescences are cut when they begin to discolor. It is not unusual for plants to rebloom in early autumn when days are warm and nights cool.

## *Salvia semiatrata* Zuccarini, Plate 75

*Salvia semiatrata* is limited in its native habitat to the Mexican province of Oaxaca, where it is found in several locations in the mountains of the Sierra Madre Sur. Usually located at elevations of 6500 ft (2000 m) or higher, *S. semiatrata* grows quite profusely at the edge of pine forests. It is frequently found on limestone cliffs and banks, and in cactus scrub areas that are dry and exposed to the elements. These high mountain areas are very cool at night and receive summer rainfall.

In the wild and under ideal garden circumstances, *Salvia semiatrata* will grow to 6 ft (2 m) in height and 3 ft (1 m) in width. However, in cultivation this shrubby plant is more likely to be half that size. Deltoid leaves under 1 in (2.5 cm) in length and a lively grassy green-yellow color lightly cover the plant. Even though they are opposite, the leaves grow in small clusters. The surface of the leaf is rugose and looks velvety; the underside is covered with short, pale cream hairs that make each vein pronounced. Inflorescences tend to be short, about 6 in (15 cm) in length, with whorls of one to three flowers in each verticil. Individual flowers are usually 1 in (2.5 cm) in length, occasionally 2 in (5 cm), and splendidly bicolored. Covered with hairs, the upper lip is a luminous dark violet and the lower lip is dusky lavender. The calyx is also covered with hairs and is 0.5 in (1.3 cm) in length. It is a rich violet color with a magenta undertone. The specific epithet, *semiatrata*, literally means half blackened or darkened, referring to the corolla tube and its two colors. Even though they are small, the individual flowers are eye catching because of the dark violet-blue blotch on the lower lip.

The culture of *Salvia semiatrata* includes fast drainage, loamy garden soil, and good air circulation. Situate the plant so that it receives sun for at least half a day during winter and summer. Deep watering at least once each week is required and a little lime sprinkled on top of the roots in late spring is helpful. Because it is a woody plant and tends to be evergreen, pinching and light pruning during the growing season is recommended. Propagation is by cuttings. I have not grown *S. semiatrata* long enough to test its ultimate hardiness, but it has wintered over in my garden with temperatures falling to 25° F (−4° C). *S. semiatrata* is grown extensively as a garden plant on the French and Italian Riviera. This salvia grows slowly, comes into full bloom for a period of time, and then rests for a period of time. It repeats this procedure from summer through autumn. A few flowers may be found during the winter and spring. Short inflorescences last well as cut flowers and look charming in small vases.

A sloping bank of plants with small-scale habit and foliage might feature three or more plants of each of the following; *Salvia semiatrata*, *Teucrium fruticans* 'Compactum', and *Lavandula angustifolia* 'Hidcote'. The gray, linear foliage of the 1 ft (30 cm) tall lavender will contrast with the green foliage of the sage and the lanceolate green-gray foliage of the 2 ft (60 cm) tall teucrium. These three plants have flowers in the purple-blue color range. All require the same culture, including moderate amounts of water.

## *Salvia sessei* Bentham

In the wild, *Salvia sessei* may be found in seven or more provinces in central Mexico. Occurring from 600–7000 ft (200–2100 m), its habitat is usually on the edge of woodlands and pine forests. The plant was first collected by the Spanish botanist, Don Martin de Sessé and his learned fellow botanist Jose Mociño, of pure Spanish descent but born in Mexico. These two were the key participants in the Royal Botanical Expedition of 1788 to 1820 commissioned by King Charles III of Spain. Plants including S. *sessei* were collected from Guatemala and a large portion of Mexico over this period of approximately 30 years. A very large herbarium was amassed and included excellent drawings by the talented Atanasio Echeverría, for whom the genus *Echeveria* is named, along with the work of another artist. This material was shipped to Spain for the purpose of preparing a *Flora Mexicana* under the supervision of the distinguished Swiss botanist, Augustin-Pyramus de Candolle. Unfortunately, the project, which involved hardship and heartbreak, was abandoned. The participants in the expedition suffered mental and physical miseries, and large numbers of their pressed plants were ravaged by insects and water. Incidentally, Sessé became one of the first professors of botany at the University of Mexico in 1788 and immediately started the establishment of a botanic garden in Mexico City.

A tree-like shrub in the wild, *Salvia sessei* will reach 15 ft (5 m) in its native habitat but in cultivation it is half that size. Leaves can be variable in size and shape but generally are 2–5 in (5–12 cm) long and deltoid in shape. They have a fresh green color throughout the growing season and cover the plant well. The color of the flowers is a remarkable blending of soft red and chartreuse that is very beautiful and similar to S. *regla*. Unfortunately, flowering stems hold up as cut flowers for only a few hours. Susceptible to cold air, S. *sessei* can be grown outdoors in mild, frost-free areas, where it tends to bloom for three months or more. The most floriferous display occurs during summer. Propagation is by cuttings taken in late August. The rooted cuttings are then placed in the greenhouse in late October or November to assure plants for the garden the following spring. The production of seed on garden plants is rare.

Full sun and a bed prepared with humus for a moist root-run are needed for this salvia. Good drainage as well as weekly water are necessities too. Growing requirements are simple in a frost-free climate. A popular plant on the French and Italian Riviera, *Salvia sessei* is often topped to about 4 ft (1.3 m) and encouraged to form a tree-like trunk. I have seen it used in this way as a hedge or background within a border. If you are able to grow the plant year round in the garden, remember to prune it in spring when active growth begins. This assures new stems that will flower during the summer and autumn.

Because it grows rapidly, *Salvia sessei* is a spectacular plant for the border. It can be shaped for the back of a perennial or shrub border, or if there is space, it can be encouraged to develop into a specimen shrub. Its upright habit is an asset in placing companions such as the 3 ft (1 m) *Nandina domestica* 'Fire Power'. The leaves of the nandina are flushed wine-red and in autumn they turn a soft orange color. The stoloniferous *Salvia blepharophylla*, with its red-orange flowers, will cover the ground and tie the composition together.

## *Salvia sinaloensis* Fernald, Sinaloa sage, Plate 76

Rarely do gardeners find a truly blue flowering plant, but several salvias from Mexico are almost true blue. *Salvia sinaloensis* has that exceptional flower color. It has been found only in the Mexican province of Sinaloa, usually in the foothills of the Sierre Madre. Introduced to horticulture in California in the 1980s, Sinaloa sage has also been available to gardeners in Britain and France since that time. Look for it when visiting the national collections of salvias in both countries. It is also available through nurseries in the United States.

*Salvia sinaloensis* is a small herbaceous perennial with many graceful stems, about 1 ft (30 cm) long, that spread on underground runners into a small, 1 ft (30 cm) wide clump. Over the summer it makes rapid growth and produces many upright flowering stems. It is a charming plant because of its growth habit and those deep, intensely blue flowers have only the slightest hint of violet. Flowering begins in summer and continues for three or four weeks with recurrent bloom in autumn.

Small lance-shaped leaves about 1 in (2.5 cm) long and 0.5 in (1.3 cm) wide are closely spaced along the stem. When new leaves first appear they are plum-purple and add a subtle shade to the small plant. They age to a mid green with a gray undertone. Plants grown in full sun retain this color but require more water. The flowers appear in whorls of six and are less than 1 in (2.5 cm) in length. They come into bloom one whorl at a time so there is never a lot of blue-violet showing at any one time. The lower lip of the flower has a spot of white and each flower is held in a wine colored 0.5 in (1.3 cm) long calyx that persists after the flowers have dropped. The calyces may be checked for seed, and if seed is forming the entire inflorescence should be left in place until maturity. In my garden, plants do produce a small amount of seed. Propagation is by seed, cuttings, or careful division of the rootstock.

Good drainage and acidic, peaty soil enriched with humus, along with a half day of sunlight is desirable. Deep watering at least once a week is needed for the plant to produce large clumps. Remember to give plants in full sun extra water. It is helpful to fertilize at least twice during the active growing season. Plants are hardy to 20° F (−7° C), perhaps even lower if given the protection of other plants. Because it does best with shelter from cold air, look for a protected nook in the garden for *Salvia sinaloensis*. Planted with large plants such as roses, it would soon make a groundcover at their base. The pale pink rose 'Souvenir de la Malmaison' or the blush-pink, lilac-striped 'Honorine du Brabant' would give shelter and shade for this delightful little salvia. To enjoy its plum-purple leaves for an extended period, plant *S. sinaloensis* at the front of a border that receives full sun and water it on a regular basis. Cool and very dry weather promote purplish leaves.

### *Salvia somalensis* Vatke, Somalia sage, Plate 77

One of the early summer blooming sages, *Salvia somalensis* usually begins flowering towards the end of May and continues, off and on, until the end of October. An aromatic shrub, reaching 4–5 ft (1.3–1.5 m) in height and 3 ft (1 m) across, it is multistemmed and rangy with an irregular outline. Endemic to Somalia, it has a limited geographical and altitudinal range. Occurring at 4000–7000 ft (1200–2100 m), it may be found at the edge of forests or as a very common or dominant undershrub in forest clearings.

Oblong, yellow-green leaves amply cover the plant. The longest and largest measure approximately 4 in (10 cm) in length and 1 in (2.5 cm) in width. The flowers are a rather pale wisteria-blue and are usually in closely spaced, many flowered whorls. The inflorescences are exceptional in that they do not all occur at the top of the stems. Even though each stem has terminal inflorescences, flowering branchlets occur along each main stem. I can think of no other salvia that flowers in this manner. Fertile seed is freely produced and propagation is easily achieved with seeds, cuttings, or divisions.

Either light shade or almost full sun is suitable for *Salvia somalensis*, along with good drainage and friable soil amended with humus. Weekly water in summer is needed. Some years ago after a hard freeze I lost this plant to 11° F (−12° C) temperatures. Luckily, and much to my amazement, seeds under the old plant germinated a few months later when warm weather arrived. My original plant came from cuttings of a plant grown by seed collected in 1973 in Somalia by the Huntington Botanical Gardens.

A combination of summer into autumn blooming plants that takes advantage of this lightly but persistently blooming salvia includes the 3–5 ft (1–1.5 m) *Lavatera maritima*, which has large, hollyhock-like, lavender flowers and gray-green foliage. A mass of the 3 ft (1 m) *Phlox carolina* 'Miss Lingard', with its large clusters of fragrant white flowers, can be highlighted with the 3 ft (1 m) *Nicotiana alata* Sensation hybrids, classified as perennial but treated as annual. These tobacco plants come in a wide range of white, pink, and rose and are pleasing when mixed throughout the planting. In the evening, they are sweetly scented. *Salvia somalensis* is also a fine companion for the stout, herbaceous, and heavy blooming *Phygelius* 'Winchester Fanfare'. The softly colored, coral-red flowers of the phygelius do not overpower the pale flowers of the salvia.

***Salvia sonomensis*** Greene, Creeping sage, Sonoma sage, Plate 78

The indigenous *Salvia sonomensis* can be found in three uncon-nected areas in California: the foothills of the Sierra Nevada, the Coast Ranges from Siskiyou County to Napa County, and from Monterey County to San Diego County. All the habitats are below 6500 ft (2000 m) and consist of dry slopes and woodland forests. The specific epithet *sonomensis* refers to the county of Sonoma, one of the plant's many native habitats.

A low-growing perennial herb that tends to form mats, *Salvia sonomensis* is called creeping sage because of its growth habit. Many different selections have been made based mainly on shape and color of leaf. These selections have been collected and propagated from numer-ous habitats but have seldom been differentiated. Two selections made by Brett Hall of the Arboretum of the University of California, Santa Cruz, were made for hardiness, appearance, and the tendency to not die back in the center of its mat. Both selections are named for their high altitude collection sites: 'Cone Peak' and 'Serra Peak'. *S. sonomensis* is highly variable: the shape of the leaf can range from long and narrow to short and almost rounded; the color of the leaves ranges from yellow-green to dusky green, even to gray-green. Flower color varies too, from pale lavender to lavender-purple; one selection has sparkling lavender-blue flowers. Plants are usually under 1 ft (30 cm) in height with 6 in (15 cm) tall inflorescences rising above the foliage.

A dry hillside that affords good drainage with light shade or high shade is needed for all selections of creeping sage. It has the reputation of being hard to grow because of susceptibility to various fungal rots. Fortunately, I have had no problems and recommend a gritty soil low in humus or organic material. I find this type of soil indispensable for a spacious and healthy groundcover. Water plants only until they become established, since this species is exceedingly drought tolerant. Creeping sage will not survive in gardens that are regularly watered or have heavy clay soil. Plants are hardy to 10° F (−12° C) or less, and do not seem to attract deer.

Easy to propagate, creeping sage tends to root as it enlarges its mat. These rooted pieces can be potted until a good root system has formed and then planted in the garden. Cuttings are the usual method of propagation and ensure the desired selection.

A hybrid of *Salvia mellifera* and *S. sonomensis* occurred in the Berkeley, California, garden of Helen Beard as a chance seedling and has been grown at the University of California Botanical Garden, Berkeley, since 1965. This hybrid has been distributed and is known as *Salvia* 'Mrs. Beard'. Growing 2 ft (0.6 m) in height and 4–6 ft (1.3–2 m) in width, it needs regular pinching to keep wood from building up in the center of the plant. Dull green leaves have a grayish cast and its tiny flowers are pale lavender. Not subject to fungal attacks, it is drought tolerant but will allow additional water if given fast drainage. This plant is an excellent choice for edging informal dry beds or paths.

*Salvia* 'Dara's Choice' is thought to be a hybrid of *S. mellifera* and *S. sonomensis*. Introduced in the 1980s, it was named by Nevin Smith of Wintergreen Nursery in Watsonville, California, for Dara Emery, who made the selection at the Santa Barbara Botanic Garden. Taller and more mounding than creeping sage, its aromatic, mid-green leaves make a fresh background for the 8 in (20 cm) tall flowering spikes. Tiny, 0.5 in (1.3 cm) long, violet flowers are held in tight, interrupted whorls. Many spikes come into bloom at the same time making what Marjorie Schmidt (1980) called a "misty effect." This hybrid is easier to cultivate than the species but is subject to verticillium wilt, a fungal problem. Branches, even whole sections, may suddenly die, but the entire plant usually withstands the attack.

If the cultural conditions set out above are observed, *Salvia sonomensis* makes a fine groundcover clambering among rocks, or a noteworthy mat for the front of a dry border. A graceful 4–5 ft (1.3–1.5 m) companion is the pink flowering currant, *Ribes sanguineum* var. *glutinosum*. Both bloom at the same time and require high shade. *Myrica californica*, the evergreen wax myrtle that responds so well to pruning, eventually reaches 10 ft (3 m) or more in height, and makes an admirable backdrop or hedge for the other plants.

## *Salvia spathacea* Greene, Crimson sage, pitcher sage, hummingbird sage, Plate 79

*Salvia spathacea* is endemic to California and can be found in the wild at low elevations in the central and coast ranges from San Bruno Mountain in the north to Orange County in the south. It is a robust herbaceous perennial with creeping rhizomes that form dense and handsome mats. In its native habitat it colonizes in soils rich with humus in the light shade of trees or on protected hillsides.

*Salvia spathacea*

Though not very well known in horticultural circles, *Salvia spathacea* has been grown in gardens in California since the 1970s. Several nurseries distribute unnamed clones that vary in intensity of flower color. Nevin Smith, a California plantsman, introduced his selection 'Kawatre' through his Wintergreen Nursery in 1979. He found it in the Santa Lucia Mountains near Kawatre, a girl scout camp. This particular selection has more deeply colored flowers than are commonly found. Smith calls crimson sage one of the most beautiful California native perennials and notes that its appearance is unlike other native California sages, but more like herbaceous sages of Europe and Asia.

A selection made by Bert Wilson of Las Pilitas Nursery in Santa Margarita, California, is called 'Powerline Pink'. The selection is notable because it stands 3 ft (1 m) tall before it flowers and its flowering stalks add another 3 ft (1 m) to the height of the plant.

The leaves of *Salvia spathacea* 'Kawatre' are evergreen and hastate. The largest measures 8 in (20 cm) in length and 4 in (10 cm) across at its base. A rich lettuce-green on the surface, the underside of the leaf is covered with short hairs and is pale pastel-green with prominent veining. The entire edge is scalloped. Flowering stalks 1–3 ft (0.3–1 m) in height form in early spring. Late February through June is the blooming period with occasional flowerings in autumn. Splendid, beetroot-purple flowers that are over 1 in (2.5 cm) in length emerge from a large, hair-covered calyx that is a dark ruby-red color. Bracts of a similar description subtend the calyces. The flowers, calyces, and bracts are in tight whorls spaced about 2 in (5 cm) apart. The calyces and bracts are predominant on the inflorescence and their whorls are the size of small lemons. Even after the flowers have bloomed and dropped, the calyces and bracts remain intact and are a handsome and interesting feature of the sage. All parts of the inflorescence that are hairy have glands that release a pleasant, fruity fragrance when stroked. Crimson sage makes a good cut flower and lasts well in fresh or dry arrangements.

*Salvia spathacea* does best with a half to full day of sun in a mild climate where temperatures remain above 20° F (−7° C). Well-draining garden soil enriched with humus will encourage colonies. Categorized as a drought tolerant plant, watering once every two weeks or so is nonetheless recommended. Propagation is by division of the rootstock, by cuttings, or seed.

Colonies of crimson sage planted on north- or east-facing hillsides along with California poppies and annual nemophilas will make a riot of color in late spring. *Nemophila menziesii* (baby blue eyes) has charming blue flowers, and the creamy white petals of *N. maculata* (fivespot) are blotched at the tips with purple or violet markings. All are plants that require the same culture, and their lengthy blooming periods overlap.

Another favorable site for crimson sage is under trees in filtered light. Planted in patches, its foliage looks handsome year round.

## *Salvia splendens* Sell ex Roenen & Schultes, Scarlet sage, Plate 80

*Salvia splendens* is found in the wild only in Brazil at altitudes of 6500–9800 ft (2000–3000 m). These particular areas are warm year round and frequently have high humidity. A popular plant, *S. splendens* is frequently planted in public and private gardens in Europe and from the United States in the north to Argentina and Chile in the southern hemisphere. Its cultivars are popular and numerous. Practically every year a new cultivar is introduced to gardeners around the world.

*Salvia splendens* was described botanically in 1822, and shortly thereafter was described in both Latin and English in James Ridgeway's *Botanical Register* and given the common name Lee's scarlet sage. The register includes the explanation that Mr. Lee from Hammersmith Nursery introduced the salvia. A beautiful hand colored drawing of the plant's inflorescence is also included. This notation may mark the beginning of *S. splendens* in horticulture. Plants were easily grown from seed and kept in greenhouses where they flowered freely for a long period of time. These plants varied greatly in size, anywhere from 2 to 9 ft (0.6 to 3 m) in height. The cultivar 'Van Houttei' (plate 80) was an early Dutch selection that was made before the short, compact forms were selected and became popular bedding plants. *S. splendens* 'Van Houttei' was named for Louis Benoit Van Houtte, the indefatigable nurseryman and editor known as "the father of Belgian horticulture." Of a gentle nature, Van Houtte had a scientific mind and pursued botany as well as art. A great traveler himself, when at home he remained in contact through letters with missionaries and far-flung botanists.

*Salvia splendens* 'Van Houttei'

A herbaceous perennial, *Salvia splendens* 'Van Houttei' has numerous, ovate, yellow-green leaves, with saw-toothed edges, that give the plant a leafy look. Plants reach 3–4 ft (1–1.3 m) in both height and width by the time they start flowering in mid to late August. Flowering continues until frost. The 2 in (5 cm) long, dark red flowers are in verticils of two to six and are held in a 1 in (2.5 cm) long calyx that is the same hue of red as the lower lip of the flower. The two reds combined produce a maroon, brownish red color. When the plant is in flower in autumn it is a stunning sight, particularly when back lit.

In a mild climate *Salvia splendens* 'Van Houttei' will develop a woody base after a few years. However, because it makes rapid growth, cuttings taken in August and wintered over in a greenhouse will flower the following August. Propagation is by cuttings. This salvia is tender and is damaged at 30° F (−1° C). In my garden in frost-free winters, 'Van Houttei' does survive but in the spring it fails to grow rapidly or develop into a fulsome plant. I advise setting out new plants grown from cuttings and getting them into the border as soon as the earth has warmed. Occasional applications of half-strength liquid fertilizer will speed 'Van Houttei' along.

Part shade is a necessity for siting *Salvia splendens* 'Van Houttei' in the garden, along with good drainage and friable soil that has been amended with humus. Regular water is needed and a mulch of humus to keep roots cool is helpful. Flowering stems hold well as cut flowers if conditioned by cutting stems under water. Cutting the flowering stems will help keep the plant shapely and in flower over a two-month period.

In an area protected by high shade, *Salvia splendens* 'Van Houttei' interplanted with the 4 ft (1.3 m) evergreen *Viburnum utile* provides the backbone of a restful and refreshing border. *Ajuga reptans* 'Jungle Beauty', the rather flat, dark green groundcover, completes the picture. Other possible groundcovers are *Heuchera micrantha* or the marble leaved hybrid, *Heuchera* 'Genevieve'. Planted in groups, either of these heucheras make 1 ft (30 cm) companions that repeat bloom off and on over a long period of time.

## *Salvia* × *superba* Stapf

Discovered as a plant of spontaneous garden origin in Europe, *Salvia* × *superba*, at the present writing, remains unseen by me, though I have long admired its cultivars. Described and named by the botanist Otto Stapf (1857–1933), the description of *Salvia* × *superba* was not published until 1961. It is a hybrid of *S. sylvestris* and *S. villicaulis*, and is a herbaceous perennial from which many cultivars and possibly hybrids have been selected. These named plants are widely distributed in Europe, Great Britain, and the United States. A few have become naturalized in small, limited areas in North America.

The cultivars and hybrids of *Salvia* × *superba* are very hardy and will easily withstand temperatures well below 0° F (−18° C). Many leafy stems elongate from the plant's base as spring turns into summer. Blooming usually begins in early summer with closely spaced whorls of small flowers held in tiny calyces subtended by small but colorful bracts. Flowers are usually a shade of violet or violet-blue, but there is a handsome white flowered form too. When seed begin to form, prune each stem to two active leaf nodes. This will encourage branching and repeat bloom. In areas with mild climates that extend into October, it is possible to induce flowering for three periods if dead-heading is regular. Spike-like inflorescences hold well in arrangements when conditioned by cutting stems under water.

The cultivars or hybrids of *Salvia* × *superba* need three-quarters to a full day of sunlight, along with deep weekly watering. A friable soil with good drainage is also desirable. Plants may be pruned to the crown when winter comes and protected with conifer boughs if temperatures fall below 0° F (−18° C). Propagation is by cuttings that can be taken in July or August.

The following list is of plants that are cultivars of *Salvia* × *superba* or S. *sylvestris*, or, possibly, hybrids. Botanists find the origin of these plants to be uncertain but gardeners find all of these plants are dependable in the border as well as being relentless bloomers. They are also good plants for attracting butterflies, bees, and other insects.

'Blue Queen', small and compact, violet flowers.
'Kew Gold', leaves gold with some green spotting.
'Lubeca', early flowering, tall, deep violet flowers.
'May Night', low-growing, dark violet-blue flowers.
'Rose Queen', small and compact, gray leaves, pink flowers, red calyces.

These plants can be very beneficial in filling niches in the garden, and the typical compact habit warrants these salvias a place or even several places in a sunny border. Raised beds in conspicuous locations might feature the continuous blooming rose 'Gourmet Popcorn', with its fragrant, semi-double white flowers with golden centers, interplanted with the dark but clear violet-blue *Salvia* × *superba* 'May Night'. Just under 2 ft (60 cm) tall, both plants are about the same height. Add the gray foliaged *Achillea* 'Anthea', with its soft yellow flowers, and the vivid, violet-blue flowered *S. farinacea* 'Victoria' for a reliably rich and pro-fusely flowering group. Gardeners who enjoy a mass of a single color can fill a large area with *Salvia* × *superba* 'Blue Queen', which is less than 2 ft (60 cm) tall. The violet flowers of this salvia are enriched by a mass of the almost single, lemon-yellow marigold *Tagetes* 'Susie Wong', which is a little over 1 ft (30 cm) in height. Its flat flowers provide a contrast in plant shape as well as color. The double flowered African-French marigold *Tagetes* 'Solar Series' gives even more color. Either the lemon-, or, for a more daring combination, orange-petaled marigold produces an arresting summertime display.

## *Salvia sylvestris* Linnaeus, Plate 81

*Salvia sylvestris* is a ubiquitous herbaceous perennial plant through-out an area that includes eastern, central, and southern Europe through central Russia and western Siberia. Known as *S. nemorosa* (Linnaeus) for centuries, Professor Gabriel Alziar's *Catalogue Synonymique des* Salvia *du Monde* recognizes Linnaeus's 1753 description of *Salvia sylvestris* and finds Linnaeus's 1762 description of *Salvia nemorosa* to be synonymous. The specific epithets *sylvestris* and *nemorosa* have similar meanings—growing in groves or woodlands; a wilding; forest loving—reflecting some of the plant's range of habitats. This salvia is indeed found in many habi-tats at many elevations, demonstrating its adaptability and hardiness.

*Salvia sylvestris*

Despite the common occurence of *Salvia sylvestris*, I find no indi-cation as to when it became a garden plant. Neither *S. sylvestris* nor *S. nemorosa* are mentioned in herbals and early gardening literature.

*Salvia sylvestris* is well-branched, and many lax stems reaching per-haps 3 ft (1 m) in length rise from its crown. These stems are covered with small, olive-green leaves that are sessile or have a short petiole. Small, barely 0.5 in (1.3 cm) long, richly colored violet-blue flowers are held in a dark violet calyx and are subtended by a royal purple bract. This species exhibits great variation in color of flowers and bracts and the colors described here are but a sample of the rich blends found in different plants. Even though the individual flowers are small, the densely packed whorls of color make a sumptuous display. Flowering begins in summer and continues for a solid two months or more and can be extended if old inflorescences are removed.

Watch for inflorescences to elongate; if they are cut back before flowers have faded and seed has formed, *Salvia sylvestris* will earn its reputation as a tireless bloomer. This dead-heading can be repeated several times during a long season of growth and will both encourage side shoots to develop and bloom and preclude seed production. *S. sylvestris* germinates readily from seed. Once I grew about 20 plants from seed collected in the wild to try to find a plant that was more upright. Unfortunately, all were lax. In the wild, plants vary greatly both in habit and flower color, which ranges from purple to violet and from white to pink. Because a great number of selections and hybrids are propagated by nurseries, the typical species is rarely found in cultivation. Jelitto and Schacht (1990) call *S. sylvestris* a wilding of little garden merit, but immediately go on to express their praise for numerous selections or hybrids of the species.

Ernst Pagles of Germany, who has been called the paradigm of plantsmen, worked for Karl Foerster, a famous German nurseryman and author. Foerster gave the young Pagles a packet of *Salvia sylvestris* seed in 1949, counseling "seek and you will find." In 1955 Pagles introduced the widely and deservedly popular selection 'East Friesland' (plate 81). Its abundant, rich violet-blue flowers are held above the crown of the plant. It repeats bloom several times if cut back. Subsequently, Pagles introduced six additional selections:

'Amethyst', blue-rose, 2.5 ft (0.8 m) tall.
'Blauhügel', (Blue Mound), clear blue, compact.
'Negrito', deep violet, broad-petaled.
'Ruegen', blue-violet with a compact habit.
'Tänzerin', deep violet, upright to 2.5 ft (0.8 m).
'Wesuwe', deep violet, early blooming.

With no cultural necessities beyond good drainage, *Salvia sylvestris* can be slipped into many spots in the garden. A half to a full day of sun and deep watering once a week will promote growth and flowering. Shade encourages more lax growth than normal. I usually cut the spent inflorescences back on the first day of the months of July, August, and September to stimulate bloom. Tolerant to 0° F (−18° C) or less, cover the crown of the plant with conifer boughs in extremely cold climates to prevent heaving.

*Salvia sylvestris* is a healthy and tough plant that easily adapts to many garden situations. It also makes a long lasting cut flower. Because of these dependable traits, it is surprising that it is seen only infrequently in gardens. Tuck it in around the base of shrub roses, where its tendency to sprawl becomes an asset. An old-fashioned border with spring flowering clumps of iris, which have sword-like foliage, and peonies, which have long-lasting, divided leaves, is enhanced by the lax, summer blooming S. *sylvestris*, whose foliage weaves between these handsome companions. As for the cultivars, their growth habit is usually reliably compact. All have rich flower color and the ability to repeat bloom. The attractive 'East Friesland' can be grown in drifts of three towards the front of a sunny border. It makes an excellent filler for odd-shaped spaces and looks handsome and healthy in large pots or raised beds with gray foliaged plants such as the California native *Artemisia pycnocephala* 'David's Choice'.

## *Salvia taraxacifolia* Hooker, Dandelion leaved sage, Plate 82

A charming herbaceous perennial, *Salvia taraxacifolia* is found in the wild only in southwest Morocco. It is found there at lower altitudes ranging from 2000–8000 ft (600–2500 m) from the high Atlas Mountains to lower elevations. Growing on rocky limestone slopes, by stony riversides, or in forest clearings, it is truly a plant adaptable to many different habitats. Given this ability, it is surprising that it has not been found elsewhere in the wild. Another peculiarity of the plant, as Ian Hedge (1974) points out, is that it has no close allies and occupies an isolated position in the genus.

*Salvia taraxacifolia*'s leaves are gray-green and remain so year round. Shaped like a lyre, they are about 3–4 in (8–10 cm) long and grow in thick basal rosettes. The dense hairs covering the back of the leaf give it a white appearance. When lightly rubbed, the glands on the hairs release an aromatic citrus odor that is most pleasing. In mild climates, where temperatures remain above 20° F (–7° C), the plant is evergreen. Rosettes of foliage are about 6–8 in (15–20 cm) across and as high. Named for the shape of its leaves, *taraxacifolia* is probably of Persian origin and means with leaves shaped like a dandelion.

Abundant upright flowering stalks, 6–8 in (15–20 cm) in height with pinkish-cream flowers, will be in bloom by the beginning of June. The flowers appear in whorls spaced about 1 in (2.5 cm) apart along the inflorescence. Because of the plant's tendency to form large mats, the numerous inflorescences and little, pale pink flowers make a pretty sight.

Dandelion leaved sage will thrive in all kinds of sites and variable conditions. To encourage matting, three-quarters to a full day of sun is recommended, along with soil enriched with humus and good drainage. Gritty soil is excellent. An application of lime once a year will help produce more robust plants; deep watering every 10 or 12 days seems to be adequate. Remove spent flowering stalks to encourage repeat bloom. Propagation is easily accomplished by seed or division.

Whether in bloom or not, *Salvia taraxacifolia* is handsome when massed as a groundcover or planted in the front of a border. Because of its gray-green leaves it blends well with most shades of green. A specific combination chosen for texture and foliage color is the mat-forming, white flowering perennial, *Arenaria montana*, which has small, rich green leaves, along with clumps of the 6–8 in (15–20 cm) grass *Festuca amethysina* 'Superba', with its finely textured, bluish looking, gray-green blades. *Salvia taraxacifolia* completes a selection of pleasing foliage.


## *Salvia thymoides* Bentham, Plate 83

A small herbaceous perennial, *Salvia thymoides* occurs at elevations of 7000–9000 ft (2100–2800 m) in two Mexican provinces, Puebla and Oaxaca. Its specific name refers to its thyme-like leaves. Described by

George Bentham in 1833, it was introduced to horticulture in California in the early 1980s, but I have been unable to learn of its introduction elsewhere.

A neat and petite plant, the gray-white leaves of *Salvia thymoides* are about 0.5 in (1.3 cm) long and lightly cover the compact plant. A modest number of minuscule violet flowers, frequently less than 0.5 in (1.3 cm) in length, come into bloom in mid-summer. The salvia continues to flower lightly throughout the autumn, and by early December the plant is in full bloom. Propagation is by seed or cuttings.

Try planting *Salvia thymoides* in early spring in order for the sage to establish a good root system before the cold weather arrives. Good drainage is essential, along with full sun. The protection of other small plants and rocks is significantly helpful in getting the salvia established. Usually, deep weekly watering is sufficient, but if the weather is windy or hot and dry, more water is necessary. In winter, this salvia may succumb to a combination of wet weather and cold air. It is probably tolerant to 25° F (−4° C) except in wet soil. Because of its small size, *Salvia thymoides* can easily be potted for a safe winter sojourn in the greenhouse.

After trying and failing many times to establish *Salvia thymoides* in my garden, I now can report success. Favorable conditions in Jardin del Viento include a south-facing rocky mound in full sun, filled with gritty soil. Even a wet and gray winter does not stop the plant from flowering. More importantly, the plant has survived these conditions and temperatures into the 20°s (around −6° C) and remained vigorous. A light yearly application of lime around the base of the plant is recommended.

*Salvia thymoides* is an appealing and interesting salvia for a collector or connoisseur of plants. Difficult to establish in most gardens, it grows well in a clay or porous container, needing only occasional observant care.

## *Salvia transsylvanica* Schur, Plate 84

A very hardy herbaceous perennial, *Salvia transsylvanica* has a wide distribution from northern and central Russia through Romania. The specific epithet, *transsylvanica*, refers to the central area of Romania, bounded on the south by the Transylvanian Alps. It was described botanically in 1853 but its introduction to gardeners (through seed catalogs) was as recent as the late 1980s.

When first becoming established, the very leafy *Salvia transsylvanica* forms a clump of leaves from which are produced many lax stems 2 ft (60 cm) or more in length. At the base of these stems the leaves are large, decreasing in size towards the top of the stem. They are dark yellow-green on top with pale undersides and prominent yellow veining. Each petiole varies in length in proportion to the size of the leaf. The beauty of the foliage is not only in its rich color and texture but also in the pronounced scalloping around the entire edge of the leaf.

Flowering begins in early summer and will continue until frost if spent inflorescences and a large portion of their lax stems are removed. The flowers are arranged in loose whorls and spaced about 0.5 in (1.3 cm) apart. Many flowers come into bloom at the same time and their rich violet color makes a lovely showing. The flowers are a good 0.5 in (1.3 cm) in length, so a lot of color can be seen on each inflorescence. These flowering stems are lax, but, even so, they make a fine display. As a cut flower this salvia lasts for many days in a bouquet.

Propagation is easiest by seed, although cuttings can be used. After the mother plant is established, self-sown seedlings may be found at its base. It takes a full year for young plants to develop a large rootstock with a tap root that will subsequently produce abundant flowering stems.

The cultivation of *Salvia transsylvanica* includes a half to a full day of sun, good drainage, and humus incorporated in friable garden soil. Deep watering once each week and a liquid fertilizer applied at half-strength several times during the growing season are recommended. Considering *S. transsylvanica*'s native habitat, plants are probably hardy to 0° F (−18° C), and quite possibly to even lower temperatures. Place conifer boughs over the crown of the plant to prevent heaving in a cold climate.

A space that measures 3 ft (1 m) is needed for the full development of *Salvia transsylvanica*. It reaches almost 2 ft (0.6 m) in height but, as previously mentioned, is lax in habit. Because of this sprawl it makes a fine companion plant and looks lovely with shrub roses. The climbing form of the old tea rose 'Mme Caroline Testout', with its subdued pink flowers, or the white flowered, upright hybrid tea 'Frau Karl Druschki' would be enhanced by S. *transsylvanica* clothing the space close by but not directly underneath the roses. All have the same cultural requirements. The front of a herbaceous border is also a desirable place for this attractive, dark green leaved salvia that repeats bloom throughout the summer as it almost crawls along the ground.

## *Salvia uliginosa* Bentham, Bog sage, Plate 85

In the early part of the 19th century, *Salvia uliginosa* was found in specific localities in southern Brazil, Uruguay, and Argentina, and was described and named by the distinguished English botanist George Bentham. In its native habitat it is found growing in bogs and wet places. In fact, the specific epithet *uliginosa* literally means of swamps and marshes.

Introduced to horticulture in 1912, *Salvia uliginosa* has steadily been gaining recognition among gardeners. And with good reason—it has beautiful sky-blue flowers, it will flourish in a multitude of growing conditions, and the rootstock is easily divided.

A herbaceous perennial that will reach 3–6 ft (1–2 m) in height in a season, bog sage spreads fairly rapidly on underground runners. It has very thin stems that are deeply grooved and its leaves are yellow-green and shaped like a lance. They are of varying sizes, serrated on the edge, and tend to grow in clusters. This gives the thin, multiple stems a fairy-like, graceful appearance, particularly when they move in a breeze. The bright azure-blue flowers are about 0.5 in (1.3 cm) in length and have a white beeline in the throat to guide insects to pollen and nectar. The flowers appear in whorls and, usually, many come into bloom at the same time. Flowering begins in summer and continues until daylight hours shorten.

Hardy to 15° F (−10° C), and probably lower, *Salvia uliginosa* is a favorite of Beth Chatto (1982), who tells of it surviving nine out of 10 winters in her cold Essex garden with a cover of litter.

As mentioned above, bog sage is far from particular about growing conditions. I recommend good drainage, garden soil enriched with humus, and infrequent watering. With little water the plant stays within the 4 ft (1.3 m) range and does not spread so rapidly. It tolerates full sun but looks prettiest with some shade. It is not evergreen and all stems should be cut to the ground in late winter or early spring. Propagation is by seed, cuttings, or division. Division is by far the easiest method. Bog sage makes a very nice cut flower throughout its long summer into autumn blooming period.

In a high shade border, *Salvia uliginosa* and white or pink Japanese anemones and the spring and autumn flowering *Geranium* 'Russell Prichard', with its reddish-rose flowers, make an attractive late summer combination. In my garden I have planted bog sage with the late spring-blooming rose 'Félicité Perpétue' to give life to the green foliage of the rose during the summer after it has flowered.

## *Salvia verticillata* Linnaeus, Plate 86

Widely distributed in the wild, *Salvia verticillata* is found across central Europe into western Asia. Naturalized in northern Europe and North America, this sage apparently adapts easily to different climates and soils. Described by Linnaeus in 1753, I find no mention of it in early gardening literature or herbals and assume that it lacks medicinal and culinary properties.

A herbaceous perennial, *Salvia verticillata* has a leafy base of mid-green leaves that are covered with short hairs, giving them a soft green appearance and making them velvety to the touch. Stems covered in leaves carry branched inflorescences that frequently reach 3 ft (1 m) in height and 2.5 ft (0.8 m) in width. Whorls of tiny, densely packed, lavender flowers are held in equally tiny calyces that are lime-green tinged with purple. The specific epithet, *verticillata*, refers to these tightly packed whorls of flowers in verticils. Graham Stuart Thomas (1990a) calls the plant stately but not showy and I would have to agree with him. However, in the early 1990s the long blooming cultivar 'Purple Rain' was introduced, and this cultivar is indeed showy. This selection was made by Piet Oudolf of the Netherlands, and is distributed from his nursery. Not as large or lax as the species, 'Purple Rain' is usually about 2 ft

(60 cm) in height, and its upright position supports whorls of small but plentiful purple flowers held in tiny violet calyces. When stems are conditioned by cutting under water, *S. verticillata* and its cultivar 'Purple Rain' (plate 86) both make fine cut flowers.

Friable garden soil improved with humus along with good drainage and water at least once a week are required for these salvias. Full sun is recommended because with shade the inflorescences tend to become leggy and lax. *Salvia verticillata* and its cultivar 'Purple Rain' are both cold tolerant to 0° F (−18° C). In a cold climate place pine boughs over the crown of plants to prevent heaving.

*Salvia verticillata* and *S. verticillata* 'Purple Rain' are good candidates for a spot in a sunny border that requires flowers of a dusky hue. An end of summer flowering border might include clumps of *Origanum laevigatum* 'Hopleys', with its vibrant pink flowers and bracts, and *Origanum* 'Santa Cruz', with its heavily flowering lilac-pink spikes. Both are about 2 ft (60 cm) in height. *Thymus vulgaris* 'Argentea', silver thyme, is less than 1 ft (30 cm), and can be interplanted to weave the composition together.

The lovely, summer blooming *Buddleja alternifolia* 'Argentea', with its silver, willow-like leaves and lilac-purple flowers, makes a fine background for drifts of *Salvia verticillata* or *S. verticillata* 'Purple Rain'. The spreading and lax *Buddleja davidii* 'Nanho Purple', which has dark red-purple flowers with an orange eye, serves the same purpose equally well. Crocus or narcissus bulbs could be included for a touch of color in early spring. The bulbs' foliage will have matured and been removed before the salvia comes into bloom.

## *Salvia villosa* Fernald

A tender and rather dainty perennial herb, *Salvia villosa* has been collected in two Mexican provinces, Coahuila and San Luis Potosi. It is handsome, and though it is not hardy, it should be known to gardeners because of its pretty, delicate appearance. It has been collected at 4000 ft (1200 m) in areas that are mainly dry and have little or no frost.

Eventually reaching 1–1.5 ft (30–40 cm) in both height and width, *Salvia villosa* is a low, mounding plant. Small, blue-green leaves, the largest about 1 in (2.5 cm) in length, hold themselves upright along the stems and amply cover the plant. The leaves are thin and covered with short hairs—the margins are outlined with tiny hairs too. The specific epithet *villosa* (hairy) refers to these soft hairs. Slender and wiry inflorescences rise above the foliage about 8 in (20 cm). Irregularly spaced verticils hold two to six flowers. The flowers are tiny, often less than 0.5 in (1.3 cm) long, but their bright violet-blue color attracts attention, particularly in the sunlight. The lower lip has a white beeline that extends into the throat. *S. villosa* never comes into what would be referred to as full bloom, but it has a few flowers continuously from spring through autumn.

Full sun and a fast-draining, gravelly soil are important conditions for this salvia. It needs regular weekly water throughout the summer. In my garden, it grows and fills out more rapidly if there are low-growing companion plants around it. Hardy to 32° F (0° C), it will survive temperatures into the high 20°s (around −2° C) for short periods of time. Propagation is by seed or cuttings. To be on the safe side, take cuttings in late August to be wintered over in the greenhouse.

A sun-filled rock garden is an ideal setting for *Salvia villosa*. A vast number of low-growing plants can be considered as companions, and I have listed below a few of varying heights. All thrive in the same culture as *S. villosa*.

> *Achillea ageratifolia,* filigree-like, silvery-gray foliage and white
>     flowers, 6 in (15 cm).
> *Achillea umbellata,* divided gray foliage and white flowers,
>     6 in (15 cm).
> *Artemisia pycnocephala,* finely cut, silvered foliage, 2 ft (60 cm).
> *Ballota acetabulosa,* handsome, rounded, gray-green foliage,
>     2 ft (60 cm).
> *Eriogonum latifolium,* flat, pearl gray foliage and pink flowers,
>     8 in (20 cm).
> *Frankenia thymifolia,* gray-blue foliage and tiny pink flowers,
>     2 in (5 cm).

*Helichrysum italicum*, bright silver, linear foliage and small, straw-yellow flowers, 1.5 ft (45 cm).

*Santolina pinnata* 'Edward Bowles', narrow, divided, gray-green leaves, 1.5 ft (40 cm). Particularly attractive pale lemon flowers.

*Tanacetum haradjanii*, finely cut, feathery, silver-white foliage, 4 in (10 cm).

## *Salvia viridis* Linnaeus, Plate 87

*Salvia viridis* is an erect herbaceous annual, occurring in the wild in a region extending from the Mediterranean into Crimea and Iran. Known as *Salvia horminum* for many years, botanists have now determined that the earlier specific name *viridis* is the correct one. In 1753, Linnaeus described *Salvia viridis* and *Salvia horminum* as separate species. *Viridis* is from the Greek and means green, covering every shade of the color. Youth and vigor are also implied. *Horminum* is the Greek for sage. Since the late 1500s, when *Salvia viridis* was brought into cultivation, many selections have been made and are named for the colorful sterile bracts that adorn each inflorescence and give the plant its unique charm.

*Salvia viridis*

This is a delightful plant for the front of a summer border, growing 1–2 ft (30–60 cm) in height and 1 ft (30 cm) in width. Because it is an annual, it develops rapidly and has a long period of bloom, lasting over a month. The colorful bracts last well as cut flowers. Nearly hidden beneath them one can find tiny, two-lipped flowers. These almost secret flowers are cream colored with a tinge of either purple or rose on the top lip, reflecting the colorful bract on top. As well as being useful in fresh arrangements, the inflorescences may be cut and dried for winter bouquets.

Three-quarters to a full day of sun, good drainage, friable soil, and moderate water are the plant's cultural requirements. Applications of liquid fertilizer are helpful to push the plants along to full bloom. In an area that has a lengthy and warm autumn, plants will bloom twice if inflorescences are cut back after they reach peak bloom. This should be done before seed production begins and probably no later than the end of July. Regular feeding and watering are recommended to encourage a second bloom.

Sow seed indoors in late March for an early jump on the season, or sow in place in the border when the soil has warmed and the danger of frost has passed. Germination takes more or less 15 days if soil temperature has reached 70° F (21° C). Seedlings are stout and transplant readily. When winters are very mild, self-sown seedlings may appear, but they should not be counted on. *Salvia viridis* used to be known as "red-topped sage," implying that the bracts were deep pink or rose. This common name was probably used to distinuish *S. viridis* from *S. officinalis* 'Purpurascens', commonly called red sage. For several centuries, both sages have been widely grown and used in Britain and on the continent. Breeders have been busy and many color selections are offered nowadays. Usually, the cultivar name describes the color of the showy bracts. I have tried and enjoyed each of the following cultivars: 'Alba', 'Bluebeard', 'Oxford Blue', 'Pink Sunday', and 'Rose Bouquet'. One British seed list offers 'Claryssa Blue', 'Claryssa Pink', and 'Claryssa White'. I have also grown these cultivars, and find them similar to the others mentioned.

Elizabeth Lawrence (1942) warns gardeners in the hot and humid southern United States that this showy annual must be grown for a late spring display. In those conditions it seldom repeats bloom in the way it does in more favorable climates.

In her extraordinary work *A Modern Herbal*, M. Grieve gives many different kinds of information on herbs and their uses. In discussing *Salvia viridis* she states the seeds and leaves used to be added to fermenting vats in order to "greatly increase the inebriating quality of the liquor." An infusion of the leaves was used for sore gums and, powdered, the leaves were used for snuff. This sage was also noted as a honey-yielding plant. Today, we no longer grow these pretty plants for their versatile, life-enhancing properties, but to enjoy their lively beauty in the garden.

If you have leggy roses, such as 'First Love' or 'Silver Jubilee', a group of *Salvia viridis* would skirt the shrubs and give additional color. Planted in drifts in the border, the colorful bracts are enhanced by the silver-gray foliage of *Artemisia arborescens* or the almost silver-white foliage of the attractive California native *A. pycnocephala*.

## *Salvia wagneriana* Polakowski

Even though *Salvia wagneriana* is found at elevations of 4000–6500 ft (1200–2000 m), suggesting cold tolerance, the climate in the mountainous areas where it is found is warm and moist. In fact, this salvia is frequently found in thickets that are both wet and warm. It is a beautiful species and very popular with gardeners in the parts of the world where it occurs naturally. Frequently found at moderate elevations in Guatemala, El Salvador, Nicaragua, Costa Rica, and the province of Chiapas in Mexico, it is one of the few salvias taken from the wild and grown in gardens in these localities. Because of its adaptability, it has escaped from cultivation and become established outside the parameters of its native habitat in many of the above mentioned areas.

Described by botanists sometimes as a herb and sometimes as a shrub, it is shrub-like in stature, attaining 3–9 ft (1–3 m) in height and 4 ft (1.3 m) or more in width. Leaves are yellowish green, sometimes with purple veins, and smooth on top. On the underside of the leaf the veins are distinctly raised. Flower color can vary from bright red to rose to pinkish cream. The bracts that cover the emerging flowers are highly colored, as are the calyces. When observed closely, flowers, calyces, and bracts are each seen to be a slightly different color. Flowers are at least 1 in (2.5 cm) in length, frequently as long as 3 in (8 cm). They are held in a calyx that is 0.75 in (2 cm) long and showy. The bracts are usually slightly darker in color than the flower and fall away as the plump flowers emerge in whorls. Seeds of *Salvia wagneriana* germinate readily and cuttings root quickly.

Blooming begins in late autumn and continues through January. Short days probably trigger flowering but the plant certainly needs warm air and soil to promote blooming. I have been able on only one occasion to bring this plant into bloom. The winter preceding bloom was without frost, allowing the plant to grow to about 3 ft (1 m) in height. The following autumn the plant reached 6 ft (2 m) and began flowering on the first of November. It was in full gorgeous bloom by Thanksgiving. Soon after that we had a killing frost and the plant melted away. In the spring there was no sign of life at its base.

Site *Salvia wagneriana* under high shade with protection from hot sun and wind. A very warm, mild climate is a prerequisite for this salvia, along with well-draining garden soil amended with humus. Mulching once a year and regular deep watering are also needed.

In a frost-free garden, *Salvia wagneriana* is a handsome partner for flowering maple (*Abutilon*), and there are many free-flowering selections from which to choose. 'Nabob', for example, is covered with dark leaves and has large maroon colored flowers. 'Pink Parasol' is charming, with satin-like leaves and almost mauve flowers. The hybrid *Abutilon* × *suntense*, so popular in Britain, has 3 in (8 cm), wide open, lavender-violet flowers. All of these plants like partial shade, water, and warmth.

# Where to See Salvias

The following are a few of the public gardens with particularly fine collections of salvias.

## UNITED STATES

Denver Botanic Gardens
909 York Street
Denver, Colorado 80206
Tel 303-331-4000

East Bay Regional Parks Botanic
    Garden
Tilden Regional Park
11500 Skyline Boulevard
Oakland, California 94619
Tel 510-562-7275

Elizabeth F. Gamble Garden
    Center
1431 Waverley Street
Palo Alto, California 94301
Tel 415-329-1356

Huntington Botanical Gardens
1151 Oxford Road
San Marino, California 91108
Tel 213-792-6141

Quarry Hill Botanic Garden
12825 Sonoma Highway
Glen Ellen, California 95442
Tel 707-996-3166

Rancho Santa Ana Botanic Garden
1500 North College Avenue
Claremont, California 91711
Tel 714-625-8767

Santa Barbara Botanic Garden
1212 Mission Canyon Road
Santa Barbara, California 93105
Tel 805-682-4726

Strybing Arboretum Society
Ninth Avenue at Lincoln Way
San Francisco, California 94117
Tel 415-661-1514

University of California Botanic
    Garden, Berkeley
Centennial Drive
Berkeley, California 94720
Tel 510-642-3343

University of California at Santa
    Cruz Arboretum
Empire Grade
Santa Cruz, California 95064
Tel 408-427-2998

Wave Hill Gardens
675 W 252nd Street
Bronx, New York 10471
Tel 718-549-3200

## BRITISH ISLES

*British National Collections*
Dyffryn Botanical Gardens
St Nicholas
Cardiff
CF5 6SU
Tel (01222) 593328

Kingston Maurward Gardens
Kingston Maurward
Dorchester
Dorset, DT28PY
Tel (01305) 264738

Pleasant View Nursery
Two Mile Oak
Near Denbury
Newton Abbot
Devon, TQ12 6DG
Tel (01803) 813388

## FRANCE

Jardin Botanique de la Ville de
    Nice
78 Avenue de la Corniche
    Fleurie
06200 Nice
Tel 93 18 03 33

*French National Collection*
Pépinière de la Foux
Chemin de la Foux
83220 Le Pradet
Tel 94 75 35 45

## AUSTRALIA

Unlimited Perennials
369 Boomerang Drive
Lavington N.S.W. 2641
Tel 060 254585

# Where to Buy Salvias

The following list contains suggestions for sources of salvias. An asterisk (*) denotes a source for seed rather than plants. A dagger (†) denotes a mail order nursery.

## UNITED STATES

Alplains*
32315 Pine Crest Court
Kiowa, Colorado 80117
Tel 303-621-2247

California Flora Nursery
Somers & D Street
P.O. Box 3
Fulton, California 95439
Tel 707-528-8813

Carman's Nursery
16201 East Mozart Avenue
Los Gatos, California 95032
Tel 408-356-0119

Berkeley Horticultural Nursery
1310 McGee Avenue
Berkeley, California 94703
Tel 510-526-4704

Canyon Creek Nursery†
3527 Dry Creek Road
Orville, California 95965
Tel 916-533-2166

Heronswood Nursery†
7530 NE 288th Street
Kingston, Washington 98346
Tel 360-297-4172

J. L. Hudson, Seedsman*
P.O. Box 1058
Redwood City, California 94064

Joy Creek Nursery†
20300 NW Watson Road
Scappoose, Oregon 97056
Tel 503-543-7474

Logee's Greenhouses†
55 North Street
Danielson, Connecticut 06239
Tel 203-774-8038

Redwood City Seed Company*
P.O. Box 361
Redwood City, California 94064
Tel 415-325-7333

The Sandy Mush Herb
    Nursery†
316 Surrett Cove Road
Leicester, North Carolina 28748
Tel 704-683-2014

Seedhunt*
P.O. Box 96
Freedom, California 95019

Sierra Azul Nursery and Garden
2660 East Lake Avenue
Watsonville, California 95076
Tel 408-763-0939

Southwestern Native Seeds*
Box 50503
Tucson, Arizona 85703

Western Hills Nursery
16250 Coleman Valley Road
Occidental, California 95465
Tel 707-874-3731

Yucca Do Nursery†
P.O. Box 655
Waller, Texas 77484
Tel 409-826-6363


## AUSTRALIA

Lambley Nursery
Lester's Road
Ascot Vic 3364
Tel 03 5343 4303
Fax 03 5343 4257

Unlimited Perennials
369 Boomerang Drive
Lavington NSW 2641
Tel 02 6025 4585

Viburnum Gardens
8 Sunnyridge Road
Arcadia NSW 2159
Tel 02 9653 2259
Fax 02 9653 1840

## BRITISH ISLES

Jim and Jenny Archibald*
'Bryn Collen'
Ffostrasol
Llandysul
Dyfed, SA44 5SB
Wales

Brian Hiley
25 Little Woodcote Estate
Wallington
Surrey, SM5 4AU
Tel (0181) 647 9679

The Beth Chatto Gardens Ltd
Elmstead Market
Colchester
Essex, CO7 7DB
Tel (01206) 822007

Chiltern Seeds*
Bortree Stile
Ulverston
Cumbria, LA12 7PB

Four Seasons
Forncett St Mary
Norwich, NR16 1JT
Tel (01508) 488344

Green Farm Plants
Bentley
Farnham
Surrey, GU10 5JX
Tel (01420) 23202

Hollington Nurseries
Woolton Hill
Newbury
Berkshire, RG15 9XT
Tel (01635) 253908

Hopleys Plants
High Street
Much Hadham
Hertfordshire, SG10 6BU
Tel (01279) 842509

Pleasant View Nursery
Two Mile Oak
Near Denbury
Newton Abbott
Devon, TQ12 6DG
Tel (01803) 813388

## FRANCE

Alain Daubas
Avenue du Bérange
34160 Saint Drezery
Tel 67 86 92 36

Pépinière de la Foux
Chemin de la Foux
83220 Le Pradet
Tel 94 75 35 45

Pépinières Filippi
R. N. 113
34140 Mèze
Tel 67 43 88 69

**NEW ZEALAND**

Bay Bloom Nurseries
Cambridge Road
Tauranga
Tel 07 578 9902
Fax 07 577 9752

Mara Nurseries
Allen Road RD 12
Hawera
Tel 06 272 2806
Fax 06 272 2033

Marshwood Nursery
Leonard Road
West Plains
Invercargill
Tel / Fax 03 215 7672

Ormonds Garden and Nursery
Kahuraniki Road RD 14
Havelock North
Tel 06 874 7820
Fax 06 874 7660

Further information on plant sources may be found in the current editions of the following books:

**North America**

*The Andersen Horticultural Library's Source List of Plants and Seeds.* Chanhassen: Minnesota Landscape Arboretum.

*Gardening by Mail* and *Taylor's Guide to Specialty Nurseries*, by Barbara J. Barton. New York: Houghton Mifflin.

**British Isles**

*The Plant Finder.* London: Royal Horticultural Society.

**Europe**

*PPP Index: European Plantfinder*, by Anne Erhardt & Walter Erhardt. Ashbourne, Derbyshire: Moorland

# Flowering Guide
# by Season

## Spring Flowering Salvias

*africana-lutea*
*apiana*
*brandegei*
*carduacea*
*columbariae*
*dominica*
*eigii*
*fruticosa*
*jurisicii*
*leucophylla*
*lycioides*
*mellifera*
*muelleri*
*pratensis*
*recognita*

*sonomensis*
*spathacea*

## Summer Flowering Salvias

Species marked * repeat bloom
in autumn

*aethiopis*
*albimaculata*
*argentea*
*arizonica**
*austriaca**
*blepharophylla**
*buchananii*
*cacaliaefolia**

*canariensis*
*cedrosensis*
*chamaedryoides**
*chamelaeagnea*
*chiapensis**
*clevelandii*
*coahuilensis**
*coccinea**
*coulteri**
*cyanescens**
*darcyi**
*discolor**
*dolomitica*
*farinacea**
*flava*
*forskaohlei**
*glechomaefolia**
*glutinosa*
*greggii**
*guaranitica**
*hians*
*hirtella**
'Indigo Spires'*
*interrupta**
× *jamensis**
*koyamae**
*lavandulifolia*
*leucantha**
*longispicata**
*macellarea**
*melissodora**
*mexicana**
*microphylla**
*moorcroftiana*
*nubicola*
*officinalis*

*patens*
*przewalskii*
'Purple Majesty'
*reptans**
*roborowskii*
*roemeriana**
*sclarea*
*semiatrata**
*sessei**
*sinaloensis**
*somalensis**
*superba**
*sylvestris**
*taraxacifolia*
*transsylvanica*
*uliginosa**
*verticillata*
*viridis**

## Autumn Flowering Salvias

*arizonica*
*austriaca*
*azurea* var. *grandiflora*
*blepharophylla*
*cacaliaefolia*
*chamaedryoides*
*chiapensis*
*coahuilensis*
*coccinea*
*confertiflora*
*coulteri*
*cyanescens*
*darcyi*
*discolor*

disjuncta
dombeyi
elegans
farinacea
forskaohlei
'Frieda Dixon'
fulgens
glechomaefolia
greggii
guaranitica
hirtella
'Indigo Spires'
interrupta
involucrata
× jamensis
koyamae
leucantha
littae
longispicata
lycioides
macellaria
madrensis
melissodora
mexicana
microphylla
miniata
muelleri
penstemonoides
polystachya
puberula
'Purple Majesty'
regla
reptans
roemeriana
semiatrata
sessei

sinaloensis
somalensis
splendens 'Van Houttei'
superba
thymoides
uliginosa
villosa
viridis
wagneriana

## Winter Flowering Salvias

africana-lutea
disjuncta
dombeyi
dorisiana
gesneraeflora
holwayi
iodantha
karwinskii
littae
purpurea
thymoides
wagneriana

# Cold Tolerance Guide

The following species are cold tolerant to 0° F (−18° C):

aethiopis

albimaculata

argentea

arizonica

austriaca

azurea var. grandiflora

cyanescens

eigii

flava

forskaohlei

glutinosa

hians

jurisicii

moorcroftiana

nubicola

officinalis

pratensis

recognita

sclarea

superba

sylvestris

transsylvanica

verticillata

# Shade Tolerance Guide

The following species are shade tolerant:

*arizonica*  
*blepharophylla*  
*buchananii*  
*cacaliaefolia*  
*chamelaeagnea*  
*chiapensis*  
*discolor*  
*dorisiana*  
'Frieda Dixon'  
*glutinosa*  

*hirtella*  
*holwayi*  
*involucrata*  
*koyamae*  
*littae*  
*miniata*  
*polystachya*  
*roemeriana*  
*sinaloensis*  
*splendens* 'Van Houttei'

# Salvias with Especially Handsome Foliage

The following species have especially handsome foliage:

aethiopis
apiana
argentea
buchananii
cacaliaefolia
chiapensis
coahuilensis
coulteri
discolor

fruticosa
interrupta
madrensis
officinalis and all its cultivars
semiatrata
sinaloensis
somalensis
spathacea
thymoides

# Salvias
# for Containers

The following salvias are well suited to container growing:

albimaculata
argentea
blepharophylla
buchananii
cedrosensis
chiapensis
discolor
dorisiana
elegans
farinacea cultivars
fruticosa
greggii

× jamensis
jurisicii
leucantha
lycioides
microphylla
   (Graham's sage)
muelleri
officinalis and
   all its cultivars
patens
reptans
roemeriana

semiatrata
sinaloensis
splendens
   'Van Houttei'
sylvestris
   'East Friesland'
taraxacifolia
thymoides
verticillata
   'Purple Rain'
villosa
viridis

# Color Designations
of Unusual Flower
or Foliage Color

The following is a list of salvias with unusual flower or foliage color. The exact or nearest possible color of flower and/or foliage is given using the Royal Horticulture Society Colour Chart, which is available from the R. H. S. Garden at Wisley in the United Kingdom.

*africana-lutea*, emerging corolla Yellow-Green Group 151B, calyx Yellow-Green Group 152A. Mature corolla Greyed-Orange Group 164A, calyx Greyed-Orange Group 176A.
*albimaculata*, corolla Violet Group 88A, spotted with white.
*apiana*, leaf surface Greyed-Green Group 190A.
*argentea*, leaf surface Greyed-Green Group 191A.
*arizonica*, corolla Violet-Blue Group 93B.
*austriaca*, corolla Yellow Group 10D.
*azurea* var. *grandiflora*, corolla Violet-Blue Group 94A.
*blepharophylla*, corolla Red Group 43A.
*brandegei*, corolla Purple Group 76B, calyx Violet Group 83B. Leaf surface Green Group 137B, underside Greyed-Green Group 191C.

*buchananii*, corolla Red-Purple Group 74A.

*cacaliaefolia*, corolla Violet-Blue Group 94A.

*canariensis*, corolla Purple-Violet Group 80B, calyx Red-Purple Group 71B.

*carduacea*, corolla Purple Group 75A.

*cedrosensis*, corolla Violet-Blue Group 93B, leaf surface Greyed-Green Group 194A.

*chamaedryoides*, corolla Violet-Blue Group 94A, leaf surface Greyed-Green Group 194A.

*chamaedryoides* 'Desert Green', corolla Violet-Blue Group 94A, leaf surface Greyed-Green Group 191A.

*chamelaeagnea*, corolla Violet-Blue Group 92A.

*chiapensis*, corolla Red-Purple Group 74A.

*clevelandii* 'Allen Chickering', corolla Violet-Green Group 88C.

*clevelandii* 'Santa Cruz Dark', corolla Violet Group 86B.

*clevelandii* 'Winnifred Gilman', corolla Violet Group 88B, stem Red-Purple Group 59A.

*coahuilensis*, corolla Purple Group 78A.

*columbariae*, corolla Violet-Blue Group 89B.

*confertiflora*, corolla Orange-Red Group, calyx Greyed-Red Group 178A.

*coulteri*, corolla Violet-Blue Group 93B.

*cyanescens*, corolla Purple-Violet Group 82C.

'Dara's Choice', corolla Violet Group 88B.

*darcyi*, corolla Red Group 45C.

*discolor*, corolla Violet-Blue Group 89A, calyx Green Group 139D. Leaf surface Green Group 139B, underside Greyed-Green 192B.

*disjuncta*, corolla Red Group 42A.

*dolomitica*, corolla Purple Group 76A with cream center.

*dominica*, corolla White Group 155C.

*dorisiana*, corolla Red-Purple Group 71B, calyx Yellow-Green Group 144B, leaf surface Yellow-Green Group 144A.

*eigii*, upper lip of corolla Red-Purple Group 74C, lower lip Red-Purple Group 62D, calyx Red-Purple Group 59A.

*elegans*, corolla Red Group 42A.

*elegans* 'Honey Melon', corolla Red Group 45B.

*elegans* 'Pineapple Sage', corolla Red Group 45A.

*flava*, corolla Yellow Group 13B with a blotch of Violet Group 83A on
the lower lip.

*forskaohlei*, corolla Violet Group 87A.

'Frieda Dixon', corolla Red Group 50B.

*fruticosa*, corolla Purple Group 75A, calyx Greyed-Purple Group 183B,
underside of leaf Greyed-Green Group 138B.

*fulgens*, corolla Red Group 45B, calyx Greyed-Red Group 178B.

*gesneraeflora*, corolla Red Group 44B, calyx Yellow-Green Group 146A.

*gesneraeflora* 'Tequila', corolla Red Group 44B, calyx Greyed-Purple
Group 187A.

*glechomaefolia*, corolla Violet-Blue Group 94B, calyx Violet-Blue Group
95C.

*glutinosa*, lips of corollas Yellow Group 9C, upper lip flecked with dots
of Red-Purple Group 59B.

*greggii* 'Purple Haze', sparkling color of corolla is not found on Chart.
The nearest is Purple-Violet Group 81A.

*greggii* 'Purple Pastel', corolla Purple-Violet Group 82B, calyx Violet
Group 83A with green.

*guaranitica*, corolla Violet-Blue Group 89C.

*guaranitica* 'Costa Rica Blue', corolla Violet-Blue Group 93B, calyx base
Yellow-Green Group 145A with purple tips.

*hians*, corolla Violet Group 87A.

*hirtella*, corolla Red Group 44B, calyx Greyed-Purple Group 183A.

*holwayi*, corolla Red Group 53B.

'Indigo Spires', corolla Violet-Blue Group 89B, calyx Purple Group 79B.

*interrupta*, corolla Violet Group 87A with 83B in center.

*involucrata*, corolla, calyx, and bracts Red-Purple Group 71B.

*involucrata* 'El Cielo', corolla Red-Purple Group 61A, calyx Greyed-
Purple Group 183A.

*iodantha*, corolla Red-Purple Group 74A.

× *jamensis* 'Cienega de Oro', corolla Yellow Group 10C.

× *jamensis* 'Sierra San Antonio', corolla Yellow-Orange Group 16C.

*jurisicii*, corolla Violet Group 83D. White flowered form Yellow-White
Group 158D.

*karwinskii*, corolla Red Group 51A, calyx Greyed-Purple Group
183A.

*koyamae*, corolla Yellow Group 12C.

*lavandulifolia* subsp. *blancoana*, corolla Violet Group 87A, leaf surface Yellow-Green Group 147B.

*leucantha*, corolla White Group 155D, calyx Purple-Violet Group 81A.

*leucantha* 'Midnight', corolla Purple-Violet Group 80A, calyx Purple Group 77A.

*leucophylla*, corolla Purple Group 78C, leaf surface Greyed-Green 189A.

*littae*, corolla Red-Purple Group 61A.

*longispicata*, corolla Violet Group 33A.

*lycioides* 'Guadalupe Mountain', corolla Violet-Blue 89B, leaf surface Green Group 138B.

*macellaria*, corolla between Orange-Red Group 35B and Red-Orange Group 43B with yellow in center of upper lip.

*madrensis*, corolla Yellow-Orange Group 16B, calyx Yellow-Orange Group 14C.

*melissodora*, corolla Violet-Blue Group 89C, lower lip Violet Group 84C.

*mellifera* 'Terra Seca', corolla White Group 155D with purple stamens.

*mexicana* 'Limelight', corolla Violet-Blue Group 89B, calyx Yellow-Green Group 144B.

*mexicana* 'Lollie Jackson', corolla Violet-Blue Group 89B, calyx green splashed with violet-blue.

*microphylla*, corolla Red-Purple Group 57C.

*microphylla* (from Belize) corolla Red Group 45A.

*microphylla* (Graham's sage), corolla Red Group 52A. *microphylla* var. *neurepia*, corolla Red Group 43A.

*microphylla* 'Rosita', corolla Red-Purple Group 57C.

*microphylla* 'San Carlos Festival', corolla Red Purple Group 61B.

*microphylla* var. *wislizeni*, corolla Red-Purple Group 67A.

*miniata*, corolla Red Group 43A.

'Mrs. Beard', corolla Violet Group 85B.

*muelleri*, corolla Purple-Violet Group 80A.

*nubicola*, corolla Yellow Group 10A with markings of Greyed-Purple Group 184B.

*patens*, upper lip of corolla Violet-Blue Group 96B, lower lip Violet-Blue Group 95B.

*penstemonoides*, corolla Red-Purple Group 72A.

*polystachya*, corolla Violet-Blue Group 89C, graduating to white at lip edge.

*pratensis*, corolla Violet Group 88A, calyx Brown Group 200A.

*przewalskii*, corolla Violet Group 88B, calyx Purple Group 79A.

*puberula*, corolla Red-Purple Group 67A, calyx Red-Purple Group 70A, bracts Red-Purple Group 67B.

'Purple Majesty', corolla Violet Group 83A, calyx Purple Group 79A.

*purpurea*, corolla Purple-Violet Group 80B.

*recognita*, upper lip of corolla Red-Purple Group 73C, lower lip Red-Purple Group 72D.

*regla*, corolla Red Group 44B, upper side of calyx Greyed-Orange Group 171A, lower side Greyed-Yellow Group 160A.

*reptans*, corolla Violet-Blue Group 96B, stems facing sun Brown Group 200B.

*roborowskii*, corolla Yellow Group 4C.

*roemeriana*, corolla Red Group 45B.

*sclarea*, corollas vary in color from Violet Group 85A to Violet Group 87C. Bracts Red-Purple Group 69A fading to White Group 155B.

*sclarea* 'Turkestanica', bracts White Group 155B edged pink, petioles Red-Purple Group 74C.

*semiatrata*, upper lip of corolla Violet Group 84A, lower lip Violet Group 83B. Calyx Purple Group 79C.

*sinaloensis*, corolla Violet-Blue Group 95A. Mature leaf Greyed-Green Group 189A. New leaf Purple Group 79.

*somalensis*, corolla Violet-Blue Group 92A.

*spathacea* 'Kawatre', corolla Red-Purple Group 71A, calyx Red-Purple Group 59A.

*splendens* 'Van Houttei', lower lip of corolla Red Group 45A, upper lip, tube, and calyx Red-Purple Group 59B.

*sylvestris*, corolla Violet-Blue Group 89B, calyx Violet Group 83B, bracts Purple Group 77A.

*taraxacifolia*, corolla Purple Group 75C, leaf Greyed-Green Group 189A.

*thymoides*, corolla Violet-Blue Group 89C, leaf Greyed-Green 191B.

*transsylvanica*, corolla Violet Group 88A.

*uliginosa*, corolla Violet-Blue Group 96B.

*verticillata*, corolla Purple-Violet Group 82C, calyx Yellow-Green Group 145A, green tinged with purple.

*verticillata* 'Purple Rain', corolla Violet-Blue Group 89C, calyx Violet Group 86B.

*villosa*, corolla Violet-Blue Group 95A.

*wagneriana*, corolla and bracts Red-Purple Group 59C, calyx Red-Purple Group 57A. Pinkish form, corolla Red-Purple Group 62A, calyx Red-Purple Group 63C, bracts Orange-White Group 159C.

# Geographical Origin of Certain *Salvia* Species

This list is included to show the reader quickly the geographical origins of a number of salvias now in cultivation. The list is not exhaustive and more detail of specific locations can be found in individual species entries. Salvias found in more than one location will be listed in the appropriate sections.

**AFRICA**
*africana-lutea*, endemic to
　　S. Africa
*chamelaeagnea*, endemic to
　　S. Africa
*dolomitica*, endemic to S. Africa
*interrupta*, endemic to Morocco
*somalensis*, endemic to Somalia
*taraxacifolia*, endemic to
　　Morocco

**ASIA**
*aethiopis*
*albimaculata*, endemic to
　　Turkey
*austriaca*
*cyanescens*, endemic to Turkey
*eigii*, eastern Meditteranean
*flava*, endemic to China
*forskaohlei*, western Asia
*glutinosa*
*hians*, endemic to the Himalayas

*koyamae*, endemic to Japan
*moorcroftiana*, Himalayas and
    northern India
*nubicola*, endemic to the
    Himalayas
*pratensis*, western Asia
*przewalskii*, endemic to China
*recognita*, western Asia
*roborowskii*
*sclarea*, southwest Asia
*sylvestris*
*verticillata*, western Asia

## CALIFORNIA

*apiana*
*brandegei*
*carduacea*
*clevelandii*
*columbariae*
*leucophylla*
*mellifera*
*sonomensis*
*spathacea*

## EUROPE

*aethiopis*, western Europe
*austriaca*, central Europe
*glutinosa*
*jurisicii*, endemic to Yugoslavia
*pratensis*
*sclarea*
*sylvestris*
*transsylvanica*
*verticillata*

## MEDITERRANEAN

*aethiopis*
*argentea*
*canariensis*
*dominica*
*fruticosa*
*lavandulifolia*
*officinalis*
*verticillata*
*viridis*

## MEXICO

*apiana*, Baja California
*arizonica*
*blepharophylla*
*brandegei*, Baja California
*cacaliaefolia*
*cedrosensis*, endemic to
    Baja California
*chamaedryoides*
*chiapensis*
*clevelandii*, Baja California
*coahuilensis*
*columbariae*, Baja California
*coulteri*
*darcyi*
*disjuncta*
*elegans*
*farinacea*
*fulgens*
*gesneraeflora*
*glechomaefolia*
*greggii*
*holwayi*
*involucrata*

*iodantha*
× *jamensis*
*karwinskii*
*leucantha*
*littae*
*longispicata*
*lycioides*
*macellaria*
*madrensis*
*melissodora*
*mellifera*, Baja California
*mexicana*
*microphylla*
*miniata*
*muelleri*
*patens*
*polystachya*
*puberula*
*purpurea*
*regla*
*reptans*
*roemeriana*
*semiatrata*
*sessei*
*sinaloensis*
*thymoides*
*villosa*
*wagneriana*

## SOUTH AND
## CENTRAL AMERICA
*cacaliaefolia*, Central America
*chiapensis*, Guatemala
*coccinea*
*confertiflora*, endemic to Brazil

*discolor*, endemic to Peru
*disjuncta*, Guatemala
*dombeyi*, Peru and Bolivia
*dorisiana*, endemic to Honduras
*guaranitica*, South America
*hirtella*, endemic to Ecuador
*holwayi*, Central America
*karwinskii*, Central America
*miniata*, Belize
*patens*, Costa Rica
*polystachya*, Central America
*purpurea*, Central America
*splendens*, endemic to Brazil
*uliginosa*, South America
*wagneriana*, Central America

## UNITED STATES
## (excluding California)
*arizonica*, Arizona and Texas
*azurea*
*columbariae*, the Southwest
*farinacea*
*greggii*, Texas
*lycioides*, Texas and New Mexico
*microphylla*, Arizona
*regla*, Texas
*reptans*, Texas
*roemeriana*, Texas

# Bibliography

Alziar, Gabriel. 1988. Catalogue synonymique des *Salvia* du monde. *Biocosme Mesogéen, Revue d'Histoire Naturelle* 5 (3–4).

Barbour, M., B. Pavlik, F. Drysdale, and S. Lindstrom. 1993. *California's Changing Landscapes*. Sacramento: California Native Plant Society.

Bawden, Harold & Joan. 1970. *Woodland Plants & Sun Lovers*. London: Faber & Faber.

Chatto, Beth. 1978. *The Dry Garden*. London: J. M. Dent & Sons.

——. 1982. *The Damp Garden*. London: J. M. Dent & Sons.

——. 1988. *Beth Chatto's Notebook*. London: J. M. Dent & Sons.

Compton, James, ed. 1992. *Salvia*. In *The New Royal Horticultural Society's Dictionary of Gardening*. New York: Stockton Press.

——. Feb. 1994a. Mexican salvias in cultivation. *The Plantsman*, vol. 15, part 4.

——. May 1994b. *Salvia darcyi*. *Kew Magazine*, vol. 2, part 2.

Epling, C. 1938. The California salvias; a review of *Salvia* section *Audibertia*. *Annals of the Missouri Botanical Garden* 25:95–152.

——. 1939. A revision of *Salvia*, subgenus *Calosphace*. *Repertorium Specierum Novarum Regni Vegetabilis, Beihefte*, vol. 110.

Grieve, M. 1971. *A Modern Herbal*. New York: Dover.

Hareuveni, Nogah. 1980. *Nature in Our Biblical Heritage*. Kiryat Ono, Israel: Neot Kedumin.

Harper, Pamela J. 1991. *Designing With Perennials*. New York: Macmillan Publishing Company.

Hedge, Ian C. 1974. A revision of *Salvia* in Africa, including Madagascar and the Canary Islands. *Notes from the Royal Botanic Garden Edinburgh* 33:1.

——. 1982a. *Flora of Turkey*, vol. 7. Edinburgh: Edinburgh University Press.

——. 1982b. *Flora Iranica*. Ed. K. H. Rechinger. Akademische Druck, Graz, Austria.

Hobhouse, Penelope. 1985. *Color in Your Garden*. Boston: Little, Brown & Company.

Illingworth, John, ed., and Jane Routh, ed. 1991. *Reginald Farrer*. Lancaster: Lancaster University.

Jekyll, Gertrude. 1908. *Colour in The Flower Garden*. London: Country Life.

Jelitto, L. and W. Schacht. 1990. *Hardy Herbaceous Perennials*. Rev. ed. Portland, Oregon: Timber Press, Inc.

Lawrence, Elizabeth. 1942. *A Southern Garden*. Chapel Hill: University of North Carolina Press.

Lawrence, Elizabeth. 1990. *Through The Garden Gate*. Ed. Bill Neal. Chapel Hill: University of North Carolina Press.

Li, Hsi-wen, and Ian. C. Hedge. 1994. *Lamiaceae*. In *Flora of China*, Wu Zheng-yi and Peter Raven. St. Louis: Missouri Botanical Garden.

Lovejoy, Ann. 1993. *The American Mixed Border*. New York: Macmillan Publishing Company.

Lloyd, Christopher. 1973. *Foliage Plants*. London: Collins.

Mattern, A., and M. Moskowitz. 1994. The life and works of Ernst Pagels. *Journal of the Hardy Plant Society*, vol. 16, no. 1.

Mitchell, Sydney. 1932. *From a Sunset Garden*. New York: Doubleday, Doran & Co.

Nottle, Trevor. 1984. *Growing Perennials*. Kenthurst, New South Wales: Kangaroo Press.

O'Brien, Bart. In press. *California Native Plant Cultivars*. Sacramento: California Native Plant Society.

Parsons, Mary Elizabeth. 1921. Rev. ed. *The Wild Flowers of California*. San Francisco: H. S. Crocker Co.

Quest-Ritson, Charles. 1992. *The English Garden Abroad*. London: Viking.

Robinson, William. 1933. Rev. ed. *The English Flower Garden*. Sagaponack, New York: Sagapress, Inc.

Rohde, Eleanour Sinclair. 1936. *Herbs & Herb Gardening*. London: The Medici Society.

Schmidt, Marjorie. 1980. *Growing California Native Plants*. Berkeley: University of California Press.

Schmidt, M., N. Smith, W. Roderick, R. Lutsko, and S. Edwards. 1990. *Native Plants for Your Garden*. Sacramento: California Native Plant Society.

Starr, Greg. 1985. New world salvias for cultivation in southern Arizona. *Desert Plants*, vol 7, no. 4. University of Arizona at the Boyce Thompson Southwestern Arboretum.

Thomas, Graham Stuart. 1990a. Rev. ed. *Perennial Garden Plants*. Portland, Oregon: Sagapress, Inc./Timber Press, Inc.

——. 1990b. Rev. ed. *Plants for Ground-Cover*. Portland, Oregon: Sagapress, Inc./Timber Press, Inc.

# Index of
# Plant Names

213